Faith and Devotion in Theravāda Buddhism

Emerging Perceptions in Buddhist Studies
(ISSN 0971-9512)

1-2. An Encyclopaedia of Buddhist Deities, Demigods, Godlings, Saints & Demons — with Special Focus on Iconographic Attributes; by Fredrick W. Bunce. 2 Vols. (ISBN 81-246-0020-1; set)

3. Buddhism in Karnataka; by R.C. Hiremath; with a foreword by H.H. the Dalai Lama (ISBN 81-246-0013-9)

4-5. Pāli Language and Literature: A Systematic Survey and Historical Study; by Kanai Lal Hazra. 2 Vols. (ISBN 81-246-0004-X; set)

6. Maṇḍala and Landscape; by A.W. Macdonald (ISBN 81-246-0060-0)

7. The Future Buddha Maitreya: An Iconological Study; by Inchang Kim (ISBN 81-246-0082-1)

8. Absence of the Buddha Image in Early Buddhist Art; by Kanoko Tanaka (ISBN 81-246-0090-2)

9. A Few Facts About Buddhism; by Gunnar Gällmo (ISBN 81-246-0099-6)

10. Buddhist Theory of Meaning and Literary Analysis; by Rajnish K. Mishra (ISBN 81-246-0118-6)

11. Buddhism as/in Performance; Analysis of Meditation and Theatrical Practice; by David E.R. George (ISBN 81-246-0123-2)

12. Buddhist Tantra and Buddhist Art; by T.N. Mishra (ISBN 81-246-0141-0)

13. Buddhist Art in India and Sri Lanka: 3rd Century BC to 6th Century AD — A Critical Study; by Virender Kumar Dabral (ISBN 81-246-0162-3)

14. The Tibetan Iconography of Buddhas, Bodhisattvas and Other Deities — A Unique Pantheon; by Lokesh Chandra & Fredrick W. Bunce (ISBN 81-246-0178-X)

15. The Dalai Lamas — The Institution and Its History by Ardy Verhaegen; (ISBN 81-246-0202-6)

16. The Tibetan Tāntric Vision; by Krishna Ghosh Della Santina (ISBN 81-246-0227-1)

17. The Buddhist Art of Kauśāmbī; by Aruna Tripathi: From 300 BC to AD 550 (ISBN 81-246-0226-3)

18. Mahāmudrā & Atiyoga; by Giuseppe Baroetto; Translated from Italian into English by Andrew Lukianowicz (ISBN 81-246-0322-7)

19. Theravāda Buddhist Devotionalism in Ceylon, Burma and Thailand; by V.V.S. Saibaba (ISBN 81-246-0327-8)

20. Faith and Devotion in Theravāda Buddhism; by V.V.S. Saibaba (ISBN 81-246-0329-4)

Emerging Perceptions in Buddhist Studies, no. 20

Faith and Devotion in Theravāda Buddhism

V.V.S. Saibaba

with a Foreword by
Sanghasen Singh

D.K. Printworld (P) Ltd.
New Delhi

Cataloging in Publication Data — DK
[Courtesy: D.K. Agencies (P) Ltd. <docinfo@dkagencies.com>]

Saibaba, V.V.S., 1947-
Faith and devotion in Theravāda Buddhism / V.V.S. Saibaba ; with a foreword by Sanghasen Singh.
xxix, 231 p. 23 cm. — (Emerging perceptions in Buddhist studies ; no. 20)
Includes bibliographical references (p.)
Includes index.
ISBN 8124603294

1. Faith (Buddhism). 2. Devotion (Buddhism). 3. Theravāda Buddhism. I. Title. II. Series: Emerging perceptions in Buddhist studies ; no. 20.

DDC 294.391 21

ISBN 81-246-0329-4
First published in India 2005

Published and printed by:
D.K. Printworld (P) Ltd.
Regd. office : *'Sri Kunj'*, F-52, Bali Nagar
Ramesh Nagar Metro Station
New Delhi - 110 015
Phones : (011) 2545-3975; 2546-6019; *Fax* : (011) 2546-5926
E-mail: dkprintworld@vsnl.net
Web : www.dkprintworld.com

Dedicated

with profound respect, loving admiration

and sincere gratitude to

My

Kalyanamitra

Padmavibhushan ***Acharya K. Satchidananda Murty***

Foreword

THE latest work of Professor Saibaba entitled *"Faith and Devotion in Theravāda Buddhism"* is an addition to his already well-acknowledged and well-recognised scholarship. It is a matter of rare opportunity for a student of Buddhological Sciences like me to express views on the work. Dr. Saibaba brilliant work is based upon his in-depth study of all available texual materials on early Theravāda Buddhism. The work has a singular distinction in providing a study on Faith and Devotion as depicted in the texts of early Buddhism. The chapters have been suitably titled as follows: Theravāda Conception of Gods and God; The Buddha in Theravāda Literature; and Saddhā and Bhatti in Theravāda Buddhism. The author has suitably added a preface in the beginning and an epilogue at the end.

The "Buddha" is the basic concept of Buddhism. Its importance can be realized in the fact that its position in the whole set of the teachings of the Buddha is unique and the uppermost. It is the first and the foremost. The other two concepts reaching the neighbourhood of the Buddha concept are the ones enumerated in the list of the Three Refuges — the Buddha, the Dhamma and the Saṁgha. There is no doubt in the fact that the position of the Dhamma and the Saṁgha were suitably raised in due course of time. But none could overstep, nor surpass the first one. Had it been so, the order of the list would have been altered, say, Dhamma, Saṁgha, Buddha or Saṁgha, Dhamma, Buddha or other combinations that arise therefrom. But it was not done; neither during the life time of the Buddha, nor thereafter. Whenever necessities arose the other two concepts were catapulted to the near neighbourhood of the Buddha concept, but never to shadow it. The efforts to equalize the position of the Dhamma with the Buddha were done by the Buddha Himself, but that was done in order to emphasize and highlight the position of the Dhamma and not to belittle the position of the Buddha concept in any way. The Buddha is reported to have said in one context that one who sees Him, in fact, sees the Dhamma (Law) and conversely one who sees the Dhamma, in fact, sees the Buddha. Secondly at the time of His Great Demise, when He was to breathe his last and had to settle the question of succession in the Order (*Saṁgha*) once for all, he did it with the help of the position of the Dhamma. He asked his disciples to treat the Dhamma as their Teacher (*Satthā*, Skt. *Śāstā*) when the Buddha was no more with them.

The second question that entails discussion on concepts like deities, god, heaven, hell and so on demand solution of the problem of stratification of the words of the Buddha and His immediate disciples as found compiled in the texts of the Tipiṭaka. The Tipiṭaka is a vast collection of the words of the Buddha, His immediate disciples and contemporaries and so on, which are found in different texts in a matter-of-fact, ad-hoc and go-ahead-manner, though the best of minds in the Order (*Saṁgha*) right from the period when the Buddha breathed His last to the period when the elders (Theras) assembled at the Kukuṭārāma (near Patna today) and gave the final shape, not only to the words of the Master, but also to the order and manner in which they were set forth for the final redaction. In view of this fact, it will be preposterous for any scholar worth the name to ascribe every word and concept as enshrined in Tipiṭaka to the Buddha. The ideas grew in succession when the historical processes took their normal course. It is a known fact that the ideas do not originate nor grow in a vacuum. First social conditions take root and expand, and thereafter and simultaneously as well ideas germinate and grow, as the social conditions too need ideas for their origin and sustenance. Thus mutual dependence is needed, but to say that the ideas originate and arise all of a sudden, without necessary and relevant conditions, is to deny the truth altogether. Thus the origin and growth of the concepts as referred to, must have originated in the society for specific needs. It is not essential to be able to explain all the causes and conditions that might have operated to cause to originate those concepts, but the causes and conditions did operate without even the slightest knowledge and awareness of any human agency whatsoever. To say so does not mean that everything in this regard was taking place with the knowledge and active participation of any other-worldly or divine agency, which gets named and specified under similar circumstances by other religious systems. Things were taking place in their normal course and continue to take place today and shall do so till the forces that arouse them do exist.

The Buddha was a very practical and pragmatic person. He knew fully well that He had to operate within a framework, which the society had provided to Him. He succeeded in making the full use of all the components available to Him around His own self. The concepts of gods, goddesses including that of God had to be used suitably and purposefully, though He was fully conscious of their non-substantiality and futility. The Buddha made them (those concepts) subservient to His cause knowing fully well that they had no role to play except that they gave some sort of moral support to those who did believe in their existence and active participation. One parallel may be drawn with the situation, which the great Urdu poet Mirza Ghalib had to face in the society he lived in. When the great rewards of prayer were being cited to him to convince him to do five timely and daily prayers to the All Mighty (Allāh), so that on the Day of Judgement he would be rewarded with the passage to the heavenly world (*jannat*), he burst into an expression and said:

> *yon to mālūm hai mujhe jannat kī haqiqat, lekin,*
> *dil ko bahalāne ko gālib ye khayāl acchā hai.*

> [Though I know fully well the truth behind the concept of heaven, Galib says, it is really a good idea to amuse one's mind.]

The philosophies during the times of the Buddha were broadly divided into two sections — the Sassatavāda (Skt. Śāśvata-vāda, Eternalism) and the Ucchedavāda (Annihilationism). The Buddha, it appears, faced a dilemma, which of the two He should opt for. If He associates Himself with the former, He would fall in the company of the eternalists probably headed by the Upaniṣadic seers and would go in for a permanent, unchanging and eternal *attā* (Skt. *ātman*, soul, self) and *loka* (world) and thus would block the path for any improvement in the lot of individuals as any amount of moral activities would have no effect on the status of the already well-framed and well-fixed shape and nature of the *attā*, while, on the other hand, if He decided to opt for the latter, He would be clubbed with those who vehemently deny the existence of *attā* as an entity and hence for them *attā* and body are not only identical, but co-terminus as well, and consequently life hereafter has no meaning for them, as it does not exist at all. In that event, what would be the fate of the monkhood life, if it was to end with the end of the body. The big question, as He gave call to the youth to leave their homes and hearths and join Him in His mission as homeless mendicants, that demanded a big answer from the Master was: why should the young men in the prime of their youth leave their homes and hearths, a life of comforts and happiness and lead the life of beggardom?

The Buddha did reject both and sought a middle course between the two. While rejecting a permanent, unchanging and eternal *attā,* He did not close the door of the life hereafter (heaven/hell) for His disciples and co-believers, but called it inferior to the final goal of *nibbāna,* the *sumum bonum* of life, which brings a permanent solution for all times to come. The fate of the gods too was viewed and preached by Him in the same framework as the one for the men. So the gods and goddesses on the one hand and the evil spirits on the other did receive no concession from the Buddha. Instead he restricted the category of the humankind to be blessed with the birth of a penultimate Buddha and debarred the gods and others from that greatest and the rarest reward. Consequently, the gods in the Buddhist texts are shown requesting the Buddha that He be pleased to take birth among men of His own choice.

The concept of God (Īssara/Mahābrahmā) too is related with the same two sections of the ancient philosophies. That which originates has to decay, (*yaṇ kiṁci samudaya-dhammaṁ sabbaṁ taṁ nirodha-dhammaṁ ti*) is one of the messages of the Buddha. The Buddha finds no exception to this rule. The God too finds place in the same category, neither lower, nor higher. In the Theory of Paticcasamuppāda or Dependent Origination too there is no scope for any supernatural power to step in, nor has it any role to play. Thus the Buddha made the so-called God job-less and purpose-less and thus place-less and essence-less altogether.

Professor Saibaba has discussed these and other related concepts in detail. I appreciate the details given by him and the discussions elaborated upon, though I do not see eye to eye with him on certain points. But on the whole the work done by Professor Saibaba is well-done and shall get acclaim from the scholars in India and abroad. Since it is a work of a very high order, I feel delighted in recommending it to the reading community for the enrichment of their knowledge on the one hand and for the clarity of their thoughts on the other. It may be further noted here that the justification for the full-throated recommendation is not based upon any subjective judgment, but lies in the fact that Professor Saibaba's present work provides an exposition of the words of the Buddha which have been acclaimed down the ages to be the ones which are devoid of all sorts of mental depravities and evilness. It will be worthwhile in this regard to quote a verse of Ācārya Dharmottara, the celebrated author of the *Nyāyabindu Ṭikā*, who, while describing the complex nature of the universe (*jagat*) hails the Buddha to be its Victor and at the same time the Enemy of all non-moral *dharma*s (elements) like *rāga* (attachment), *dveṣa* (avarice) and *moha* (ignorance, infetuation). The *śloka* (verse) under reference runs as under:

> *jayanti jāti-vyasana-prabandha-prasūti-hetor jagato vijetuḥ* ।
> *Rāgādhyarāteḥ sugatasya vāco manas-tamas-tānavam ādadhānāḥ* ॥

Date 11/06/2005 **Sanghasen Singh**
199 Vaishali Enclave
Pitam Pura, Delhi - 110 088

Preface

THIS is an analytical study of faith, devotion and worship in the Theravāda School of Buddhism. It attempts to analyse and elucidate these concepts and deals with their objects, viz., gods in general and the Buddha in particular, their nature, attributes and functions. Although on the one hand Theravāda Buddhism has the authentic tradition of philosophical and doctrinal discourses, yet it should not be misunderstood as a mere academic school since it is a tradition in which monks and laity live the actual lives of various religious practices and struggle to realize the Buddhist ethical ideals. Thus, faith and devotion underlie the whole Buddhist Tradition.

The book which is divided into three chapters respectively deals with the Theravāda conception of (i) Deities and supernatural, (ii) the exalted personality of the Buddha, and (iii) the concept of '*saddhā*' and '*bhatti*.' Of these, Chapter One examines the conception of "the deities" and "the supernatural" in the Pāli canon. It attempts to elucidate the Theravāda attitude towards the *deva*s of higher and lower status with reference to their attributes, knowledge, powers and functions. It further discusses the role of these deities as the objects of contemplation (*devānussati*) and the benefits that can be derived from. It further delineates the fervent devotional attitude of Buddhist deities towards the Three Refuges (*tisaraṇa*). It also makes a comparative study of some Vedic and Brāhmaṇical gods with Buddhist deities.

In contrast to the polytheistic gods of pre-Buddhistic Indian religion, the deities in Pāli canonical texts of Theravāda

School are distinguished as much inferior to the Buddha as well as other *arhants* in respect of their virtues, knowledge, and power. In view of their absolute dependence on the Buddha as the learners of *dharma* and seekers of salvation, the Buddhist deities are made subservient to the Buddha — who attained the highest perfect enlightenment (*sambodhi*). They are the foremost beings who recognize his supremacy, admire and pay their highest reverence and devotion. Thus, they are portrayed as promulgators and heralders of the Buddhist faith and devotion.

It endeavours to point out how as a non-theistic religion Theravāda rejects all forms of theism and how its basic tenets, viz., noble truth of suffering, the doctrines of *aniccā, anatta, paticcasamuppāda,* the cyclic theory of universe, and the *summum bonum* of *nibbāna* are inconsistent and incompatible with the hypothesis of an Absolute, Omniscient, Omnipresent and Omnipotent Creator God. The important aspect of Buddhist conception of the ultimate and supernatural is suggested indirectly in the Pāli canon of Theravāda Buddhism by its doctrine of *nibbāna,* by its non-denial of Upaniṣadic *Brahman* and by the Buddha's silence on metaphysical issues. These imply the fact that Lord Buddha had a clear conception of the "Transcendental reality" which he did not positively assert.

Chapter Two throws light on the exalted personality, supernormal and supramundane character of the Buddha and how he is portrayed in the Pāli canonical and post-canonical literature as super-eminent over all the sentient beings, the rest of all mankind, all the Buddhist deities, saints of different gradations of spiritual eminence including those of *arhant* and *pratyekabuddha* by virtue of his special attributes, knowledge, powers and functions. The Buddha's pre-eminence is further revealed by his self-proclamation, by the conception of the members of the Buddhist Order and by the several numinous epithets attributed to him.

In the Theravāda Pāli canonical, post-canonical and commentarial literature there is a substantial doctrinal basis for the idealization and spiritualization of the Buddha, in his identity with truth (*dhamma*), in his transcending the cosmic law (*kamma*), in his personification of enlightenment (*nibbāna*) and finally in his conception of prototype of the Transcendental absolute. Consequently, similar to non-Theravādins such as Mahāsāṁghikas and its sub-sects, Theravādins too had to allow in their religio-philosophical framework docetic and Buddhological speculations. All this ultimately led towards the Transcendental conception of the Buddha who became an object of highest reverence, adoration, irreversible faith (*saddhā*) and devotion (*bhatti*).

Chapter Three discusses the origin, nature and scope of faith and devotion for the Buddha in Theravāda Pāli canonical, and post-canonical literature thereby elucidating how and why Buddha has been regarded as the object of Faith and Devotion; how he came to be regarded as the object of absolute confidence (*saddhā*), as an object of recollection and contemplation (*buddhānussati*) and as an object of fervent devotion (*bhatti*) and worship (*pūjā*).

In Theravāda Pāli canon, the Buddha is conceived as an object of absolute confidence (*saddhā*), primarily in his role of Teacher of gods and men (*sattha deva-manussanam*) and also as the *ācāriya* — he was the first religious guardian of the Buddhist Order as well as the centre of the entire monastic life. The Buddha is also regarded as an object of meditation and contemplation. Recollection of the Buddha (*buddhānussati*) is the basic constituent of the Buddhist devotion. The Buddha plays a significant role among the Three Refuges (*tisaraṇa*), as the guide' and the "revealer of the truth" (*dhamma*) and the founder-father of the Buddhist Order (*saṁgha*). Although according to Pāli canon, the Buddha alone can serve as the true refuge,' as the Compassionate and Omniscient Teacher, nevertheless, his saviour role is restricted in the framework of Buddhist doctrines. Yet in Theravāda Buddhism the Buddha is conceived both as mundane and supramundane ideal.

As *saddhā* in the Buddha is the merit-producing act, it serves as the means to overcome fetters, to attain heavenly birth and to attain ecstasy and concentration and as the basic ingredient and foundation of the whole Buddhist ethics, it ultimately leads an aspirant to the realization of the higher truth. Further, *saddhā* in the sense of *pasāda* (*pasāda-saddhā*) is stated as the indirect means for the attainment of *nibbāna*. The rise of the divine conception of the Buddha is coupled with the transformation of Buddhist conception of *saddhā* into *bhatti* which we find in the later Pāli canonical works, wherein the uniformity in the meaning of *saddhā* is lacking. It is also probable that with the growing number of laity *saddhā* had begun to be valued as *bhatti*. This is plausible mainly because the large number of Buddhist laity belong to different religious sects prior to their entering the Buddhist Order. Probably their sectarian notions of faith and devotion have been insinuated into Buddhism in practice. It should be noted that all the modes of paying devotion and worship to the Buddha and other objects of faith are non-Buddhistic reverential gestures. The Buddha did not prescribe any mode of devotion and worship for the Buddhist laity as there was no necessity of emotional form of devotion from his doctrinal standpoint. However, he had approved their adopted modes of paying homage and worship. The Buddha was so liberal that he did not interfere with the religious practices of Buddhist laity. He just preached the *dhamma* and left it for their understanding. His non-interference led them to freely adopt ritualism and ceremonialism in their personal lives. It is an uncontroversial fact that the Buddhist order could not have survived till this day without the support of the Buddhist lay followers. It is also possible that laity of other religious sects who later became the adherents of Buddhism might have misinterpreted the specific and special connotation of the Buddhist concept of *saddhā*.

The Pāli word *bhatti* is differently meant as 'devotion' and also "attachment and fondness" in the *Khuddaka Nikāya* works of the Pāli canon, viz., the *Theragāthā*, the *Jātakas*, the *Mahāniddesa* and in the works of the *Abhidhamma Piṭaka*. Buddha-*bhatti* is emphasized in the later Pāli canonical works like the *Jātaka*s and the *Thera-Therīgāthā*. The Buddhist vows in the *Therīgāthā* have great resemblance to the prayers of theistic religions. Later Pāli canonical works like the *Udāna*, the *Buddha-vaṁsa*, the *Apadāna* and the *Vimānavatthu* refer to loving devotion towards the Buddha.

By the age of later Pāli canonical works and Pāli commentaries Buddhist conception of *saddhā* had become the seed-bed of *bhatti*. The *Saṁyutta*, the *Aṅguttara* and the *Khuddaka Nikāyas* of the Pāli canon refer to the different derivatives of the word *pūjā* such as *pūjita*, *pūjanīya*. *Buddha-pūjā* which was initially conceived as a "mental act," came to mean as a "ritual performance" in the works like the *Dhammapada* when it was associated with Buddhist offerings and is understood as *stūpa* and relic worship in the works like the *Vimānavatthu* and the *Apadāna* of the *Khuddaka Nikāya*. The *Mahānidessa* of this collection used the Buddha's epithet "Bhagavā" in the sense of honoured and worshipped.

The *Majjhima*, the *Saṁyutta* and the *Aṅguttara Nikāyas* record that learned brāhmaṇas of orthodox type such as Jānussoni, Brahmāyu, Pokkarasādi, kings like Bimbisāra of Magadha and Pasenadi of Kosala expressed their *bhatti*, showed their profound humility and paid affectionate obeisance by prostrating with their heads and kissed the feet of the Buddha. The Buddha did neither criticize nor reject such homage paid by them.

According to Ācārya Buddhaghoṣa's *Puggala Pannati* commentary *saddhā* could be developed into *bhakti*, by constant practice. The *Dīgha Nikāya* commentary, the *Visuddhimagga* and also its commentary, viz., the *Paramatthamañjūṣā* of Ācārya Dhammapāla interpreted the word "Bhagavā" as *bhattavā* (worshipful or adored and possessor of devotees respectively). All this leads us to conclude that in Theravāda Buddhist perspective the Buddha is *bhagavā*, the Blessed Lord and embodiment of Great compassion. Hence, modern scholars like Prof. B.M. Barua, Trever Ling and Jack Donald Van Horn in their writings contend that Buddhism had been regarded as a form of Bhagavatism since the time of Indian Emperor Aśoka.

Visakhapatnam
23-05-2005

V.V.S. Saibaba
Professor
Dept. of Philosophy & Religious Science
Andhra University

Contents

Foreword — Sanghasen Singh vii

Preface xiii

Acknowledgements xxv

Abbreviations xxvii

1. Theravāda Conception of Gods and God 1

Meaning of the Word Deva 1

Buddha's Attitude on the Existence of Devas, their Place in his Doctrine 3

Buddha's Utterances (Buddha Vacana) on the Existence of "Devas" 3 3

Buddha's Conception of "Devas" and their Place in his Doctrine 6

Various Means to Attain Devahood 8

General Characteristics of Deva in Theravāda Buddhist Perspective 10

Devotional Attitude of the Devas of Higher and Lower Status 15 15

Devas of Higher Status 15

The Attributes of the Devas 16

The Knowledge of the Devas 19

The Powers of the Devas 23

The Functions and the Role of the Devas 25

The Devotional Attitude of the Devas of Higher Status Towards the Buddha and His Order 28

Devas of Lower Status 32

The Nature and Attributes of the Devas 33
The Knowledge and Powers of Devas 34
The Functions and Role of Devas of Lower 35
Māra 37
Recollection and Contemplation on Devas (Devānussati) 38
The Object of Recollection of Devas 39
Method of Recollection of Devas 40
Fruits of Recollection and Contemplation of Devas 40
A Comparative Study of Some Buddhist Devas Vedic and Brāhmaṇical Gods 42
Buddhist Devas as Distinguished from Vedic Gods 42
Comparison between Buddhist Devas of Higher Status and Vedic Gods 43
Vedic and Buddhist Brahmā 43
Vedic Indra and Buddhist Sakka 44
Vedic and Buddhist Yama 45
The Other Popular Gods 45
Comparison between Buddhist Devas of Lower Status and Vedic Gods 46
The Buddhist Conception of Creator God, the Absolute and the Supernatural 46
Buddha's teaching on the Belief of Creator God 47
How Theravāda Buddhism is Non-theistic 49
Theravāda Buddhist Criticism of Theism 51
Refutation of God as First Cause 51
Refutation of God as "Being" and "Force" 53
Refutation of God as Eternal, Absolute and Ultimate Reality 54
Refutation of God as Omniscient and Omnipresent 56
Refutation of God as Personal and Impersonal 56
Refutation of God as Active Agent 57
Refutation of God as Creator 58

The Puppet Argument 60
The Ontological Argument 60
The Cosmological Argument 60
The Argument from Design 60
The Argument from Utility/Fruit Test 60
The Theistic God is Indistinguishable 61
The Conception of God is Unintelligible 62
The Conception of God is Inexplicable 62
Refutation of God as Sustainer and Destroyer 62
Refutation of God as Benevolent 64
Doctrinal Points which are Inconsistent and Incompatible with the Conception of Creator God or the Absolute 66
Doctrine of Aniccā (Impermanence) 66
Doctrine of Anattā (Not-self or unsubstantiality) 67
Doctrine of Paṭiccasamuppāda (Dependent Origination) 67
Doctrine of Kamma 68
Doctrine of Nibbāna 68
The Cyclic theory of Evolution 68
The Chief Purpose of Buddha's Teaching 70

2. The Buddha in the Theravāda Literature 73
Meaning of the word 'Buddha' 73
The Exalted Personality of the Buddha 74
The Supernormal Knowledge of the Buddha 76
The Omniscience of the Buddha 77
Five Eyes (Pañca-Cakkhūni) 79
Special Knowledge 81
Ten Kinds of Knowledge 81
Three-fold Knowledge (Tevijjā) 83
Buddha's Knowledge of the Past 84
Buddha's Knowledge of Heavens and Hells 84
Buddha's Knowledge of Others' Mental and Spiritual Attainments 85
Buddha's Great Compassion 86

The Supernormal Powers of the Buddha 87

Powers of Intelligence (Ñāṇabala) 89

Power of understanding other's Mental Reflexions 90

Buddha s Physical Strength and Faculty of Movement 91

Clairvoyant Powers 91

Prophetic Powers 92

Miraculous Powers 93

Powers to Walk on Water and Travel by Air 95

Power to Visit Deva Realms 96

Power to Appear and Disappear 96

Power of Freedom from Environmental Disturbances 96

Power to Overcome Suffering, Sickness and Death 96

Power to Conquer the Wicked, Superhuman, Human and Sub-human Beings 97

Saviour Powers 98

Powers of Healing and Wish-fulfilling 98

Buddha's Special Powers 99

The Functions of the Buddha 101

The Supremacy of the Buddha 102

Buddha's Supremacy, Over all other Human Beings 102

Buddha's Supremacy Over Deities 103

Buddha's Supremacy Over all Other Holy Persons 104

Buddha as Distinguished from a Paccekabuddha 104

Buddha as Distinguished from an Arhant 105

Buddha as Distinguished from the Members of the Order in General 107

Gautama Buddha's Supremacy Over other Buddhas 108

The Pre-eminence and the Divinity of the Buddha 109

Buddha's Self-assertion about his Pre-eminence 109
Buddha Regarded as Pre-eminent by Others 111
Buddha's Pre-eminent Place in the Order 112
The Buddha's Epithets 113
Buddha as Superman 116
The Divinity of the Buddha 117
The Transcendence of the Buddha 118
Theravāda and Docetism 123
Buddhology 123
Unity in the Plurality of Buddhas 124
The Identity of Buddha and Dhamma 125
The Identity of Buddha and Nibbāna 127
The Buddha and Tathāgata 129
The Buddha and Absolute Truth 130
The Buddha as Immeasurable, Unthinkable and Infinite 130

3. Saddhā and Bhatti in Theravāda Buddhism 133

Part A - Saddhā

The Meaning and Scope of Saddhā 133
Types of Saddhā 136
Aveccappasāda 138
Saddhā — its Scope and Limitations 140
Faith in the Buddha as the Satthā 144
Faith in Buddha as Compassionate Protector 147
Saddhā in the Ti-Saraṇa (Three Refuges) 148
The Origin of "Ti-saraṇa" and its Meaning 149
The Meaning of the word "Buddha" in "Ti-saraṇa" 150
The Place of the Buddha in the Ti-saraṇa 151
Advantages of Taking Refuge in the Buddha 154
Means of Cultivation of Saddhā 155
Cultivation of Saddhā by means of Buddhānussati 155
Benefits Derived from The Practice of Buddhānussati 157

Advantages of Cultivation of Saddhā 159
Disadvantages of Lack of Saddhā 163
Disadvantages of Disrespect, Disregard, Irreverence and harming the Buddha 165
Harming the Buddha and its Retribution 166

Part B - Bhatti

Origins and Meaning of Bhatti in the Pāli Canon 167
Pāli terms used in the Canon for Constituents of Devotion 169
Nature and Scope of "Bhatti" 169
Objectives of Buddha-Bhakti 170
Buddha as Bhagavā 172
Devotional Attitude of Laity and Monks in the Pāli Canon 174
Acts of Devotion 179
Buddha-Pūjā 179
Buddha-accanā 181
Buddha-patthanā 185
Buddha — thava and Thuti 186
Buddha as object of Devotion 187
after His Parinibbāna 187
Advantages of Devotion 188
Fruits of Devotion of Laity 190
Disadvantages of Lack of Devotion 191

Epilogue **193**

Bibliography **203**

Index of Buddhist Works **217**

Index of Buddhist Words and Proper Names **223**

Acknowledgements

I AM deeply grateful to my most revered teacher Padmavibhushan Professor K. Satchidananda Murty, formerly Vice-Chairman, UGC, Govt. of India and Professor in the Department of Philosophy, Andhra University whose profound scholarly lectures delivered during 1972-73 and my PhD. project, completed was successfully under his competent supervision, forms the basis of this book. Professor Murty has also inspired me to make an intensive study of the Pāli Canonical and Post-Canonical works of Theravāda Buddhism dealt in this work.

Professor Sanghasen Singh formerly Professor and Head of the department of Buddhist Studies, University of Delhi has laid me under a debt of obligation by specially writing a valuable foreword containing many important points connected with the theme of this book. I deem it obligatory on my part to claim my indebtedness to my sister Dr. V. Vizialakshmi, Associate Professor and Head, Department of Hindi, Pondicherry University for her constant encouragement; my wife Smt. Jaya, my two sons Srinivasa Vijayaditya Satchidananda Murty and Vijaya Manjusri Maitreya for their enthusiastic push and keen interest to bring this publication into light. I especially appreciate Dr. K. Ramesh Babu, Yoga Instructor, Extension Wing, Institute for Yoga and Consciousness, Dr. P. Kishore Kumar, Department of Philosophy, Andhra University for all their assistance, rendered in processing the typescript.

I would be failing in my duty, if I don't express my grateful thanks to Shri Susheel K. Mittal of D.K. Printworld (P) Ltd., New Delhi for his continued efforts in expediting the printing and publication of this work.

Visakhapatnam
23-05-2005

V.V.S. Saibaba
Professor
Dept. of Philosophy & Religious Science
Andhra University

Abbreviations

AKK	:	*Abhidharmakoṣa Kārikā*
AN	:	*Aṅguttara Nikāya*
B	:	*The Buddhist*
BB	:	*The British Buddhist*
BE	:	*Buddhism in England*
BIR	:	*Buddhism an Illustrated Review*
BPS	:	*Buddhist Pub. Society*
BR	:	*The Buddhist Review*
BVA	:	*Buddhavaṁsa Aṭṭhakathā*
Cn	:	*Cullaniddesa*
DhS	:	*Dhamma Sangani*
DN	:	*Dīgha Nikāya*
DNA	:	*Dīgha Nikāya Aṭṭhakathā*
DP	:	*Dhammapada*
DS	:	*Devata Saṁyutta*
DPA	:	*Dhammapada Aṭṭhakathā*
DPL	:	*A Dictionary of the Pāli Language*
EB	:	*The Eastern Buddhist*
Ency Bsm	:	*Encyclopaedia of Buddhism*
EPD	:	English Pāli Dictionary.
ERE	:	*Encyclopaedia of Religion and Ethics*
GS	:	*Gradual Sayings*

HJ	:	*The Hibbert Journal*
IPA	:	*Indian Philosophical Annual*
IPC	:	*Indian Philosophical Congress*
IT	:	*Itivuttaka*
J	:	*The Jātaka*
JBORS	:	*The Journal of the Bihar and Orissa Research Society*
JDL	:	*Journal of the Department of Letters*
JRAS (GB & IR)	:	*The Journal of the Royal Asiatic Society of Great Britain and Ireland*
KP	:	*Khuddakapāṭha*
KS	:	*The Book of Kindered Sayings*
KV	:	*Kathāvatthu*
KVPA	:	*Kathāvatthuppakaraṇa Aṭṭhakathā*
MA	:	*Mahāniddesa Aṭṭhakathā*
MB	:	*The Mahā Bodhi*
Mn	:	*Mahāniddesa*
MLS	:	*Middle Length Sayings*
MN	:	*Majjhima Nikāya*
MNA	:	*Majjhima Nikāya Aṭṭhakathā*
MP	:	*Milindapañha*
PA	:	*Paramattha Jotikā*
PB	:	*Prabuddha Bhārata*
PDS	:	*Petakopadesa*
PP	:	*Puggala Pannati*
PSM	:	*Patisambhidamagga*
PSMA	:	*Patisambhidamagga Aṭṭhakathā*
PTS	:	Pali Text Society
SBE	:	Sacred Books of the East

Sn	:	*Sutta Nipāta*
SnA	:	*Sutta Nipāta Aṭṭhakathā*
SN	:	*Saṁyutta Nikāya*
SNA	:	*Saṁyutta Nikāya Aṭṭhakathā*
ThA	:	*Theragāthā Aṭṭhakathā*
U	:	*Udāna*
UA	:	*Udāna Aṭṭhakathā*
UCR	:	*University of Ceylon Review*
VA	:	*Vibhaṅga Aṭṭhakathā*
VM	:	*Visuddhi Magga*
VV	:	*Vimānavatthu*
VVA	:	*Vimānavatthu Aṭṭhakathā*
WB	:	*World Buddhism*
YS	:	*Yakkha Saṁyutta*

1

Theravāda Conception of Gods and God

Meaning of the Word Deva

ETYMOLOGICALLY the Pāli word *deva* (god) appears to have been derived from the root *div* which is meant as "playing, sporting or amusing oneself."[1] The word is related to Latin word *deus*.[2] The word *deva* literally means "a shining or radiant one"; a "deity" or "celestial being" who is regarded as "trans-human"[3] in Pāli Buddhist literature. But due to its different connotation in Pāli canon, the word *deva* is not equivalent to the English term "god,"[4] chiefly because, Pāli *deva* does not give the sense of either an absolute supernatural being transcending space-time, who is omniscient, omnipresent and omnipotent, or of a "Creator" or "First cause" of the universe. Further the word

1. Rhys Davids and Stede (ed.), *Pāli-English Dictionary* (hereafter abbreviated as *PTS Dictionary*), p. 329a, (s.v.) *Deva*; According to the Khuddakapāṭha Commentary on the word *deva*, the *devas* play with the five strands of sensual desires (*MN*, Sutta XIII) or they glitter with their splendour, (see, Ñāṇamoli (tr.) *The Illustrator of Ultimate Meaning* (*Paramatta Jotika*, Part I) Commentary on the Minor Readings by Bhadantacariya Buddhaghoṣa, p. 133.
2. Brandon (ed.), *A Dictionary of Comparative Religion*, p. 233b; see also, Nyāṇātiloka (ed.), *Buddhist Dictionary*, p. 45.
3. *PTS Dictionary*, p. 329a.
4. C.A.F. Rhys Davids, "Was Original Buddhism Atheistic," *The Hibbert Journal*, vol. XXXVII, October 1938-July 1939, pp. 118-19.

devā (pl. of the word *deva*) cannot be rendered as gods since they are neither eternal nor immortal. The English word "God" which is primarily defined variously as "The Supreme Being, the creator and ruler of the universe" or a "male deity presiding over some portion of worldly affairs;"[5] or a "Superhuman being worshipped as having power over nature and human fortunes"[6] differs in meaning from the word *deva*, since in the vocabulary of Pāli language, distinct linguistic forms, viz., *nimmātu*; *vidhātū*; *Issara* (masculine) denote the English word "Creator,"[7] but not *deva*. Hence renowned Pāli scholars like R.C. Childers,[8] T.W. Rhys Davids, Stede,[9] and Ven. Buddhadatta Thera,[10] distinguished the word *Issara* from *deva* holding that the former's meaning is only limited to "Lord, ruler, chief, king, creative deity," etc. Strictly speaking the Pāli *deva* cannot be translated as "divine being," for in Buddhist canonical texts the word "divine" is being used as an "expression of perfection."[11] In other words, the meaning of the word "divine" changed its pre-Buddhistic meaning in the perspective of Buddhist cosmology and ethics.[12] *Abhidhānappadīpikā*, the first Pāli lexicon probably composed in thirteenth century AD gives

5. Stuart Berg Flexner (ed.), *The Random House Dictionary of the English Language*, p. 565a.
6. H.W. Fowler & F.G. Fowler (eds.), *The Concise Oxford Dictionary of Current English*, pp. 516-17.
7. Buddhadatta (ed.), *English-Pāli Dictionary* (hereafter abbreviated as *EPD*), p. 115a.
8. Childers (ed.), *A Dictionary of the Pāli Language* (hereafter abbreviated as *DPL*), p. 160b.
9. *P.T.S. Dictionary*, p. 123b.
10. *Supra*, 7.
11. In Early Buddhism the word "divine" neither refers to *deva* nor a Brahmā; See, H.G.A. Van Zeyst, "Atheism," *Encyclopaedia of Buddhism* (*Ency Bsm*), vol. II, Fasc. 2, p. 305b.
12. *Devadhamma Jātaka*; also see *World Fellowship of Buddhists Review*, vol. XII, no. 5 (September-October 1975), p. 22.

sura, amara and *tidasa* as the masculine forms of *deva* and *devatā* and *devakanna* as its feminine forms.[13]

While R.C. Childers and T.W. Rhys Davids, and Nyānatiloka maintain that the word *deva* is collectively applied to all the inhabitants of twenty-six heavenly worlds of the *devas* (*devā*) of sense-desire sphere, the Fine-material sphere and Immaterial sphere, the latter two are of the opinion[14] that the world also includes all *devatās* (f. *deva*) who comprise all deities (i.e., subordinate deities and demon spirits), who are worshipped or to whom gifts are offerings are given.

Buddha's attitude on the existence of Devas, their place in his Doctrine and the means to attains the State of Devahood

BUDDHA'S UTTERANCES (BUDDHA VACANA) ON THE EXISTENCE OF "DEVAS"

There are only two *Suttas*, i.e., (1) *Kaṇṇakatthala Sutta* (*MN*, XC) and (2) *Saṅgārava Sutta* (*MN*, C) where Buddha has been directly questioned about the existence of *devas*. In both these *Suttas*, the Buddha did not respond by direct assertions, but his answers, suggest that he agreed upon the existence of Buddhist conception of the *devas* only.

In the *Kaṇṇakatthala Sutta* in the dialogue between king Pasenadi of Kośala and the Buddha when the king asked, "Sir, are there *devas*?" According to the commentary,[15] Buddha's counter question "Why do you Sir, ask thus . . ."[16] does show neither his assertion nor a denial on the existence of gods. When the king again interrogated, "Be it so, Sir, do these

---

13. See, "Abhidhānappadīpikā, 14, lines 11 and 12," in Dr. B.C. Jain (ed.), *Pāli Kośa Sangaho*, p. 4.
14. Childers, *DPL*, p. 115b; *P.T.S. Dictionary*, p. 329 a and p. 330a.
15. *Majjhima Nikāya Aṭṭhakathā* (*MA*), III.359f.
16. *MN*, II.130; *Middle Length Sayings* (hereafter abbreviated as *MLS*), II.311.

devas come to be reborn here (in this world) or do they not?"[17] Buddha in his reply distinguishing *devas* who are malevolent from benevolent *devas* said that the former will be reborn in the world and the latter will not reborn here but will be reborn in happier realms. This makes it clear that Buddhist conception of *devas* differs from the Vedic conception of gods. In this *sutta* when the king's minister Viḍuḍabha inquired the Buddha, "Whether such malevolent *devas* can banish or drive away the non-malevolent deities?"[18] Ānanda intervenes and instead of the Buddha answers the question whose purport is to point out the ethical distinction between the benevolent and malevolent *devas* and to emphasize the supremacy of the former who are morally perfect over the latter who are morally imperfect. In this *sutta* lastly king Pasenadi makes a vain attempt to know about the existence of *devas* by means of another question, "Rev. Sir, is there a Brahma?" and Buddha similarly avoided the question, by answering in the same way.

In the *Saṅgārava Sutta*, when the brāhmaṇa youth Saṅgārava questioned the Buddha on the existence of *devas*,[19] the Buddha gave a puzzling reply[20] which is variously translated[21] into English, viz.,

(i) "In the above context, Bhāradvajā, I have found that there are gods."
(ii) "I know on good grounds . . . that there are gods."
(iii) "I knew offhand there are gods."

Prof. Jayatilleke while interpreting the significance of this assertion of Buddha writes that

17. *MN*, II.130; *MLS*, II.312.

18. *Ibid*.

19. *MN*, II.212.

20. *MN*, II.212: *thānaso me taṁ bhāradvāja, viditaṁ yadidaṁ atthi devā ti.*

21. M.M.J. Marasinghe, *Gods in Early Buddhism*, pp. 127-28; K.N. Jayatilleke, *Facets of Buddhist Thought*, p. 12; Lord Chalmers (tr.), *Further Dialogues of the Buddha*, vol. II, p. 122.

> Buddha holds that there are devas not because of a popular or traditional belief, which he took for granted, but because he was personally convinced of their existence on good grounds.[22]

According to Marasinghe, in the above assertion, Buddha has accepted the existence of only Buddhist "gods" for the context of the assertion precedes, the account of an anxiety of Buddhist gods over the weak physical condition of Gautama in his pre-enlightenment period.[23]

Bhikkhu Nāṇajīvako commenting on the *sutta* holds[24] that the question of Saṅgārava on the existence of *deva*s was a wrongly fromulated one which arose from the epistemological distinction connected with the perfection of knowledge calimed by three types of teachers of religious life, explained by the Buddha at the beginning of *Saṅgārava Sutta*. According to Nāṇajīvako, of the three types of teachers, the first two types, i.e., those who claim perfect knowledge by means of "heresy" and "logical analysis" have no direct access of perception and knowledge on the existence of gods. The third type of teachers like the Buddha who are enlightened have no need to consider such supra-sensible phenomena like "gods" as a matter of belief or of reasoning like the above two types of teachers.[25] By the above assertion of the Buddha on the existence of gods in the *sutta*, it is shown that he had direct knowledge about their existence by an "immediate, prereflexive pure experience."[26] In this *sutta* in reply to Saṅgārava's queries, the Buddha made it clear by categorically

22. K.N. Jayatilleke, *Facets of Buddhist Thought*, p. 13.
23. M.M.J. Marasinghe, *op. cit.*, p. 127.
24. Bhikkhu Nāṇajīvako, "Why is Buddhism a Religion," *Indian Philsophical Annual*, vol. VI, 1970, pp. 139-40.
25. *Ibid.*, p. 140.
26. *Ibid.*, p. 138.

stating that any intelligent person would grasp the meaning of his assertion that there are gods, and the world is loud in agreement that there are gods.[27] Because the Vedic and Buddhist concepts of *deva*s are altogether of different character, in Ven. Nāṇajīvako's words they are

> two incommensurable value aspects which cannot be admitted both at a time and hence one's admittance necessarily implies the denial of the other.[28]

Dr. Marasinghe points out[29] that in both the above *sutta*s Buddha spoke only of *deva*s according to Buddhist concept, and agreeing with Nāṇajīvako he concludes that the admittance of Buddhist concept of *deva*s implies a denial of the validity of gods of the Vedic character.

BUDDHA'S CONCEPTION OF "DEVAS" AND THEIR PLACE IN HIS DOCTRINE

It is enunciated in *Vibhaṅga*[30] that to aspire for *devahood* is one among the eighteen occurrences of craving in connection with internal aggregates. It is further said in this context that to assert oneself as *deva* comparing oneself with a *deva*; to assert or deny that he is a *deva* or he is "not a *deva*;" to aspire that he "shall be a *deva*" are some among the eighteen occurrences of craving in connection with internal aggregates. Similarly, to think that "by means of this I am a *deva*," or to aspire that "by means of this I may be a *deva*" or to intrrospect or interogate in oneself that "by means of this, would that I may be a *deva*" are some of the eighteen occurrences of craving in connection with external aggregates. It is further stated that the last of the five types of mental bondage is to become a *deva* in future

27. *MN*, II. 213; *MLS*, II. 402; see also, Lord Chalmers (tr.), *Further Dialogues of the Buddha*, vol. II, p. 123.
28. Nāṇajīvako, *op. cit.*, pp. 140-41.
29. M.M.J. Marasinghe, *op. cit.*, p. 128.
30. Thittila (tr.), *The Book of Analysis* (*Vibhaṅga*), pp. 504-07.

life by means of the religious practices in the present life.[31] The *Peṭakopadesa* asserts on the basis of *Nikāya* evidence that if one wishes to become some god or other by means of practising a "virtue or duty or divine life," he subjects himself by corruption of wrong view.[32] According to Theravāda Buddhist doctrine the false notions of "all is permanent" and "survival of the self" are the basis for human belief and reliance on the supernatural assistance.[33]

Further in the *Cetokhila Sutta* (*MN*) Buddha instructs that to except rebirth as a *deva*, when one is leading the spiritual life is not conductive to the attainment of *arhant*-hood. Describing an *arhant*'s attitude towards *deva*s in *Mūlapariyāya Sutta*,[34] Buddha contends that having full knowledge of the *deva*s as *deva*s (*deve devato abhijānāti*), and knowing them as impermanent, liable to suffering and void of self and substance, an *arhant* does not imagine anything about *deva*s. In other words he does not possess craving, conceit and wrong views about *deva*s (*deve na maññati*), does not imagine himself among the *deva*s (*devesu na maññati*), does not imagine himself as originating from a *deva* (*devato na maññati*), does not imagine that "mine are the *deva*s" and lastly he does not find delight in *deva*s. Moreover even the lowest state of four saints of Holiness is superior to the *deva* status. According to the *Dhammapada*,[35] the reward of the first step on the path of Holiness (Sotāpannahood) is higher than that of heavenly attainment. Therefore in early Buddhist teaching to aspire to become like

---

31. *Vibhaṅga*, 941. *ibid.*, tr., p. 488.
32. *Peṭakopadesa*, 82; Ñāṇamoli (tr.), *The Piṭaka Disclosure* (*Peṭakopadesa*) according to Kaccāna Thera, tr., pp. 34-35.
33. Alicia Matsunaga, *The Buddhist Philosophy of Assimilation*, pp. 5, 8-9.
34. See, Nyānaponika thera (ed.), *Buddhism and the God-Idea*, pp. 17-20.
35. *Dhammapada*, Verses 178, 187.

a *deva* is not the highest goal or ultimate objective, because those who are subjected to ignorance (*avijjā*) and craving (*taṅhā*) are destined to repeatedly born in the six realms of existence including that of *deva*s and when compared with extinction, all kinds of reappearance are viewed as bad destination.[36]

VARIOUS MEANS TO ATTAIN DEVAHOOD

In early Buddhist ethics, the better (higher) the deed, the higher the *deva* status attained by a person, or conversely the graver the sin, the graver the suffering in any of the four states of misfortune. According to *Dīgha* and *Majjhima Nikāyas*,[37] a person is born in some heavenly state only after the dissolution of the body. The *Sāleyyaka Sutta* (*MN*) gives reasons why some beings go to heaven, and some to hell. The Pāli *Nikāya* texts in general say that one special advantage of practising moral religious life is, it gives one the freedom to elect one's future state of existence which includes *deva* status of one's choice. The four *Nikāya* texts in Pāli canon gives an account of a number of meritorious deeds which lead persons to different *deva* realms.

There is substantial evidence in early Buddhist texts[38] that one's rebirth in a particular realm of *deva*s largely depends on one's inclination for a particular form of *deva*-hood. The paramount importance of volition (*cetanā*) or inclination is such that an offering of food or gift with different intentions, i.e.,

36. Ñāṇamoli (tr.), *The Guide* (*Nettippakaraṇaṁ*) according to Kaccāna Thera, tr., pp. 120, 69-70; *Nettippakaraṇaṁ* 499 and 250.

37. See, *DN*, II: *Janavasabha Sutta*, p. 212; *Sakkapanha Sutta*, p. 271; *Pāyasi Sutta*, p. 357; *DN*, III: *Udambrīkāsīhanāda Sutta*, p. 52; *MN*, I; *Bhaya-Bherava Sutta*, pp. 22-23; *Cula-Dhamma Samādāna Sutta*, pp. 307-9; *MN*, II: *Raṭṭhapāla Sutta*, p. 73, etc.

38. "I shall become a god or someone or other of the subordinate gods, angles (*devo vā bhavissāmi devaññataro vā ti*, *SN*, IV. 180; *AN*, IV. 461); (I shall become) a Gandhabba, Māra, Brahmā (*Dhammapada*, 105); *yakkho vā devo vā* (*Peṭavatthu Aṭṭhakathā*, 16); (q.v.) *PTS Dictionary*, p. 329b.

either to be reborn as one among the four Great Kings or to calm one's mind, gives corresponding heavenly births.[39] The *Sankhāruppatti Sutta* (*MN*) also shows that according to one's wish or desire a person can be born either as one among any of the *deva*s of the, twenty-six heavens, or by the same wish or offering of gift, a person can even extinguish the cankers (*āsava*s) and thereby win the goal of *nirvāṇa*. Thus, an individual who leads a moral religious life can excercise his own right to wish for himself and obtain a particular form of rebirth.

In the *Aṅguttara Nikāya* texts much more than any other virtue, liberality (*dāna*) as a means of heavenly reward is quite frequently mentioned. For instance the giver of food is said to receive five things, i.e., long life, beauty, ease, strength and intelligence in his rebirth among *devas*.[40] In the *Aṅguttara Nikāya*, of those who attain different states of *deva*-hood, a special privilege is given to the disciple of a Buddha when compared to an ordinary individual (*puthujjana*). If the person who attains the *deva* state is a disciple of Buddha, after spending his entire life span he will pass away in those realms; but if he is an ordinary individual after the exhaustion of merit he will be reborn in the three states of misery (i.e., *niraya, tiracchāyoni,* or *pettivisaya*). For instance, the Buddha distinguishes a *dāyaka* from non-*dāyaka,* when enquired about the future destiny of two individuals of equal faith (*saddhā*) by saying that though as a result of their morals both of them will be reborn in heaven (*sagga*), still the *dāyaka* excels the non-*dāyaka* in five places, viz., in divine *āyu, vaṇṇa, sukha, yasa* and *ādhipateyya*.[41]

It is stated in some *Khuddaka Nikāya* texts[42] that by accumulating extraordinary merit one attains a state of *deva*-

39. See, *AN*, IV.60.
40. See, *AN*, III.42.
41. See, *AN*, III.33.
42. See, *PTS Dictionary*, p. 330a.

hood. In the *Vimāna Vatthu*, *cetanā* (volition) is considered as the important factor which governs an action in deciding the nature of the ensuing retribution. Upon the enquiry of monks on the rewards of alms-giving, the Buddha affirms that charity does not become especially productive of reward merely by efficiency of the gift, but through the efficiency of thought and efficiency of the field of merit (i.e., efficiency of the field of those to whom the alms are given). According to the *Pañcagati-dīpanā*,[43] a post-canonical work, observation of precepts is the means to heaven, meditation is the means to Brahmā worlds and true knowledge is the means to *nirvāṇa*. Therefore, all these *Nikāya* accounts show that *deva*-birth is neither an inevitable occurrence nor an accident, nor it does entirely depend on the intensity of one's actions, but is the result of one's inclination for particular form of rebirth as a *deva* coupled with the nature of worthiness of moral action which has three components, i.e., efficiency of thought, efficiency of the gift and efficiency of the field of merit.

The various moral religious practices which lead to *deva* births are the accessories in formulating the doctrinal truths of Buddhist philosophy, because they show the efficacy of moral precepts which are comprised in *pañcasīla dasa-sīla* in early Buddhist ethics.

While certain virtues are means of *deva*-hood, the Immoral action (*akusalas*) corresponding to them cause rebirth in *niraya*.

General Characteristics of Deva in Theravāda Buddhist Perspective

According to the popular cosmography of the early Buddhism recorded in the *Abhidhammattha Saṅgaha*,[44] the four-fold rebirth of the Buddhists comprise the following:

---

43. *Pañcagata dīpāna*, p. 160; (q.v.) Law, *Heaven and Hell in Buddhist Perspective*, pp. 19-22.

44. See, Kosambi (ed.), *Abhidhammaṭṭha Saṅgaha*, Chap.V.

I. Four states of misfortune (four *apāya bhūmīs*), viz.,
   (i) The plane of misery (*nirayō*)
   (ii) The plane of animal kingdom (*tiracchānayōni*)
   (iii) The plane of *petas* (*petti visayo*)
   (iv) The plane of *asura* demons (*asura kāyo*)

II. Seven states of fortunate sense-experience (*kāmāvacara bhūmis*)

III. Sixteen states of form sphere or *rūpaloka* (*rūpāvacara bhūmis*)

IV. Four formless spheres or *arūpaloka* (*arūpāvacara bhūmis*)

All the above-mentioned diverse classes of beings have been born in their respective worlds by reason of moral or immoral actions performed as the human beings in their worldly activity. When the *karmic* result current is exhausted then beings pass away and are reborn elsewhere.

In the Theravāda tradition the *deva*s are objects of Buddhist mystical belief.[45] Except their being recognized as part and parcel of the cosmic scenery *deva*s in early Buddhism have no ultimate priority or significance. In the special Buddhist context they are only superior personages of some kind, when compared to human beings. This is evident from Pāli *Nikāya* texts[46] according to which the word *deva* always implies a kinship and continuity of life with humanity and other beings. They are regarded as "superior species who gain their status due to their self-efforts." Their birth as *deva*s is not as a consequence of their having been Buddhists, for any human being irrespective of his faith or creed is reborn as a *deva*, simply by means of some good action or the other. Hence, they carry with them numerous beliefs of their past earthly existence both of true and false.

---

45. Dr. Vishwanath Prasad Varma, "Early Buddhist Mysticism," *The Mahā-Bodhi*, vol. 67, no. 1, p. 12.

46. *DN*, I. 17; *SN*, III.85.

The Buddhist *deva*s are just superhuman in respect of their powers, knowledge, life-spans and the celestial happiness. They are characterized by physical and psychological attributes in the exposition on the *Viññānaṭṭhiti*s.[47] They have different radiant bodies, both in its purity and in its extent as well which are resulted from the extent of purity in their actions of past earthly existences.[48] Their council is accessible without physical migration[49] to those earthly beings who possess the "Divine Eye" (*Dibba-cakkhu*) and "Divine Ear" (*Dibba-sota*) which are two among the six higher powers (*abhiññā*) and one of the three kinds of Higher knowledge (*Te-vijjā*).

The Buddhist *deva*s resemble the Greek deities in being neither all-knowing (omniscient) and all-powerful (omnipotent) nor free from the law of causality. They exhibit many of the human weaknesses by possessing many of the infirmities and disabilities.

All the *deva*s are finite and conditioned as they share the three characteristics of existence and are thus subjected to the universal laws of suffering (*dukkha*), impermanence (*anicca*) and non-substantiality (*anattā*). Even though the *deva*s do not suffer from old age and its accompanying ailments, they are subjected to death.[50] Despite their tremendous length of life-spans,[51] all the power, glory and falicity of these heavenly inhabitants would come to an end soon after the exhaustion of their merits according to the Buddhist law of impermanence of all compounded things. For instance the *Itivuttaka* (*Khn*) makes a mention of five signs of warning at the time of a *deva*'s fall from his heavenly state.

---

47. See, *AN*, IV.39.
48. See, *MN*, III.147; *AN*, IV.241.
49. See, M.M.J. Mārasinghe, *op. cit.*, p. 95.
50. See, *Nettippakaraṇaṁ* 131; Ñāṇamoli (tr.), *The Guide* (*Nettippakaraṇaṁ*) according to Kaccāna Thera, tr. p. 39.
51. See, *SN*, III.86; *AN*, II.33.

> Monks, when a *deva* is destined to fall from a company of *devas*, five signs of warning are shown forth: his flowers fade, his garments are soiled, sweat exudes from the armpits, an ill-colour pervades the body and the *deva* takes no delight in his *deva*-seat.[52]

Further owing to the mysteries of retribution a *deva* may be reborn as an inhabitant of hell. All long-lived blissful *devas* tremble like the animals on hearing a lion's roar,[53] when they are disillusioned by the Buddha's doctrine of the personality, its origin, its cessation, the way to its cessation[54] and realize their evanescent and non-eternal nature. They are beset by fear, agitation and are troubled by anxiety (*parināmaduḥkhatā*).

The *devas* in general are at a disadvantage when compared to men in some respects. They are hindered by two views,[55] viz.,

1. Some cling to human sensuous delights and "becoming."
2. Some stick to annihilationistic views and not-becoming.

According to the *Kathāvatthu* (I.3)[56] no *deva* can practise the renunciation of the world, though they are not in general forbidden to practise the "path culture" *Dīgha Nikāya* states that some *devas* of the sky and earth who are conscious of the earth are subjected to grief and lamentation like ordinary mortals whereas the *devas* who are free from attachment are not subject to grief.[57] Those *devas* whose lives are without

52. F.L. Woodward (tr.), *Itivuttaka: As it was said* (*The Minor Anthologies of the Pāli Canon,* Part II), pp. 171-72.

53. See, *AN*, II.33.

54. *AN*, *Cātuka-nipāta* (*The Fours*) No. 33.

55. *Itivuttaka*, tr. p. 147.

56. Shwezan Aung and Mrs. Rhys Davids (tr.), *Points of Controversy* (*Trans. of Kathāvatthu*), p. 214; According to *Kathāvatthu*, the "Path Culture" is forbidden only to those of the *Asaññasattha devas*.

57. *DN*, II, p. 108; (q.v.) Law, *Heaven and Hell in Buddhist Perspective*, p. 12.

hindrance lacked the incentive to practise virtue, unlike human beings who alone are capable to practise such virtue amidst temptations and hindrances. Therefore in the *Itivuttaka*[58] it is further stated that other *devas* cheer the falling *deva* wishing him that he might be born among human beings, practise the Buddhist doctrine and thereby get benefitted by the *dhamma* by establishing himself in it.

Because of this advantage of human world over that of the *devas* and their inability to produce fresh wholesome *kamma,* they are compelled to acquire further merit through "Transfer of merit" (*anumodana*) performed by human beings. As intention is the basis of all activity (i.e., volitional activity where *kamma* is generated, those *devas* who are aware of the moral law of causality are able to produce in themselves good natural impulses (*kusala-citta*) by approving the good actions of Buddhist monks and laymen who invites *devas* to share the merit of a charity given or some good performed by them.[59] For instance, at the special request of *deva Sakka,* the Buddha is stated to have enjoined all devotees of faith on all occasions to transmit the merit of their good deeds to the *devas* and other beings.[60] In Theravāda Buddhism, the enlightened beings, i.e., *arhats, Pacceka Buddhas* and the Buddhas have been categorized under the classification of *devas* as being divine by purity (*visuddhi deva*). Except the *devas* by purification (i.e., *visuddhi devas*) all the rest of *devas* of all kinds[61] are themselves in *saṁsāra* and are in need of salvation.[62] Portrayed as lay

58. *Supra*. 52.
59. G.P. Malalasekera, "Buddhism and Problems of the Modern Age-II," *World Buddhism,* vol. XXI, no. 5 (December 1972), p. 111.
60. Arya Dharma, "The gods and their place in Buddhism," *The Mahā-Bodhi,* vol. 47, no. 5 and 6 (May & June 1939), p. 237.
61. See two types of classification of *devas* in *PTS Dictionary,* pp. 329a and 330b.
62. *Ibid.*, p. 329a.

Buddhists and devout adherents of the faith they are said to have attained the fruition of the four holy paths by following the Buddhist doctrine. These include also the *deva*s of higher status, Brahmā and Sakka who attained the first stage of sanctification. A discourse of Buddha[63] shows that the *deva*s have not attained such tranquillity of mind attained by *arhant*s.

According to early Buddhist epistemology *nirvāṇa* is a far higher goal than the attainment of any heaven, and all human beings are potentially capable to rise to greater heights than *devas*[64] by developing their minds through the practice of *jhāna* and hence will be regarded far superior than the *deva*s and will be respected. As a consequence of this all *deva*s of higher status were made much inferior to Buddhas, Pacceka Buddhas, *arhants*, because of the latter's perfection in virtue, knowledge and Enlightenment. For example, the *Visuddhimagga* (xiii. 414) shows that in all his three domains, viz., "Birth domain" (*janma khetta*) which comprises 10,000 worlds; "Authority domain" (*ājña khetta*) which comprises a hundred thousand times ten millions of worlds; and "knowledge domain" (*visaya khetta*) which is without limit, all the *deva*s are infinitely inferior to a Buddha. Whereas the *deva*s of higher status are also inferior to other Buddhist monks and laymen who have attained the four stages of holiness of Sotāpañña, Sakadāgāmin, etc., the *deva*s of lower status have become far inferior to even the ordinary Buddhist laymen.

Devotional attitude of the Devas of Higher and Lower Status

DEVAS OF HIGHER STATUS

Different planes of existence and levels of consciousness

---

63. See, *AN*, I.63; *Gradual Sayings* (*GS*), I.60, note. 4.
64. Manoj Kumar Barua, "God in Buddhist Philosophy," *The Mahā-Bodhi*, vol. 56, no. 7 (July 1948), pp. 244-45.

which are superior to the terrestrial world and to the average human consciousness are recognized in early Buddhism. The inhabitants of these higher planes of existence are the "*Deva*s Proper" (*Upapattideva*s) who comprise the *deva*s of Sense-desire sphere (*Kāmāvacara*), Fine-Material sphere (*Rūpāvacara*) and Immaterial sphere (*Arūpāvacara*). The *deva*s of Sense-desire sphere who comprise six lowest celestial realms are, viz., the Four Great kings, The thirty-three *deva*s, the Satisfied or blissful, *deva*s enjoying pleasure and *deva*s enjoying their creations and other's creations. These enjoy the five-fold divine sense-pleasures in a grander scale than those of earthly beings, but are not enlightened.

The *deva*s of Fine-Material sphere who comprise the next sixteen higher celestial realms are, viz., Retinue of Brahmā, Ministers of Brahmā, The Great Brahmās, Brahmās of Minor Lustre and Infinite Lustre, Radiant Brahmās, Brahmās of minor aura, infinite aura and steadfast aura, Greatly rewarded Brahmās, Sensationless Brahmās, Immobile, Serene, Beautiful, Clearsighted and Supreme Brahmās. In these *deva*s material qualities are absent and all sexual distinctions are obliterated. The *deva*s of Immaterial sphere who comprise the last four highest formless celestial realms are, viz., *deva*s of spheres of "Infinite of Space," "Infinity of Consciousness," the Knowledge of "No-thingness," and of "Neither-perception-nor-non-perception." These are spiritually superior to the above two kinds of *deva*s, who have consciousness without material body and who are pure contemplative formless beings.

The Attributes of the Devas of Higher Status

The Buddhist Sakka, as a king of the Tāvatiṁsa *deva*s is inferior to Buddhist *deva*s of higher status like Mahā Brahmā. According to the *Kulāvaka Jātaka* (*J.*, vol. I., no. 31) there are multiple number of Sakkas in different world systems which are thousands in number.[65] He is said to be possessed with passion, hatred and delusion,[66] ignorance, timidity and cowardice.[67] He is subjected to birth, old age, death,[68] lamentation, sorrow, dejection and despair.[69] In some places he is portrayed as malign, jealous[70] who tries to dissuade the righteous,[71] encourages animal sacrifices.[72] But mostly he is seen as a *deva* of high character, kindly and just. He is depicted as compassionate[73] and sympathetic towards the human sufferers.[74] He is a supporter[75] and protector of righteousness,[76] and also a rescuer of good.[77] He plays the role of a Tester[78] and restorer of righteousness[79] by converting

---

65. B. Jayawardhana, "Cakkavāḷa," *Ency Bsm*, vol. III, Fasc. 4, p. 570b.
66. *AN*, vol. I, pp. 144-45.
67. *SN*, I.219.
68. *Mandhātu Jātaka* (*J*., vol. II, no. 258).
69. *AN*, I.144.
70. *J*. vol. II, no. 281.
71. *J*. vol. V, no. 526.
72. *Lomassa Kassapa Jātaka* (*J*., vol. III, no. 433).
73. *Kulāvaka-Jātaka* (*J*., vol. I, no. 31).
74. *Bhadra-Ghaṭa Jātaka* (*J*., vol. II, no. 291); *Somadatta Jātaka* (*J*., vol. III, no. 410); *J*., vol. III, no. 372.
75. *Kaccāni-Jātaka* (*J*., vol. III, no. 417).
76. *Guttila-Jātaka* (*J*., vol. II, no. 243); *J*., vol. II, no. 194; *Keli-Śīla-Jātaka* (*J*., vol. II, no. 202).
77. *Dhammaddhaja-Jātaka* (*J*., vol. II, no. 220); *J*., vol. III, no. 386; *Canda-Kinnara-Jātaka* (*J*., vol. IV, no. 485); *J*., vol. V, no. 92, Verse 284; *J*., vol. III, 146, Verses 181-82.
78. *Kurudhamma-Jātaka* (*J*., vol. II, no. 276); *Vaka-Jātaka* (*J*., vol. II, no. 300); *Kaṅha Jātaka* (*J*., vol. IV, no. 440).
79. *Mahākanha-Jātaka* (*J*., vol. IV, 469).

the unrighteous and wicked,[80] keeping them in right path. He acts as the destroyer of heresies[81] and teaches lessons to the wicked and persons who are lack of character.[82] The Buddhist Sakka is a bestower of desires and gifts to the worthy and pious.[83] In numerous lives of the *bodhisattva* in the *Jātaka*s Sakka personally intervenes and by honouring the *bodhisattva*[84] serves him in many ways.[85] Thus Sakka has been humanized and moralized[86] in the Pāli texts.

In early Buddhist texts, the Brahmās replace the creator-God of Vedic and Brāhmaṇic religion. There is a plurality of Brahmās and also Mahā Brahmās who are stated as enjoying positions of pre-eminence.[87] The Chief Brahmās are flattered by the prayers of ignorant people although they cannot help them. They entertain the false belief that their existences are everlasting due to the extreme length of their life-spans and fail to see that they are evanescent. But they too are subjected to the laws of *kamma* shared by other worldlings. All the Brahmās as well as the Mahā Brahmās are subject to change

80. *Bilāri-Kosiya-Jātaka* (*J.*, vol. IV, no. 450); *Kumbha Jātaka* (*J.*, vol. V, no. 512); *J.*, vol. V, no. 535; *Vighāsa-Jātaka* (*J.*, vol. III, no. 393); *Khadiraṅgara Jātaka* (*J.*, vol. I, no. 40).

81. *Dhajavihaṭha Jātaka* (*J.*, vol. III, no. 391).

82. *J.*, vol. II, no. 228; *Culladhanuggaha Jātaka* (*J.*, vol. III, no. 374); *Mahā-Paduama-Jātaka* (*J.*, vol. IV, 472).

83. *Suruci Jātaka* (*J.*, vol. IV, no. 489); *J.*, vol. VI, no. 538; *Vidurapaṇḍita-Jātaka* (*J.*, vol. VI, no. 545).

84. *Sādhina-Jātaka* (*J.*, vol. IV, no. 494); *J.*, vol. VI, no. 538; *Nimi-Jātaka* (*J.*, vol. VI, no. 541).

85. *Kuddāla-Jātaka* (*J.*, vol. I, no. 70); *J.*, vol. IV, no. 489; *Culla-Suttasoma-Jātaka* (*J.*, vol. V, no. 525); *J.*, vol. VI, no. 538.

86. *University of Ceylon Review* (hereafter abbreviated as *UCR*), April 1945, p. 68.

87. See, G.P. Malalasekera (ed.), *Dictionary of Pāli Proper Names*, vol. II, 336; In *Kannakatthala Sutta* of *MN*, Brahmā is referred as *adhideva* or "Super God" (s.v.) *'Adhi,'* in *PTS Dictionary*, p. 27a.

and are bound by the limitations of individuality.[88] The Brahmās are not all-powerful because of their mortality and transitoriness and like other mortals they too are subjected to Māra's power.[89] The Brahmās are inferior to the Buddha and *arhants* in many respects. Just as there are malign and benign Sakkas, malign Brahmās have been distinguished from benign Brahmās.[90]

The Knowledge of the Devas of Higher Status

The shorter of the two conventional formulas which describe the significance of Buddha's attainments shows that Buddha as the teacher of *devas*[91] surpass all *devas* in possessing the higher knowledge. It is further stated that the knowledge of all *devas* is transcended by the enlightened Buddha who is endowed with purity or clarity in the eight-fold series of knowledge and insight. By virtue of possessing such a penetrative and analytical knowledge, the Buddha is described as attained a full and complete knowledge, understanding, and insight into the nature and the character of all the *devas* as well as the entire universe.[92] But *devas* have no such knowledge about the Buddha's enlightenment and are also ignorant about cosmic truths and about their origin.

The *Itivuttaka* of *Khuddaka Nikāya*,[93] one of the later books

88. *Brahmalokopi āvuso anicco addhuvo... sakkāya-pariyāpanno...* (*SN*. v. 410).
89. See, *DN*, II, p. 263.
90. See, *Kaṇṇakatthala Sutta* (*MN*, XC).
91. *itipi so bhagavā arahaṁ sammā-sambuddho vijjācaraṇa-sampanno sugato loka-vidū anuttaro purisa-dhamma-sārathi satthā deva-manussānaṁ buddho bhagavā ti.* — *DN*, I. 49; *DN*. I. 112; *DN*. III.5.
92. *yato ca kho me bhikkhave evaṁ aṭṭhaparivaṭṭaṁ adhidevañāṇa dassanaṁ suvisuddhaṁ ahosi, athāhaṁ bhikkhave sadevake loke samārake sabrahmake . . . sammāsambodhiṁ abhisambuddhoti paccññāsiṁ* — *AN*, IV.304; *GS*, IV.202.
93. *Itivuttaka*, tr., p. 155.

of the Pāli canon also testifies to the above fact by stating that the *deva*-eye and the eye of flesh as means of knowledge are inferior to and surpassed by the Buddha's eye of wisdom. Hence, neither a *deva*, Brahmā nor Māra can with justice claim to challenge the validity or the truthfulness of whatever the Buddha declares to have obtained the understanding of.[94]

The knowledge of *deva*s and their ability of attaining their heavenly status results from their higher religious accomplishments,[95] which does not help them to attain *nirvāṇa* or enlightenment. All *deva*s are said to possess only partial knowledge of *dhamma*. For example, Brahmā Tissa explains to Ven. Moggalāna that those *deva*s of six sense-desire realms, who possess the four attributes of a stream winner[96] or who have imperfect faith in Triple refuges (*ti-saraṇa*)[97] only have the knowledge of Stream-winning and others have such knowledge. According to the above Brahmā some *deva*s of the Brahmā realms know of a monk's emancipation and the precise nature of his attainment,[98] of the first six stages of holiness which comprise the three supramundane paths and the corresponding three Fruitions, viz., that of Stream-winner, Once-Returner and Non-Returner.

It is evident from the *Saṁyutta Nikāya*[99] that *deva*s differ in possessing different degrees of insight. For instance, some *deva*s had only partial understanding of the doctrine of Buddha as in *Bhaddekaratta Sutta* (*MN*, CXXXI). When Ven. Vakkali was on his deathbed two *deva*s approached the Buddha and one

---

94. *sammāsambuddhassa te paṭijānato ime dhammā anabhisambuddhā ti tatra vata maṁ samaṇo vā brāhmaṇo vā devo vā . . .* — *AN*, II.9; IV.83, etc.

95. *DN*, I.215; *DN*, II.205; *DN*, II.329.

96. *AN*, III.331.

97. E.M. Hare (tr.), *The Book of the Gradual Sayings*, vol. III, p. 234.

98. *AN*, IV.74.

99. *SN*, III.121.

reported to him that Vakkali was bent on release, whereas the other told that Vakkali would win complete emancipation. Not only Māra,[100] but even the most powerful and intelligent *devas* (Sa-Brahmakā) of the cosmos are unable to trace the transcendental one's consciousness or can locate the mind of a *fully emancipated* monk. The Buddha's affirmation on the subject of omniscience in the *Kaṇṇakatthala Sutta* (*MN*, XC), viz., that "no Brāhmaṇa or Śramaṇa (including himself) can claim the omniscience in the sense of knowing and seeing everything at one and the same time" may also be extended to the *devas*. It may also be added that among the *devas* of twenty-six Buddhist heavens, the *devas* in a particular realm do not have the knowledge and understanding of the *devas* of all above higher realms right from their next higher heaven.

More than half of the eighty-one *Suttas* in *Devatā Saṁyutta* contain questions claimed to have been asked by the *devatās*. Some *suttas*[101] which raise queries on verification of doctrinal points show the ignorance of *devas* and how the Buddha corrected them. They hold erroneous views such as attachment brings delight to beings; worldly possessions such as sons and cattle, etc., are the best and the highest of things; and wrongly evaluate the worldly things such as clan, kine, wife, etc.

The limited knowledge of the *devas* is reflected in their various questions[102] like how one crosses the flood of *saṁsāra*?; to know about the end of *saṁsāra*; to know how freedom from ills be attained?, etc.; or their verification of doctrinal truths[103] such as meritorious actions that bring bliss; the impermanence

100. Māra's effort to locate Godhika's and Vakkali's consciousness (*SN, Māra Saṁyutta*, 3.3); *SN*, III.124.

101. See, *Devatā Saṁyutta* (hereafter abbreviated as *DS*), (*SN*) *Vaggas* and *Suttas*: 2.2; 2.3, 2.4, 3.1, 3.4.

102. *Ibid., DS*, 1.1., 3.7; 3.10.

103. *Ibid., DS*, 1.3; 1.4; 4.1.

of life, by associating with good people one attains the end of all suffering; their posing riddles or enigmas to Buddhas[104] such as How many things do light up the world?; What is it that is most valuable to me?; and What is it that is hard for thieves to take away?; What sustains all that lives on earth?; What is it that gives man rebirth?; What undergoes the round of births and deaths?.

In early Buddhist texts Sakka is regarded as a religious aspirant who hears Buddha's discourses;[105] approaches the Buddha to clarify his doubts.[106] On one occasion he was described as "not ripe enough to understand the *dhamma*;"[107] yet on some occasions[108] he used to clear the doubts and remove the heresies on religious issues. He led a pure life for a long time and became a Sotāpanna.[109]

In early Buddhism Brahmās are shown as lacking full and accurate knowledge regarding their states of existence, though some of them had much more knowledge and learning than *deva*s like Sakka and Māra. They had misconceptions that they were creators of living beings;[110] entertained pernicious views that their world was everlasting, eternal and complete itself with no rebirth, decay, death and no other salvation beyond it;[111] thought that no recluse or brāhmaṇa can enter their abode.[112] The Pāli canon also reports that a Brahmā understood

104. See, *DS*, 3.6; 6.1; 6.4; 6.5.

105. See, *Cula-Taṅha-Saṅkhaya Sutta* (*MN*, XXXVII).

106. *DN*, II.263f; esp. 276f. *The Sakkapañha Sutta* (*DN*); *SN*, I.232, 233; *SN*, IV.101f.

107. See, *Dīghanikāya Aṭṭhakathā* (*DA*) on *DN*, II, pp. 271.

108. *Nimi-Jātaka* (*J.*, vol. VI, no. 541).

109. See, *DN*, II.275.

110. See, *Brahmajāla Sutta* (*DN*, I).

111. *Brāhma-Nimantaṇika Sutta* (*MN*, XLIX).

112. *Brahma Saṁyutta* (I.5) of *SN*.

the transient nature of himself and his heaven and admitted that he no longer claimed to be permanent and eternal.[113] Another Brahmā confesses his ignorance of cosmological facts when questioned by a monk and sends the questioner to the Buddha whom (Brahmā) frankly admits to be wiser than himself.[114] Of all the Brahmās, Brahmā Sahāmpati, who was the seniormost of all Brahmās and the Mahā Brahmā of the world system during Gautama's life appears to be more learned,[115] intelligent,[116] and possess greater understanding of Buddha's teaching.[117] He admits the Buddha as the attainer of the Highest Truth.[118]

Yama, one of the *deva*s of higher status and the ruler of Yama-heaven, intends to learn *dhamma* from the Buddha in order to improve his own condition.[119] This reveals that he too is not the attainer of the Highest Truth.

The Powers of the Devas of Higher Status

According to Geoffrey Parrinder,[120] the Buddhist *deva*s are only spectators and cannot act independently of the Buddha.

---

113. *MN Sutta*, no. 50.

114. *Kevaddha Sutta* (*DN*, XI); According to *Potthapāda Sutta*, the Brahmā does not know where the primaries composing his creation can cease.

115. At *DN*, II, p. 157, on the occasion of Buddha's *parinibbāna*, Brahmā Sahāmpati recites a verse which is learned and philosophical in context in comparison with the verse recited by Sakka.

116. The first use of the word *tathāgata* in addressing the Buddha is attributed to Brahmā Sahāmpati in *Ariyapariyesana Sutta* (*MN*, I, p. 168).

117. See, B. Jayawardhana, "Brahma," *Ency Bsm*, vol. III, Fasc. 2, p. 299b.

118. T.W.R. Davids and H. Oldenberg (tr.), *Vinaya Texts, Part I*, p. 86.

119. F.L. Woodward (tr.), *The Book of the Gradual Sayings*, vol. I, p. 125.

120. Parrinder, *Avatar and Incarnation*, p. 132.

They are not empowered to raise human beings to a higher status. They had no power to affect any person's salvation, for they had to seek their own salvation. Yet it is stated by the Buddha himself on several occasions that by customary acts of reverence and offerings to *devas*,[121] the people in return will be protected by them. It is further said that the *devas* protect a person who sleeps with mindfulness[122] and who develops in *metta*.[123] The *Accariyabhuta dhamma Sutta* (*MN*, CXXIII) tells us that the *devas* from the four quarters guarded the *bodhisatta* and his mother against human or non-human foes. In the *Ātānātiya Sutta* (*DN*, XXXII) the four great kings, the guardian kings of the four quarters, uttered protective charms which will guard the Buddhist order. *Deva* Viṣṇu is also charged with the commission of protecting the Buddha *sāsana*.[124]

The Buddhist *devas* can cause this earth to violently tremble and shake by intense meditation which is in accordance with Buddhist technique of meditation. But no *deva* can hinder the progress of *dhammacakka*[125] or can turn back the wheel of the *dhamma*.[126] According to the *Māra Saṁyutta*, even Māra utterly failed in his ignoble attempts to frighten, to shake confidence and conviction, or to entangle to Buddha[127] and his disciples in the sensual desires, to abandon the path of emancipation

121. *DN*, II.75; See also *Dialogues of the Buddha*, II.80; *Mahāparinibbāna Sutta* (*DN*, II.88). (q.v.) *The Mirror of the Dhamma*, p. 35.

122. *AN*, III.251.

123. *AN*, IV.150.

124. Arya Dharma, "The Gods and their place in Buddhism," *The Mahā-Bodhi*, vol. 47, no. 5 and 6 (May & June 1939), p. 236.

125. See, *SN*, V.420f.

126. *taṁ hoti dammacakkaṁ appaṭivattiyaṁ samaṇena vā brāhmaṇena vā devana vā* . . . — *AN*, I.110; *AN*, III.148-49.

127. See also, Mrs. Rhys Davids (tr.), *Dhammapada* (*The Minor Anthologies of the Pāli Canon, Part I*) verse 8.

and to advocate false doctrines. According to the *Bhikkhuni Saṁyutta* too, his efforts to divert the *bhikkhunis* from the path were futile.

In the *Brāhmaṇimantaṇika Sutta* (*MN*. XIIX), it is shown how Brahmā Baka in spite of his best efforts was unable to vanish from the Buddha, but the latter succeeded in disappearing before the eyes of Brahmā and his host, thereby establishing his supremacy over the Brahmā in knowledge and power. The physical inferiority of Brahmās to Buddha can be inferred from Buddha's assertion to Cunda that Cunda's meal cannot be partaken by anyone including Brahmās.[128] Several other passages in *Nikāyas*[129] show that even Mahā Brahmās are physically and morally inferior to the Buddha.[130]

The Functions and the Role of the Devas of Higher Status

The functions of Buddhist *devas* are limited to their heavens and are transient, and hence the ultimate goal of Buddhists is not any of their heavens but *nirvāṇa*. Since they do not fulfil any important functions like helping the aspirants towards salvation, they are not indispensable.[131]

The *devas*' role in early Buddhism is limited to instructing non-Buddhists and laymen in Buddhist doctrine and also wishing their spiritual progress. They act as proclaimers of important doctrines like *Dhammacakkappavattana Sutta*, which shows their keen interest in hearing the doctrine. Some *devas* including Brahmā help the aspirants by directing them either to lead the hermit life[132] or to the Buddha enabling them to

---

128. B. Jayawardhana, "Brahma," *Ency Bsm*, vol. III, Fasc.2, p. 295b.
129. *DN*, II, p. 150; *SN*, I, p. 138, etc.
130. B. Jayawardhana, "Brahma," *Ency Bsm*, vol. III, p. 296a.
131. L. De La Valle Poussin, "Nature" (Buddhist)," *ERE* vol. IX, p. 209b.
132. *Ency Bsm*, vol. III, Fasc. 2, p. 300b.

become the members of the order.[133]

The *devas* are delighted to talk to a person who has faith in the triple refuges and possessed of Āryan virtues[134] and when a disciple attains *arhant*-hood.[135] According to the *Itivuttaka*,[136] they make three utterances on three occasions: i.e., when an Ariyan disciple renounces the world; when he endeavours to develop seven factors of Enlightenment and when he releases himself by insight. The *devas* also inform the Buddha about monks' spiritual progress.[137]

The *devas* requested the *bodhisattva* to be reborn as a human being to that he might become a Buddha.[138] The four sons of *devas* received the baby *bodhisattva* at the time of his birth.[139] They are sympathetic not only towards the Buddha in attending on the Buddha during the times of his physical suffering,[140] but also towards their earthly relations of their past existences.[141] Some of the *devas* known as Lokābhyūhas warn the world about the forthcoming calamity of the "Age of destruction" before a hundred thousand years.[142]

In the *Nikāya* texts the Brahmās who played the active role are Brahmā Sahāmpati, Brahmā Sanankumāra, Subrahmā, Suddhāvāsa, Tudu and Tissa. Of the above, Brahmā Sahāmpati,

---

133. D.M. Strong (tr.), *Udāna*, p. 9.

134. F.L. Woodward (tr.), *The Book of Kindered Sayings* (hereafter abbreviated as *KS*), Part V, p. 338.

135. *AN*, IV.117.

136. *Itivuttaka*, tr. pp. 170-71.

137. *Udāna*, Chap. III. tr. pp. 31-32.

138. Mrs. Rhys Davids (tr.), *Psalms of the sisters* (*Psalms of the Early Buddhists I*), pp. 3-4.

139. See, *Mahāpadāna Sutta* (*DN*, XIV).

140. *SN*, I.27.

141. *Matta-Kuṇḍali Jātaka* (*J.*, vol. IV.449).

142. L. De La Valle Poussin, "Ages of the World," *ERE*, vol. I, p. 188b.

the chief of the Brahmās presented himself in all the principal incidents of Buddha's life. His visits to the Buddha on twelve occasions shows the great concern of Brahmā and his keen interest in the Buddha as well as his order.

Just as Sakka and other *devas*, Brahmās support the Buddha and his order. Out of compassion for the worldly beings, Sahāmpati requested the Buddha to preach the doctrine and succeeded in persuading the latter.[143] He approves the thoughts of Buddha when the latter thought himself that it would be fittest if he live under the norm, honour and respect it.[144] He requested the Buddha to patronize the monks or departed almsmen and succeeded in mollifying the Buddha.[145] He informs the Buddha about a Bhikkhu's future state of rebirth.[146] He shows great concern when Devadatta caused dissension in the Buddhist order[147] and expresses his sorrow at Buddha's passing away.[148] The part played by the Mahā Brahmā in Buddha Gautama's life was the same in the lives of the all-preceding Buddhas of the past.[149]

As distinguished from Brahmā Sahāmpati, Brahmā Sanankumāra is noted for his psychic powers, poetic abilities and for his voice. He also plays a teacher's role in early Buddhism.[150] Brahmā Tudu tries to advice Kokālika *bhikkhu* not to hold wrong views about the two chief disciples of the Buddha. In the *Mahānārada Kassapa Jātaka*[151] the great Brahmā

143. *Vinaya Texts*, Part I, tr. p. 86.

144. Mrs. Rhys Davids (tr.), *The Book of Kindered Savings*, Part I, p. 176; also see *GS*, vol. III, p. 21.

145. *Cātuma-Sutta* (*MN*, LXVII); *SN*, III.92.

146. *Brahma Saṁyutta* (*SN*), I.10

147. *Ibid.*, (2.2).

148. *Ibid.*, (2.5).

149. *Ency Bsm*, vol. III, Fasc.2, p. 298a.

150. *Ibid.*, pp. 299b-300a.

151. *J.* vol. VI, no. 544.

Nārada, in response to the prayer of a king's daughter, converted the king by teaching him righteousness.

Sakka plays the role of an exemplary lay follower of the Buddha. He visits the Buddha nine times,[152] and also the *arhant*s and other good men.[153] He honours the Buddha, *arhant*s and also the lay Buddhists, although he himself is being worshipped by brāhmaṇas and others.[154] He asserts himself as an attendant of the Self-controlled Buddha.[155] Sakka knows when a mighty or virtuous being prays him.[156] Thus, being aware, when need arises he fulfils the wants of Buddha[157] and also plays a role of Vajirapāni when the Buddha intends to convert non-Buddhists.[158]

The role of Buddhist *deva*s is well compared by J.F. Mckechnie[159] with the "Fellow-Voyagers" of human beings on the same ship of conditioned existence who occupy first class cabins, distinguishing themselves from human beings who travel in the third class cabins. They are not revered as the Buddha, the supreme pilot of the ship and perfect Master in navigation, since without the aid of his *dhamma* they do not know how to navigate the ocean of conditioned existence.

THE DEVOTIONAL ATTITUDE OF THE DEVAS OF HIGHER STATUS TOWARDS THE BUDDHA AND HIS ORDER

Among all beings, the Buddha is most honoured, revered and beloved by the *deva*s. His supremacy over all the *deva*s is well

152. See, *DN*, II.269f; *MN*, I.251; *SN*, I.233; *SN*, IV.101, 109, etc.

153. *MN*, II.179; *AN*, IV.165.

154. See, *SN*, I.226.

155. *Vinaya Texts*, tr. Part I, pp. 141-42.

156. *J.*, vol. IV, no. 440.

157. *Vinaya Texts*, tr. Part I, pp. 126-27.

158. *Ambaṭṭha Sutta* (*DN*, I .95).

159. J.F. Mckechnie, "God and Gods," *The British Buddhist*, vol. II (September 1928), p. 8.

established in Early Buddhist texts. For instance, Sakka realized the greatness of the Buddha when he discovered the increasing number of new *deva*s appearing in his realm outshining others as a result of the practice of Buddha *dharma*.[160] His great adoration to the Buddha is shown in a *Dīgha Nikāya* hymn (*DN*, II.208):

> Indeed, Sir, The Thirty-three gods
> With their leader rejoice,
> Honouring the Tathāgata
> and the good nature of the teaching.[161]

Sakka is a pupil of the Buddha[162] and in the guise of a young brāhmaṇa he walks in front of the Buddha reciting verses of praise.[163] In one of his visits to the Buddha, having intended not to disturb Buddha who was absorbed in meditation, Sakka departs silently asking Bhuñjati, to salute the Buddha on his behalf.[164]

According to *Brahmanimantaṇika Sutta* (*MN*, XLIX), Buddha is described as mighty and exalted above all *deva*s including the Mahā Brahmā. It is also stated in this *sutta* that the "Reality" attained by the Buddha is beyond the ken of the highest Brahmā. In the *Brahmā Saṁyutta* (I.6), two Brahmās went to another Brahmā realm and having convinced him on the Buddha's supremacy over all Brahmās, directed him to the Buddha. Just as in the case of Sakka referred above, two Brahmās went away without disturbing the Buddha who was engaged in meditation.[165]

---

160. *DN*, II.208.

161. *modantivata bho devā tāvatiṁsā sahindaka, tathāgatam namassantā dhammassa ca sudhammatam* — *DN*, II.208; (q.v.) Jack Donald Van Horn, *Devotionalism in Early Buddhism*, p. 126.

162. *DN*, II.284.

163. *Vinaya Texts*, tr. pp. 141-42.

164. *DN*, II.270.

165. *SN*, I.146.

In the *Ātānāṭiya Sutta* (*DN*, XXXIII), the Four Guardian Kings visited the Buddha and paid their respects. The Buddha is held in high esteem as "supreme of all the *devas*"[166] and as the "highest blessing,"[167] by *devas* Mānava-Gāmiya and Mahāmaṅgala respectively. In *Devatā Saṁyutta* (*SN*, Suttas 1.9 and 1.10), the *devas* Candima and Suriya when seized by Rāhu sought refuge in the Buddha who protected by freeing them.

It is significant to note that in the *Vinaya* and the *Suttapiṭakas*, we find the *devas*, not only treating the Buddha with highest respect, but they are also devoted to the other *arhants* of the Buddhist order. All the *devas* of twenty-six Buddhist heavens salute and pay their respects when they approach Buddha and other *arhants*. Their mode of salutation to the Buddha is similar to that of the disciples of the Buddha, who adjust their upper robes to cover one shoulder and putting their right knee on the ground, raising their joined hands towards the Buddha. Before they depart, "they pass round him their right side toward him" and thus with a circumambulatory gesture disappear from the Buddha.

In *Sakkapañha Sutta* (*DN*, XXI) Sakka pays homage to the Buddha. In *Dīgha Nikāya* (II, 284ff), Sakka recites a hymn of praise expressing his attitude of devotion and worship towards the Buddha.[168]

---

166. *SN*, tr. p. 92.

167. V. Fausböll, *The Sutta Nipāta*, pp. 43-44.

168. (i) *yadā ca buddhaṁ addakhiṁ vicikicchāvitāraṇaṁ* ।
samhi vitābhayo ajja, sambuddhaṁ payirupāsiya ॥

(ii) *tanhāsallassa hantāraṁ, buddham appaṭipuggalaṁ* ।
ahaṁ vande mahāvīraṁ, buddham ādiccabandhuṇam ॥

(iii) *yaṁ karomasi brahmano samanaṁ devehi mārisa* ।
tad ajja tuyhaṁ dassāma, handa sāmaṁ karoma te ॥

(iv) *tvam eva asi sambuddho tuvaṁ satthā anuttaro* ।
sadevakasmim lokasmim, natthi te paṭipuggaloti ॥

(q.v.) Jack Donald Van Horn, *op. cit.*, p. 128.

When I saw the Buddha,
doubt was overcome,
today, free from fears,
I am worshipping the Fully Enlightened one.

The destroyer of the dart of desire
The Enlightened one without a rival,
The Great Hero, Enlightened one,
Kin-of-the Sun I adore,

The level of Brahmā
established by the gods, O Sir,
that now we see as yours
Lo! we worship you.

You indeed are the Fully Enlightened one!
You the Leader unsurpassed!
In the worlds with their devas
You have no rival!

Even on such occasions, when he goes to the celestial gardens for enjoyment, Sakka would extend his clasped hands towards the direction of the Buddha, *arhants* and other good *upāsakas*.[169] In the *Majjhima Nikāya* (*MN*, III, 178ff), *deva* Yama also desires to attend upon or worship (*payirupāseyyam*) the Buddha.

In the *Saṁyutta Nikāya*,[170] Kokanadā — the daughter of cloud king Pajjunna — worships the Buddha. In the *Devatā Saṁyutta* (*DS*, 4.7), when the Buddha was at Mahāvana in Kapilavatthu, all the *devas* in all the *lokadhātus* came and paid their reverence to the Buddha and the order. *Devas* from all world-systems paid their last respects before Buddha's *parinibbāna* and honoured him by showering a rain of heavenly flowers and by playing celestial music, out of reverence for the successor of the Buddhas of the past.

169. *SN*, I.234-36.

170. *SN*, I.4.10; Mrs. Rhys Davids (tr.), *KS*, Part I, pp. 40-41.

Not only the Buddha, but the *arhants* too were held superior to the *devas* who worship them. All *arhants* such as Moggalāna, Kassapa, Kappina, Anuruddha are superior to *devas*.[171] Even the great *devas* like Brahmā and Sakka worship the *arhants* from afar. It is stated that on different occasions Sakka with other *devas* visited Elders Uttara, Sunīta and Theri Subhā to whom they paid homage with clasped hands and worshipped them.[172] Many *devas* are found worshipping the saints in *Theragāthā* and *Therigāthā*.[173] The *Paramaṭṭhadipanī* (*Theragāthā Aṭṭhakathā*), refers to several instances of *devas* approaching an *arhant* in a worshipful attitude "waiting on him morning and evening, out of gratitude."[174]

DEVAS OF LOWER STATUS

Abhidhānappadīpikā, the Pāli lexicon in its definition of the word *devayoni* mentions several deities of lower status as belonging to *deva* origin[175] and it also refers to such *devatā*s, viz., Gandharvarāj, Kinnara, Vasuki, etc., in different places of the lexicon.[176] The *Pāli-English Dictionary* apart from the *bhummadevas* (i.e., Nāga, Suvaṇṇā, Yakkhā, Asurā, Gandhabbā) adds the following under the *devas* of lower status.[177] They are: Tree gods or dryads (*rukkha-devatā*), Earth gods (*vatthu-devatā*), wood nymphs (*vana-devatā*) and Water-spirits (*samudda-devatā*). In addition to these according to R.C. Childers there are tutelar deities of certain town (*nagara*

---

171. *SN*, I.146.

172. See, *AN*, IV.163; *Theragāthā*, I.64; *Therigāthā*, 2.158.

173. (s.v.) "Deva" in *PTS Dictionary*, p. 329a.

174. H.G.A. Van Zeyst, "Atheism," *Ency Bsm*, vol. II, Fasc. 2, p. 306b.

175. *siddho bhuto cha gandhabbo guhyakō yakkha-rakkhasa kumbhāndo cha pisachādi nidiṭṭha deva yoniyo* — *Abhidhānappadīpikā*, 13; see, *Pāli Kosa Sangaho*, Part I, p. 4.

176. *Ibid*., pp. 7, 9, 117.

177. *PTS Dictionary*, p. 330b; (s.v. *Devatā* (f)).

devatayo) or guardian *devas* of a town,[178] deities of families, tree nymphs, deities who reside in rocks, genii of a particular locality, those who dwell in air or cloud.[179]

The Nature and Attributes of the Devas of Lower Status

In the *Āṭānāṭiya Sutta* (*DN*, XXXII) King Vessavana characterizes the *yakkhas, gandhabbas, kumbhāṇḍas* and *nāgas* as "not humane, but as rough, irascible and violent." According to *Gandhabbakāya Saṁyutta* (*SN*, XXXI, Khaṇḍavagga), the *devas* who dwell in the fragrance of the root-wood, heart-wood, pith, bark, sap, leaves, flowers and scents, belong to Gandhabala group. Similarly it is stated in *Valāha Saṁyutta* (*SN*, XXXII), the *devatās* embodied in cool-clouds, hot-clouds, clouds of thunder, wind and rain belong to the *devas* of cloud-group (*valāhaka-kāyika*).

The *petas* and the *kumbhāṇḍas* are the two types of non-human beings. The *petas* live almost throughout the world of men, but especially in the kingdom of Yama situated 500 leagues below Jambudīpa. The *asuras* live underneath the Seat at different depths of 20, 40, 60 and 80 leagues in the four towns ruled by four kings.

There are infinite number of *yakkhas*, terrestrial, atmospheric, etc. According to *Abhidharmakosa* (iii.56), three categories of *yakkhas* occupy a special place as inhabitants of Mount Meru.[180] The *yakkhas* are non-human beings (*amanussa*) who are half deified and endowed with great power by which they influence people partly helping and partly hurting. The malign *yakkhas* are referred in some *Jātakas*.[181] The Sun, the

178. Childers, *DPL*, p. 115b.

179. *Ibid.*, p. 116a; (s.v.) "Devatidevo."

180. L. De La Valle Poussin, "Cosmogony and Cosmology (Buddhist)," *ERE*, vol. IV, p. 134a.

181. *Ayakūṭa-Jātaka* (*J.*, vol. III, no. 347); *Vidurapandita-Jātaka* (*J.*, vol. VI, No. 545).

Moon and the stars do not form a special class of *devas*.[182]

The Knowledge and Powers of Devas of Lower Status

The majority of 127 visits of *devas* of lower status, to the Buddha are to clarify their doubts. Some of these *devas* such as *ārāma devatā, vana-devatā* and *rukkha-devatā* possess poor knowledge, compared to Buddha's disciple *citta* whom (when he was on death-bed) they asked to wish to be reborn as an Emperor in his next life.[183]

The *Yakkha Saṁyutta* (*SN*, Sagathavagga, X) refers to various *devatās* who approach the Buddha either to put some queries or to listen his sermons. The *yakkhas*' lack of knowledge on doctrinal truths is shown in *suttas* of *Yakkha Saṁyutta*[184] wherein they seek verification on the correct view on various topics such as on the nature of consciousness of the *jīva* on the source of passion, hatred, repulsion, love, excitement, etc.[185] Some of the *yakkhas* posed riddles to the Buddha trying to frighten him if he could not answer them.[186] Some of the *yakkhiṇīs* attentively heard the doctrine quietning their children.

There are a very few instances of the malevolent spirits[187] who tried in vain to tempt the disciples of the Buddha. The malign *yakkhas* made futile attempts[188] to possess the lay disciple's children, or to frighten the Buddha[189] or even to kill the *bodhisattva* in his past existences.[190] Satisfied with the

182. See, *Abhidharmakosa Vyākhyā*, iii:60.
183. See, *SN*, IV.302.
184. See, *Yakkha Saṁyutta* (*YS*), Nos. 1 and 3.
185. *Ibid.*, *Suttas* 6 and 7.
186. *SN*, I.207, 214.
187. *Vana Saṁyutta of SN*, *Sutta* No. 6.
188. *Yakkha Saṁyutta of SN*, *Sutta* No. 5.
189. Mrs. Rhys Davids (tr.), *The Book of the Kindered Sayings*, Part I, p. 265.
190. *J.*, vol. III, no. 347; *J.*, vol. VI, no. 545.

Buddha's doctrine, some like *yakkha* Hemavata sought the refuge of the Buddha with his large retinue.[191]

The *peṭas* and *kumbhāṇḍas* had no power to harm the Buddha and *arhants* or even the lay disciples of the order. In *Vinaya*[192] the Buddha asserts that there are powerful fairies, fairies of middling power and of inferior power who bend the hearts of the powerful, middling and inferior kings to build the dwelling places. Nāga Mucilinda, the serpent king who served the Buddha in his post-enlightenment period, by protecting him from the stormy weather is one of the best examples of the good natured *devas* of lower status.[193] The friendly nature of *nāgas* is shown in some *Jātakas*.[194]

The Functions and Role of Devas of Lower Status

The *devas* of lower status play a role of good-intentioned friends (*kalyānamittas*) with regard to *bhikkhus* as well as the lay-disciples of the Buddha. In *Vana Saṁyutta* they are described as "kind and sympathetic beings" (*anukampikā atthakāmā deva*).[195]

The *devas* of lower status also act as messengers of the *dhamma* (*dhammadūtas*) by posing riddles to *bhikkhus* on *dhamma*, or questioning them on the analysis of the doctrine, thereby revealing the *bhikkhus*' ignorance to them.[196] Some *devas* of Jambūdīpa act as proclaimers, by announcing the proper time for the recital of *Vinaya*.[197]

---

191. Fausböll, *The Sutta Nipāta*, Sec. IX.
192. T.W. Rhys. Davids and H. Oldenberg (tr.), *Vinaya Texts*, Part II, p. 101.
193. *Udāna*, tr., Chap. II, p. 13.
194. *Kharaputta Jātaka* (*J.*, vol. III, no. 386).
195. *SN*, I.199.
196. *MN*, III.192f; *MN*, III.199f.
197. *DN*, II.49.

The *deva*s of lower status voluntarily approach the lay disciples of the Buddha to offer helpful suggestions for their future well-being, by directing some to the Buddha so that they may become Buddha's disciples,[198] and by advising their past earthly relations to offer food to the chief disciples of the Buddha.[199] Some of the *yakkha*s praised the lay followers when the latter offered alms and robes to *bhikkhus*.[200]

The *deva*s also act as beneficiaries to the Buddhist order by pointing out transgressions of the monks and exhorting them to follow and practise the doctrine attentively. They come and exhort the *bhikkhu*s at the latter's slightest faltering in meditation, to take heed lest they may fail in attaining their goals. They watch and ward the *bhikkhu*s of the order, when the latter entertain evil thoughts whilst in meditation or when they spend much time in households which is not in consonance with the monastic rules of the Buddhist Saṁgha.[201] The *Vana Saṁyutta* (*SN*, Sagathavagga, IX) narrates some forest deities who put the ill-behaved *bhikkhu*s on the right path. They often remind the *bhikkhu*s of the latter's mission to live higher life.[202] The *devatā*s are also fond of the company of *bhikkhu*s which is evinced from the expression of their sorrow on the departure of the *bhikkhus* who spent their rainy season in the forest abodes.[203] In a nutshell, the Buddhist *deva*s of lower status are alert to prevent the *bhikkhus* from deviating from the correct path. Their attempts are always successful for their advices were followed by the members of the Buddhist order.

The *deva*s of lower status also adore and worship the

---

198. *Sutta Nipāta*, 91f. Where the *deva*s asked the merchants Tapussa and Bhallika to offer food to Buddha after his enlightenment.
199. *AN*, IV.63.
200. *Yakkha Saṁyutta of SN*, *Sutta*s 10 and 11.
201. *SN*, I.197; *SN*, I.200 and 201.
202. *Vana Saṁyutta of SN*, *Sutta*s 1, 2, 5, 11 and 13.
203. *Ibid.*, Sutta No. 4.

Buddha by admitting his supremacy over all of them.

Glory to you, well-bred of Men!
Glory to you, highest of men!
With what goodness you contemplate!

Even non-humans worship him thus:
The conqueror Gotama you should worship.
The conqueror Gotama we worship;
He accomplished in wisdom and morality,
The Buddha Gotama, we worship.[204]

From the above study, it may be concluded that the *devas* of lower status in Early Buddhist texts are portrayed as more or less equals with the Buddhist laity who endeavoured to promote the Buddha's teachings.

MĀRA

Māra occupies an interesting position in Buddhism. There are some accounts which describe him as the ruler of the six sensuous spheres (Kāmadeva *lokas*); dividing his sovereignty of Kāmāvacara *devaloka* along with Sakka. While he is said to have obtained his high position due to the practice of supreme *dāna* in a previous existence and possesses vast power, he is an evil one and gloats in sensual pleasures.[205] He is sometimes spoken of as a deity and sometimes as just as personification of evil and death.[206] While gods encourage spiritual progress Māra attempts to obstruct it in every way.[207] Trevor Ling concludes that Māra is "the supreme head of all the forces

204. *namo te purisājañña, namo te purisattama* ।
kusalena samekkhasi, amanussāpi taṁ vandanti ॥
sutaṁ netaṁ abhiṇhaso, tasmā evaṁ vademase ।
jinaṁ vandatha gotamaṁ, jinaṁ vandāma gotamaṁ ।
vijjācaraṇa sampannaṁ, buddham vandāma gotamaṁ ॥
(q.v.) Jack Donald Van Horn, *op. cit.*, p. 131.

205. R.C. Childers, *DPL*, pp. 240-41.

206. Nyāṇatiloka, *Buddhist Dictionary*, p. 97.

207. M.M.J. Marasinghe, *op. cit.*, pp. 210-12.

that militated against human well being and holy living." He is the cause of all evil, and he has been conquered once for all by the Buddha.[208]

Recollection and Contemplation on Devas (Devānussati)

In Theravāda Buddhism the *deva*s are not the objects of adoring devotion for the Buddhists, in view of their inferiority to the Buddha and his order in their virtues, knowledge and power. Hence they are not entitled to worship (*pūjā*) or to sacrifice (*homa*). The Buddhist attitude towards the *deva*s is based on the altruistic principle of Buddhist ethics. By showing expanding sentiments of compassion and benevolence in the ten cardinal directions, the Buddhist monk ought to maintain social relations with all beings including the *deva*s of all kinds.[209] Thus, the Buddhist *deva*s of both higher and lower status were to be treated only with goodwill, friendliness[210] and love.[211] It is stated in *Dīgha Nikāya*[212] that a Buddhist monk must honour the *deva*s who haunt his dwellling place, and the best way to honour them is by way of transferring to them the merit of his gifts to the self-controlled brethren.

Although no *sutta* in the Pāli canon points out the usefulness of *deva*-worship,[213] yet meditation on the virtues, knowledge and liberality of the *deva*s known as *devānussati,* is given considerable importance. The word *anussati* which is derived

---

208. Trevor Ling, *The Buddha*, p. 75.

209. L. De La Valle Poussin, "Nature (Buddhist)," *ERE*, vol. IX, p. 209b.

210. C.A.F. Rhys Davids, "Love (Buddhist)," *ERE*, vol. VIII, p. 161a.

211. According to *Ekādasa Nipāta of AN*. XI, a person who cultivates *metta* (loving kindness) wins the love of spirits and is protected by them; see, also D.K. Barua, *An Analytical Study of Four Nikāyas*, p. 596; *Return to Righteousness*, ed. Ananda Guruge, p. 160.

212. *DN*, II. 88f; Rhys Davids, *Dialogues of the Buddha*, ii. 93f.

213. *Supra*, 213.

from Sanskrit *anusmṛti* means "remembrance, recollection, thinking of, mindfulness."[214] If strictly defined, the word *anussati* does only give the sense of "recollection and contemplation" and not "mindfulness."[215] Buddhaghoṣa in the Exposition of the Six Recollections of his *Visuddhimagga* (Chap. VIII) defines *anussati* as "from arising in places where it ought to arise, is suitable for a well-born man who has entered the religious life through faith."[216]

Devatānussati which is meant as "remembrance of the gods,"[217] or "Recollection of heavenly beings"[218] has for its objects one of the six things to be meditated upon, or kept in mind or recollected (six *anussatiṭṭhānāni*). The method of concentration is common to all the six recollections with the variation of object.

THE OBJECT OF RECOLLECTION OF DEVAS

To the question of "Why should one meditate or recollect on the reward in celestial spheres following a virtuous life?" the *Aṅguttara Nikāya* responds that *deva*-recollection is a means to "cleanse the vicious or defiled mind by effort,"[219] by developing which one is established in the five states of faith, energy, mindfulness, concentration and understanding.[220] According

214. *PTS Dictionary*, p. 45a.

215. H.G.A. Van Zeyst, "Anussati," *Ency Bsm*, vol. I, Fasc. 4, p. 778b

216. Pe Maung Tin (tr.), *The Path of Purity*, Part II, a tr. of Buddhaghoṣa's *Visuddhimagga*, p. 226.

217. *PTS Dictionary*, p. 330b; (s.v.) "Devatānussati."

218. Childers, *DPL*, p. 45a.

219. "*Upakkhiliṭṭhassa cittassa upakkamena pariyodapana;*" This type of cleansing the mind is explained as living with the *devatās*, calming of the mind on account of the *devatās*, etc. (*ayaṁ vuccati ariyasāvako devatūposathaṁ upavasati, devatāhi saddhiṁ saṁvasati, devatā c'assa ārabbha cittaṁ pasīdati pāmujjaṁ uppajjati, ye cittassa upakkiḷesā te pahīyati* — *AN*, I.211), see M.M.J. Marasinghe, *op. cit*. p. 272.

220. Pe Maung Tin (tr.), *The Path of Purity*, Part II, tr., p. 261.

to the *Anussati Sutta*, one who develops such qualities in himself as that of the *devas* of different heavenly realms by means of *deva*-recollection will secure rebirth as *devas*.[221]

METHOD OF RECOLLECTION OF DEVAS

A passage from *Aṅguttara Nikāya* shows how a noble disciple, who is endowed with such qualities as faith, etc., in seclusion and solitude recalls these qualities, placing the *devas* as witness:

> There are the heavenly beings of the retinue of the Four Great Kings, the heavenly beings of the world of the Thirty three, the Yama devas . . . and there are heavenly beings besides. Such faith, such morality, such knowledge, such liberality, such insight, possessed of which those heavenly beings, after vanishing from here, are reborn in those worlds, such things are also found in me.[222]

In the dialogue of *Mahānāma Sutta* (*AN*, III. 284) the Buddha affirms that one who wishes to develop recollection of *devas*, should call his own faith and other virtues to mind and adduce those of the spirits as witnesses. Thus when the disciple first of all recalls the qualities of the *devas* and afterwards those that exist in himself, viz., faith, virtues, learning, liberality and understanding, his mind is not invaded by lust, hate or delusion, but is upright with reference to the *devas*.

FRUITS OF RECOLLECTION AND CONTEMPLATION OF DEVAS

The fruits of the practice of the recollection and contemplation of *devas* is explained in some passages of the *Aṅguttara Nikāya*.[223]

---

221. *Anussati Sutta* of Anuttarīya Vagga (*AN*, III.312); (q.v.) W.G. Weeraratne, "Anussati Sutta," *Ency Bsm*, vol. I, Fasc. 4, pp. 778b 779a.

222. (q.v.) Nyāṇatiloka, *Buddhist Dictionary*, pp. 17-18; also see, Pe Maung Tin (tr.), *The Path of Purity*, Part II, tr., pp. 259-60.

223. *AN*, III.312; *AN*, V.329, 332, 34, etc.

According to *Mahānāma Sutta*, relinquishment of the hindrances by means of recollection of *devas*, gives rise to the *jhāna*-factors. But the *jhāna* without attaining to ecstasy attains only to access because of depth of one's qualities of faith and so on or from one's intentness of their recollection. This *jhāna* known as recollection of *deva*s serves as an indirect means to Higher Path.[224] The recollection of *deva*s cannot help us to reach any stage of absorption because "the concentration of mind is not sufficiently unified, but occupied with special qualities of *devas*."[225] Hence, recollection of *deva*s results in bringing about the state of *devas*.[226]

A person who applies his mind to recollection of *deva*s becomes dear and beloved of the *deva*s. He attains abundance of faith, virtue and other qualities. He abides, fully rapturous and joyful. He is bound for a happy destiny even though he fails to proceed further. By recollection of *devas*, one obtains the knowledge about *deva*s, and becomes mighty and majestic like those *deva*s. In the discourse of Buddha to Visākhā, in the *Uposatha Sutta*,[227] the *deva*-recollection along with others is described as "a station for meditation on the purification of the mind of the noble disciple who keeps *uposatha*" "Fasting Day" (*Sabbath*) and thus it indirectly brings great fruits of the Fasting Day. *Deva*-recollection along with others is further characterized as the "way of the attainment of opportunity through a noble disciple's worthiness in absolute purity."[228] The recollection of *deva*s also purifies the noble disciple's mind

---

224. Pe Maung Tin (tr.), *The Path of Purity*, Part II, tr., p. 260.
225. Ñāṇamoli (tr.), *The Path of Purification*, p. 244; VII.117.
226. Pe Maung Tin (tr.), *The Path of Purity*, Part II, tr., p. 261.
227. *AN*, I.206f; see, Pe Maung Tin (tr.), *The Path of Purity*, Part II, p. 261.
228. *Sambādhokāsa Sutta* (*AN*, III.314), (q.v.) *The Path of Purity*, Part II, tr., p. 261.

for the futher attainment of absolute purity.[229] By recalling the qualities of different realms of *devas*, even the mind of the average man becomes clear. Through this power he discards the hindrances and thereby strives for insight and the realization of saintship. Thus recollection of *devas* is only an indirect means to attain *nirvāṇa*.

A Comparative Study of Some Buddhist Devas and Vedic and Brāhmaṇical Gods

BUDDHIST DEVAS AS DISTINGUISHED FROM VEDIC GODS

The Theravāda Buddhists not only adopted and adapted the Buddhist heavens from the Brāhmaṇic religion,[230] but also modelled some of their important *devas* of higher status like Brahmā, Sakka (Indra), Yama and *devas* of lower status such as *gandhabbas, ārāma devatā, rukkha devatās* and *vana devatās* from the pre-Buddhistic Vedic and Brāhmaṇic mythology. But the character and functions of Buddhist *devas* differ from those of Vedic and Brāhmaṇical gods, as the former are portrayed to suit the doctrinal context of Theravāda Buddhism and thus serve as instruments to prove the truth of the teachings of the Buddha. When we compare the nature and role of the Buddhist conception of *devas* with the Vedic and Brāhmaṇical gods, we find the following differences:

1. Unlike the anthropomorphic gods of Vedism, the status of Buddhism *devas* is due to their past meritorious actions.
2. The Buddhist *devas* who attain their *deva* status by purification are superior to those of Vedic and Brāhmaṇical gods by birth and tradition.[231]

---

229. *Gedha Sutta* (*AN*, III.312); (q.v.) *The Path of Purity*, Part II, tr., p. 261.

230. L. De La Valle Poussin, "Abode of the Blest (Buddhist)," *ERE.*, vol. II, p. 687a.

231. See, *Mahāsamaya Sutta* (*DN*, XX).

3. Unlike the Vedic gods like Prajāpati, Hiraṇyagarbha, Indra, Varuṇa and others who are eternal and immortal, the Buddhist *deva*s are neither eternal nor immortal, but are subjected to disease, decay and death.
4. The Buddhist *deva*s are not omniscient, omnipresent and omnipotent like Vedic and Brāhmaṇical gods (e.g., Viṣṇu, Śiva).
5. Unlike Vedic and Brāhmaṇical gods who crave for their share in the rituals and sacrifices, the Buddhist *deva*s live in accordance with the *dhamma* and admire others who lead virtuous lives.
6. Unlike Vedic and Brāhmaṇical gods, the Buddhist *deva*s are not the objects of any cults or rituals. In Theravāda Buddhism *dāna* (charity) is substituted to Brāhmaṇic *yannā* (sacrifice).
7. In regard to their role, the Buddhist *deva*s differ from the Vedic and Brāhmaṇical gods who were sovereigns over their subjects' life, prosperity and salvation. The Buddhist *deva*s behave more or less as lay-disciples and play the role of protectors and propagators of Buddhist religion.
8. The favours and grace of Buddhist *deva*s need not be sought like those of their Vedic counterparts by means of sacrifice and prayer, for they can neither save others by blessing them with liberation nor can lead the aspirants to the goal of salvation or *nibbāna*.

COMPARISON BETWEEN BUDDHIST DEVAS OF HIGHER STATUS AND VEDIC GODS

Vedic and Buddhist Brahmā

B. Jayawardhana[232] thinks that the conception of "Buddhist

---

232. B. Jayawardhana, "Brahma," *Ency Bsm*, vol. III, Fasc. 2, p. 291a.

Brahmā" is drawn from the conception of Brahmā of the transitional stage of the *Sūtra* period of the *Brāhmaṇas*.[233] The word "Brahmā" which indicates a single supernatural heavenly being in Vedic philosophy, denotes in Theravāda Buddhism a number of species of *devas* inhabiting one of the sixteen heavens of the world of Form, as well as their chiefs known as Mahā Brahmā who illusorily claimed to be the creator-gods. In *Brahmajāla Sutta* (*DN*, I.18) the term Mahā Brahmā has been used to describe the first being who comes to be reborn at the beginning of each evolutionary cycle of this universe. He is spoken as the highest denizen of thousandfold world system (*AN*, V.59). There are a great number of Mahā Brahmās, seventy-two in number[234] one in each cycle. The Buddhist texts mention[235] different names of Mahā Brahmās, viz., Nārada, Ghatikāra, Upāka, Phalagaṇḍa, Pukkusāti, Bhaddiya, Khaṇḍadeva, Bāhuraggi, Piṅgiya, Sanankumāra and Sahāmpati, who figured in important events in Buddha's life. But remarkably nowhere in the Pāli canon, the Mahā Brahmā (neuter) is identified with Upaniṣadic *Brahman* (Impersonal Ultimate).

Vedic Indra and Buddhist Sakka

The Buddhist Sakka differs from his Vedic counterpart Indra, who had been depicted as a great helper and giver of boons to his supplicants and increases wealth of those who offers sacrifices and praises him. In contrast to this Vedic war god, the Buddhist Sakka is portrayed as humane, kind-hearted, admirer and supporter of Buddha and his order. Unlike the anthropomorphic god of Vedism, the *deva* status of Buddhist

---

233. See, *Śatapatha Brāhmaṇa*, XII, 8, 29.

234. *dvāsattati gotama puññakammā, vasavattino jātijaraṁ atītā, ayam antimā vedagū brahmuppatti, asamābhijappanti janā anekā ti* — see, *SN*, I.143; *KS*, I.180.

235. B. Jayawardhana, "Brahma-kayika Deva," *Ency Bsm*, vol. III, p. 312a.

Sakka resulted from the seven qualities of a good layman. In Pāli canon he appears as a voluntary intruder who serves the Buddha and his order without being prayed to or offered any sacrificial offerings. Thus, as Charles Godage well observes,[236] the Vedic Indra is transformed in the ethical cosmology of Theravāda Buddhism.

Vedic and Buddhist Yama

The Vedic Yama who was the king of the dead is transformed into the mere *deva* king of Yama heaven who is no more a ruler of the Niraya. Especially in post-*Nikāya* Buddhist literature he did not preside over the judgement over the dead and also was not incharge of the punishments inflicted in the Niraya. He just witnesses the operation of the law of *karma*.[237] In the *Aṅguttara Nikāya* commentary,[238] the Buddhist Yama even intends to explore the means of averting the suffering in Niraya.

The Other Popular Gods

The other popular gods of Vedism like Agni, Varuṇa and Soma were cast in an inferior role in Theravāda Buddhist texts. For instance, Varuṇa's moral greatness of Vedic age had been overshadowed in the Pāli canon where he is given a minor role.[239] The Vedic wine-god Soma also is seen in a lowly status in the Pāli texts. The *Tevijja Sutta* (*DN*) discusses the futility of invoking gods like Soma as a means to attain union with Brahmā and relates the efficacy of cultivating the divine life as the right means to attain the fellowship with Brahmā. The position of Varuṇa is sometimes degraded even to the rank of fairies

236. Charles Godage, "The Place of Indra in Early Buddhism," *UCR*, vol. III, no. I, (April 1945), pp. 71-72.

237. See, *Devadūta Sutta* of the Tika Nipāta (*AN*, I.138).

238. *Manorathapūraṇī*, II.231.

239. See, *DN*, I.244; *DN*, III.204; *SN*, I.219.

and other common spirits like guardians.[240]

COMPARISON BETWEEN BUDDHIST DEVAS OF LOWER STATUS AND VEDIC GODS

When we turn to Buddhist *devas* of lower status, the Buddhist *gandhabbakāyika devas* are mere counterparts of Vedic *gandharvas* whose conception according to Prof. Wijesekara[241] is borrowed from Atharvavedic religion. The belief in several other deities like *ārāma devatā*, *rukkha devatā* and *vana devatā* also seems to have had its parallel[242] in the Vedic religion, since mountains, planets, trees, etc., have been anthropomorphized into gods and goddesses in the Vedic hymns.

The above study of the comparison between some Buddhist *devas* and Vedic gods shows that as distinguished from the gods of Vedic and Brāhmaṇical philosophy, the *devas* in Theravāda Buddhist perspective are adapted to suit the special requirements of "doctrinal necessity."[243] It also appears plausible that the Buddha endeavoured to tame the frightful, covetous, capricious gods and to convert them along with the benevolent gods by teaching the former the elements of morality and leading the latter to higher rungs of the ladder of spirituality.

The Buddhist Conception of Creator God, the Absolute and the Supernatural

The Pāli word *issara* is primarily meant as "lord, ruler, master, chief" and in its secondary sense, it denotes a creative deity, Brahmā.[244] R.C. Childers, following *Abhidhānappadīpikā* adds

---

240. See, *Mahāsamaya Sutta* (*DN*, XX); *DN*, III.204.

241. Prof. Wijesekara, "Vedic Gandharva and Pāli Gandhabba," *UCR* (April 1945), p. 76.

242. Macdonell, *The Vedic Mythology*, p. 154f.

243. M.M.J. Marasinghe, *op. cit.*, p. 65.

244. *PTS Dictionary*, (s.v.) *Issara*, p. 123b.

to the word[245] two other English renderings, viz., "King;" "Civa." Besides *issara*, the words *nimmāta* and *vidhātu* are also used as Pāli equivalents synonymous to the word "Creator."[246]

BUDDHA'S TEACHING ON THE BELIEF OF CREATOR GOD

In the Theravāda Buddhist teaching, the belief in a Creator-God or World-Soul (*pradhāna*) who is a designer and controller of the world is described as one of the wrong views (*micchā-diṭṭhi*)[247] or pernicious views. By cultivating one of the five kinds or stages of Right views known as *kammassakata sammā diṭṭhi*, a disciple of the Buddha casts away the erroneous views that all sentient beings are created and conditioned by *Īśvara*, Brahmā or Creator God. He understands that the origin of universe is due to dependent origination and correlation.[248]

In *Brahmajāla Sutta* (*DN*), the belief in a Creator God is shown to be the outcome of a confusion of Mahā Brahmā himself made between his "partial realization of truth" (*pacceka sàcca*) on the Brāhmaṇic planes of existence distinguished from the fuller realization of the transcendental *nibbāna*. The belief that the *saṁsāra* is created by a Creator God is an illusory product of ignorance (*avijjā*), but for an *arhant* who has fully comprehended the four noble truths, it is a myth.[249] For instance, in the *Mūla-pariyāya Sutta* (*MN*) it is shown how an *arhant* who has full knowledge of Lord of creatures or Brahmā does not imagine that the Lord of creatures (Brahmā) is permanent and immutable, free from evil, etc. An *arhant* does not also imagine that he is created or emanated from the

245. *Supra*, 8.

246. Buddhadatta Mahathera, *EPD*, p. 115a.

247. B.M. Barua, "Buddha's greatness and Role," *The Mahā-Bodhi*, vol. 52, nos. 5-6 (May-June, 1944), p. 132.

248. Dr. C.L.A. De Silva, "The Three Fold Views," *The Mahā-Bodhi*, vol. 48, nos. 5-6 (May and June 1940), p. 173.

249. Francis Story, *Gods and the Universe in the Buddhist Perspective*, p. 85.

Brahmā; he does not crave by taking delight in the Brahmā or entertain the wrong views such as that Brahmā is his Lord, Master and Creator God because he is freed himself by extinction of three fetters, i.e., greed, hatred and delusion.[250]

The belief in the theistic conception of Creator God expresses one's craving for either of the heavens of sense-sphere or "Fine-material sphere." If the assumption of Creator God (*Issara*) as the cause of the world, which rests on the false belief in an eternal self[251] is not abandoned by the understanding of the noble truths of suffering and impermanence, it brings out definite bad results (*Niyata Micchādiṭṭha*) owing its effect on the ethical conduct of a person. By the belief in a Creator God as solely responsible for the happiness and misery in the world, a person lacks the impulse and effort to act which consequenty leads him to inaction.[252] The Buddha criticized Makkhali's theism, on the ground that it gave a false sense of security to people and encouraged complacency by denying freewill and the value of human effort.

In *Vibhaṅga* of the *Abhidhamma Piṭaka*[253] also the view of Creator God as a Supreme deity responsible for the pleasure and pain of beings is stated as one of the three bases of heresy.

When we turn to the commentaries, it is stated in the *Sammohavinodinī* (*Vibhaṅga Commy.*) of Buddhaghoṣa, that the false belief in a Creator God is removed by the acquisition of the knowledge of the real cause of misery.[254]

---

250. Nyāṇaponika Thera (ed.), *Buddhism and the God-Idea,* pp. 17-20.

251. See, *Vasubandhu's Abhidharma Kosa,* 5, 8 (vol. IV, p. 19; *Sphutārtha,* p. 445, 26) (q.v.) Nyāṇaponika Thera, *op. cit.,* p. 24.

252. *AN* (*The Threes,* No. 61); see, *The Wheel,* No. 1 55/58, p. 43.

253. See, *Vibhaṅga,* 923; *Vibhaṅga* tr., p. 477.

254. *samudayanānaṁ issara padhāna kalasabhāvādīhi lokopavattati akārṇe kāraṇābhimānappavattaṁ hetumhi vippaṭipattim . . . nivatteti —*
→

It is further asserted in the *Kaṅkavitaraṇa Niddesa* of *Vibhaṅga Commentary* that in order to acquire the mental serenity called *Kaṅkavitaraṇa Visuddhi*, a monk should cultivate such an attitude that he should remove all kinds of doubts including the one that the body is created by *Issara* or God, or the other that Mind and Matter (*nāmarūpa*) is God itself.[255]

The belief in Creator God is also rejected as false in the *Visuddhimagga* of Buddhaghoṣa:

No God, no Brahmā can be found,
Creator of saṁsāra's round;
Empty phenomena roll on,
Subject to cause and condition.[256]

HOW THERAVĀDA BUDDHISM IS NON-THEISTIC

Theravāda Buddhism is called "homo-centric"[257] as opposed to "theo-centric." It is a form of non-theism or atheism[258] only so far as it denies that the universe is a product of an eternal omnipotent Godhead or a personal God who is its creator, ordainer and destroyer. It is consistently non-theistic, for it declares that human being has the potentiality of attaining the highest spiritual goal without any external assistance of deity[259] or Creator God to whom he can complain about his

→ *Visuddhimagga*, 511; Ñāṇamoli (tr.), *The Path of Purification*, p. 584. see also, R. Siddhartha, "Buddhism and the God Idea," *The Buddhist Anuual of Ceylon*, vol. III, no. 3, pp. 204-05.

255. *na tāvidam nāmarūpam. . . imassatāvarupakāyassa evam hetuppaccayepárigāṇhāti* — See, R. Siddhartha, *op. cit.*, pp. 204-05.

256. *na h'ettha devo brahmāvā saṁsārass'atthi kārako, suddha dhammā pavattanti hetusambhāra paccayāti.* — *Visuddhimagga*, XIX

257. Narada Maha Thera, "Buddhism: The Golden Mean," *World Buddhism* (hereafter abbreviated as *WB*), Ceylon, vol. XVIII, no. 10 (May 1970), p. 253.

258. K.N. Jayatilleke, *The Message of the Buddha*, p. 105.

259. J.T. Mitchell, "The Theist and the Buddhist: An Examination of Some Relative Positions," *W.F.B. Review*, vol. XII, no. 5 (September-October., 1975), p. 20.

dissatisfaction, or before whom he can repent for is sinful actions.[260]

H.G.A. Van Zeyst defines Buddhist non-theism or atheism as the negation of a "philosophical conception of 'Deity' as the single, personal, ultimate cause of the universe and source of all existence, distinct from polytheism and pantheism."[261]

Buddhism is atheistic, if atheism is denial of "God," the omniscient and omnipotent source of the world and the author of salvation.[262] But it is to be distinguished from materialistic atheism which denies survival, recompense and responsibility as well as moral and spiritual values and obligations.[263] It neither accepts any form of animistic theories, nor natural theistic determinism, nor total indeterminism.[264]

Prof. Jayatilleke holds[265] that Buddhism is non-theistic in the following four senses:

(i) if theism is affirmation of God's existence;

(ii) if atheism is denial of God's existence;

(iii) if scepticism or agnosticism means, it is not possible to know God; and

(iv) if positivism is that which states that the question is meaningless, since the meaning of the term "God" is not clear.

In Theravāda Buddhism non-theism, or rejection of

260. S. Tachibana, "What is Karma," *The Buddhist*, vol. IX, no. 12, (April 1939), p. 208.

261. H.G.A. Van Zeyst, "Atheism," *Ency Bsm*, vol. II, Fasc. 2, p. 306b.

262. Howell Smith, "The Christian and Buddhist Conception of Love," *The Buddhist Review* (hereafter abbreviated as *BR*), vol. I, no. 2, pp. 124-25.

263. Jayatilleke, *The Message of the Buddha*, p. 114.

264. *Ibid.*, p. 109.

265. Jayatilleke, *Facets of Buddhist Thought*, pp. 17-18.

ultimacy of any one supreme being, is linked with or based upon its several doctrinal aspects, viz., radical pluralism, the signata (i.e., *dukkha*, *aniccā* and *anattā*); all beings as compounded things; the cyclic theory of evolution of the universe; and the doctrines of *kamma* and *nibbāna*.

Theravāda Buddhist Criticism of Theism

Theravāda Buddhist metaphysics rejected all forms of theism. It refuted different aspects of theistic conception of God, viz.,

(1) God as First Cause,
(2) God as "Being" and "Force,"
(3) God as Eternal, Absolute and Ultimate Reality,
(4) God as Omniscient and Omnipresent,
(5) God as Personal and Impersonal,
(6) God as Active agent,
(7) God as Creator,
(8) God as Sustainer and Destroyer, and
(9) God as Benevolent.

REFUTATION OF GOD AS FIRST CAUSE

According to the Theravāda Buddhist doctrine, the world is not created by any absolute first cause. From the Buddhist point of view the 'Absolute' is not the First Cause. It is a "No-thing" which contains the effect of its previous emanations which in turn becomes the cause of a further emanation.[266]

Buddhism does not oppose 'God' as such, but God as a Supreme and First Cause.[267] For it, the law of causation (*idappaccayatā*) can alone explain the cosmic series of changes. The theory of empirical causation and causal regularities also explain the causal series. The Buddha emphasized that one

266. J.E. Ellam, "Practical Buddhism," *The Buddhist Review*, vol. XI, 1921, p. 77.

267. HG.A. Van Zeyst, "Atheism," *Ency. Bsm.*, Vol. II, Fasc. 2, p. 307b.

has to stop at the fundamental laws of nature and regularities of causation. To go beyond that would be both unnecessary and wrong.[268] According to Buddhaghoṣa, there are five root causes which constitute the cause and condition of a material body, viz., ignorance, craving, clinging, *kamma* and nutriment (as its condition).[269]

Theravāda Buddhism rejected the notion of any effect being caused solely by a single cause for it is incompatible with the relative universe which is conditioned by pluralism and multiple conditions governed by law of dependent origination.[270] As our minds are conditioned to spatio-temporal relativity, we ignorantly look for first causes. The doctrine of Buddhist genesis in *Agganna Sutta* only explains the mundane life on this planet, but the actual origin of the beginning of life cannot be traced. The *Anamatagga Saṁyutta*[271] which shows that the beginning of a person is cloaked in ignorance and cannot be known[272] underlies the denial of First Cause as the originator of beings.

So too is the case with the universe. In the Theravāda Buddhist cosmogony from the standpoint of cyclic theory of evolution of the universe it is absurd to look for any First Cause in the "curved space-time complex" and in a "curved

---

268. G. Dharmasiri, *A Buddhist Critique of the Christian Concept of God*, p. 44 (see, 2.21).

269. *Ibid.*, p. 34, fn. 12.

270. Dolly Facter, *The Doctrine of the Buddha*, p. 64; see also, T.R.V. Murti, "Buddhism and Vedanta," *The Indian Philosophical Congress* (29th session at Ceylon, 1954), p. 68.

271. See, *Nidāna Vagga* of *SN*, Part II, pp. 178-93.

272. *anamattaggāyam bhikkhave saṁsāro pubbhakoṭi na paññayati avijjānīvaraṇānaṁ sattānaṁ taṅhāsamyojanānaṁ sandhāvataṁ saṁsarataṁ* — see, especially *Tiṇakaṭṭha Sutta* and *Puggala Sutta* which describe the beginninglessness of a person through analogies.

construction of inter-relationships" where there can be no point of origin or departure.[273]

In the XVII section of the *Khuddaka Vibhaṅga* the views concerning the ultimate beginning and end of beings are described as wrong views.[274] That the universe was without first cause and without known beginning (*anamatagga*) is also evidenced from the fact that the Buddha could see worlds without limit "as far as he liked" (*yātatā ākaṅkheyya*)[275] and could also probe into the past without limit.[276] Francis Story succinctly states the Buddhist view:

> The question of a First Cause does not enter into the Buddhist view of the cycles of becoming (*Saṁsāra*), nor of the universe. When the process of incessant arising and passing away is seen as a complex of interrelated conditions, any theory of a primal cause becomes irrelevant. In the logic of causality there can be no absolute beginning, for each cause is seen to be the effect of a preceding cause. So a Creator God must himself have had a creator; if he had not, the argument for his existence on the basis of causality collapses.[277]

REFUTATION OF GOD AS "BEING" AND "FORCE"

The Buddha refuted God as 'Being' by criticizing the term 'Being' as a meaningless term and also as a gramatically illegitimate construction. According to him, by viewing God as Being we overstep the limits of conventional usage.[278] Prof.

---

273. Francis Story, *Gods and The Universe in Buddhist Perspective*, pp. 70-71.
274. U. Thittila (tr.), *The Book of Analysis* (*Vibhaṅga*), see Introd., p. ixvii and 899th *Vibhaṅga*, tr. p. 467.
275. *Niddesa*, I, vol. II, 356.
276. Jayatilleke, *The Message of the Buddha*, p. 98.
277. Francis Story, *The Four Noble Truths*, p. 37.
278. *MN*, III, pp. 230; 234; (q.v.) G. Dharmasiri, *op. cit.*, p. 224, fn.12.

Jayatilleke holds that the very concept of 'Being' is not possible without a violation of the convention. If we mean by 'Being' only 'Present,' then it does not constitute 'past' and 'future.' But if we define 'Being without a time reference, we are violating the convention for it means that past and future have also 'existence' in the sense of "present has existence."[279] The implied inconsistency in the assumption of God as 'Being' appears to be that there cannot be the element of permanency and unchangeableness in 'Being.' Similarly no where in the Pāli canon, the Buddha has admitted Creator God in the form of 'Force.'

REFUTATION OF GOD AS ETERNAL, ABSOLUTE AND ULTIMATE REALITY

According to the Theravāda Buddhist doctrine, things which are productive, are not eternal. Because the God (of Theists) is productive (for he able to create), he is not eternal. The *Brahmajāla Sutta* (*DN*, I) states that it is the lack of insight, or the inability to recollect their previous existences, which made some to eternalize, the Brahmā world and treat Brahmā as 'Primordial.' The four kinds of partial Eternalists mentioned in the above *sutta* belong to this category. The *Pātika Sutta* (*DN*, III.28) maintains that certain recluses and teachers ignorantly declared in their traditional doctrine that the world was the handiwork of a Supreme Creator or Brahmā.[280]

Theravāda Buddhism recognized the concept of Mahā Brahmā who is morally perfect and has very great knowledge. In the *Tevijja Sutta* (*DN*, XIII) Buddha contends that the Brahmā ideal is the highest spiritual goal for those who are faith-dominated (*saddhādika*) in the Buddhist sense. The Buddha asserts that the Brahmā state is the highest spiritual ideal[281]

---

279. Jayatilleke, *Early Buddhist Theory of Knowledge*, pp. 316-17.

280. Jayawardhana, "Ābhassara," *Ency Bsm*, vol. I, Fasc. 1, p. 14b.

281. See, expressions like *brahma-bhuta* (*Brahmā* become, *MLS*, iii.195- →

for those who are inclined to follow or are incapable of pursuing the rigorous path of *nibbāna*. But even such a great Brahmā who is spoken of as the highest denizen of the thousandfold world system (*sahassa lokadhātu*) is subject to change,[282] and the Brahmā realms are also stated to be non-eternal and transient.[283]

Moreover, if we recognize an unconditioned, imperceptible eternal principle either as object (God) or subject (*ātman* or soul), renunciation of life would be unthinkable and impossible.

From the Theravāda Buddhist standpoint things which are not omnipresent cannot be 'absolute.' Because God is not omnipresent, He is not the 'absolute.' Theravāda Buddhism refutes God as 'absolute' because it holds that "any concept must stand in relation to its object in one or more of the many modes" (*paccaya*) of conditionality, association, dependence, predominance, foundation, etc. As such relationsip is inherently impossible in the 'absolute,' so, for Buddhism God as 'absolute' is an impossibility as well as a self-contradiction. Theravāda Buddhist atheism rejects not only the "personal elements of devotion and emotion," but also "superhumanized omnipotence, omniscience, omnipresence and eternity,"[284] falsely ascribed to the absolute.

The union of the Brahmā (*Brahmā sahāvyata*) which was the ultimate state of spirituality of Brāhmaṇic religions is not the *summum bonum* (highest good) of Theravāda Buddhism.

→ 96); *Brahmapatha* (the way to Brahmā, *SN*, I.141); and *Brahmapatti* (attainment of Brahmā, *SN*, I.169).

282. *mahābramuno pi bhikkhave atthi'eva aññathattaṁ atthi viparināmo. . .* — *AN*, V.60.

283. *brahmaloka pi āvuso anicca addhuvo sakkāya pariyāpanno. . .* — *SN*, V.410; *KS*, V.35.

284. H.G.A. Van Zeyst, "Atheism," *Ency Bsm*, vol. II, Fasc. 2, pp. 305a-b.

It is merely a form of celestial existence obtainable by the cultivation of the four *brahma-vihāras* and is very much an inferior state to *nibbāna*. Hence, as H.G.A. Van Zeyst rightly observes, there is no scope in Buddhism "for either a goal of divine union or a scheme of salvation in which man has to co-operate with the divine."[285]

REFUTATION OF GOD AS OMNISCIENT AND OMNIPRESENT

Another aspect of theism rejected by the Buddha was God's "Omniscience." The Buddha criticized the idea of God's Omniscience for the Buddhist doctrine of freewill negates it. The Buddha views all Pre-Buddhistic forms of omniscience as necessarily involving determinism. Man's actions are conditioned but not determined by external and internal stimuli. The concept of divine providence or divine omnipresence is incompatible with the notion of human freedom.

The Buddha also denied that he was 'omniscient' in the theist's sense of the term. He regarded that even the Mahā Brahmā is not omniscient,[286] omnipresent, and omnipotent. Buddha's protest against the idea of God as 'omniscient' is based on the argument that if there were an omniscient God, moral discourse in the world would become impossible and meaningless.

REFUTATION OF GOD AS PERSONAL AND IMPERSONAL

Theravāda Buddhism has refused to accept God as a Personal or impersonal or supermundane or antemundane principle. In Theravāda Buddhist metaphysics, even the highest mystic states do not provide any evidence for the existence of a Personal God or an Impersonal Godhead.[287]

---

285. H.G.A. Van Zeyst, "Atheism," *Ency Bsm*, vol. II, Fasc. 2, p. 308a.

286. See, *Kevaddha Sutta* (*DN*, XI) and *Brahmanimantaṇika Sutta* (*MN*, XLIX).

287. Nyāṇaponika Thera (ed.), *Buddhisam and the God-Idea*, p. 5.

In the Pāli canon, Personal God Creator external to the universe is denied.[288] The sixty-two theories mentioned in the *Brahmajāla Sutta*, condemned by the Buddha as heresies, include the monotheistic speculation (viz., "that God is eternal but not the individual"), and also different forms of polytheistic theories (viz., "that all the gods are eternal, but not the individual souls" and that "certain illustrious gods are eternal, but not the individual souls").

All forms of impersonal aspects of Creator God are excluded from the Buddhist metaphysics by the Buddhist doctrine of *anatta* (not-self or unsubstantiality). Despite the absence of any reference to the Upaniṣadic *Brahman* in the Pāli canon,[289] in the *Milindapañha*, there is an important question raised by king Milinda, is answered by Ven. Nāgasena, denying God as the eternal unchanged being (i.e., *Brahman*). In reply to Milinda's question "What are the things that do not exist?" Ven. Nāgasena asserts that three things do not exist, viz.,

1. Anything that is not subject to decay and death,
2. Anything that is eternal, and
3. A reality (a soul) in beings.

Since Theravāda Buddhism accepts only the reality of 'Becoming' and the causality of act-force and not any kind of 'Being,' we can take it for granted that it implicitly denied the *Brahman* concept of Upaniṣads, especially as impersonal creator God and origin of all things.[290]

REFUTATION OF GOD AS ACTIVE AGENT

Theravāda Buddhism refuted the idea of God as an active

---

288. Allessandro Costa, "Buddhism: An Agnostic Religion," *Buddhism an Illustrated Review*, vol. II, no. I (October 1905), pp. 85-86.

289. See, J.E. Carpenter, *Theism in Medieval India*, p. 26; also Parrinder, *Avatar and Incarnation*, p. 131.

290. Sir Monier-Williams, *Buddhism in its Connexion with Brahmanism and Hinduism and its contrast with Christianity*, p. 118.

agent who can function as an evolver, designer and controller, because an active agent must be an individual, finite, conscious and composed of the mental and material qualities. But God cannot be conceived as individual and finite because such limitation destroys the ideas of omnipresence and omnipotence.

If God were to maintain his individuality he becomes subject to troubles and sufferings caused by "mental co-efficients" (*saṅkhāra*). If he were to be conceived as conscious, he can neither be perfectly happy nor eternal, because he will be subject to the law of *kamma* due to which will arise mental activities that beget pleasure, pain and indifference. If he were to be composed of the mental and material qualities, he will be subject to laws of mutation that operate on both.[291] Moreover, the laws of action (*kamma-niyamā*) in Buddhist doctrine is not laid down by a supreme law-giver, but is independent of any external conscious agent. It is only governed by conditionality and impermanence.

REFUTATION OF GOD AS CREATOR

Three *Sutta*s in the *Nikāyas*, viz., *Brahmajāla* (*DN*, I), *Pāṭika* (*DN*, III.28) and *Aggañña Sutta* (*DN*, III.84) explain almost in the same way how the misconception of Brahmā as Creator God arose. They all agree that the *ābhassarā* world is the one in which beings are born when the world system begins to passs away in its course of evolution (*vivaṭṭa*) and involution (*saṁvaṭṭa*). The *Brahmajāla* and *Pāṭika Sutta*s maintain that the world system begins to re-evolve after this involution, and a being dying through the exhaustion of his merits or his life-span[292] in the *ābhassarā* world is reborn in the Brahmā world.[293]

291. Dr. D.G. DE. S. Kularatne, "Existence and Creation," *The Mahā-Bodhi*, vol. 57, no. 7 (July 1949), p. 222.

292. *āyukkhayā vā puññākkhayā* — *DN*, I, p. 17.

293. Jayawardhana, "Ābbassara," *Ency Bsm*, vol. I, Fasc. I, p. 14a.

According to the *Brahmajāla* he dwells with his mental body (*manomaya*) in the empty Brahmā *vimāna*, living in joy, lustrous in body and moving in the sky. When he feels lonely and wishes for companions, coincidentally and not by his will, other *ābhassarā deva*s also make their appearance in the Brahmā world,[294] which lead the first *ābhassarā deva* to think that he is the Great Brahmā the Creator of others; and others are under the impression that the first *ābhassarā deva* having been in existence before them think he must have been their lord and originator. Some of the Brahmā *deva*s on account of loss of life or merit happen to be reborn in the world of mortals, and through meditation, etc., visualize their former existences up to their birth in the Brahmā world and conclude that Mahā Brahmā who was existing when they were first born was the creator of all beings and was eternal, whereas the beings who were born after him were created by him and hence impermanent. They believe that such a Brahmā is omnipotent (*abhibhū anabhibhūto*), omniscient (*aññadatthudaso*), the Mighty Lord (*vasavatti issaro*), maker (*katta*), creator (*nimmāta*), the most Perfect (*seṭṭho*), the Designer (*sañjitā*) and that they are creatures.

The hypothesis of the Creator God does not fit in the doctrinal framework of the Theravāda Buddhist metaphysics, for it is unnecessary in view of the beginningless and endless universe.[295] It cannot be even argued that the universe could have been created in the immense past by God, because, since the origin of universe goes to an infinite past and as it is everlasting, the problem of creation becomes completely redundant.[296] Furthermore, the idea of Creator God is not only incompatible with the Buddhist conception of universe

---

294. Brahmakāyika Bhumi, see *Sumaṅgalavilāsinī*, I, p. 410.

295. Hewavitarne, "The Unknown," *The Mahā-Bodhi*, vol. XXII, no. 7, (July 1914), p. 162.

296. Dr.G. Dharmasiri, *op. cit.*, p. 39 (2.13).

which is devoid of a prior cause, but is also irreconcilable with the existence of evil in the world on the empirical level.

Therevāda Buddhism rejected several theistic arguments which are directed to prove the existence of Creator God.

The Puppet Argument

According to the Buddha, if theists maintain that everything is the creation of a Supreme Being who is responsible for everything (viz., the glory and misery, the good and the evil acts of human beings), then the latter are only instruments of God's will. It further implies that the human being is not responsible for his actions,[297] which is false.

The Ontological Argument

This argument which supports theism is rejected on the ground that they mistakenly regarded existence as an attribute.

The Cosmological Argument

This is denied on the ground that it postulated an uncaused cause or using the word 'cause' in a non-significant sense contradicting its own premise.

The Argument from Design

It is rejected as superficial, for God could not be regarded as a successful and efficient designer who has created evil, waste and cruelty in the world.

The Argument from Utility/Fruit Test

The advantages resulting from a belief in a Creator God do not prove his existence. Further, the history of world religions shows that different theistic religions did not permanently create any sense of security and inspiration, but instead of them have brought evil by wars.

---

297. *issaro sabbalokassa sace kammaṁ kalyānapāpakaṁ niddesakāri puriso issaro tena lippati.* — *Mahā Bodhi Jātaka, J.*, vol. V. no. 528; H.T. Francis (tr.), *The Jātaka*, vol. V, pp. 122-23.

One sort of theistic evolutionism presupposes that the world is a part or aspect of the Creator God, and links the salvation of the individual with the knowledge of the world's evolution. As against this, Theravāda Buddhism does not see any necessary connection between the two ideas and therefore held that the world is without a refuge and without God (*attāno loko anabhissaro*). Further, like some theistic systems, Theravāda Buddhism does not connect concept of *deva*s with a supreme Creator God. The existence of a Creator God and creation by him is rejected by the Buddha in the *Titthāyatana Sutta* (*AN*, Tikanipāta). Buddhaghoṣa also holds that the knowledge of origin forestalls wrong theories of cause such as that the world originates due to a overlord (*issara*) or omnipotent being.[298]

The Theistic God is Indistinguishable

According to the Buddha, the theists cannot furnish any criteria for discriminating God from other entities. Hence, as the delineating criteria which makes a concept "meaningul" is lacking, Buddha called the talk about Creator God or Brahmā and the ways of attaining union as meaningless statements (*appāṭihīrakataṁ*). In the *Tevijja Sutta* (*DN*, XIII), Buddha found from the *Brahman* Vāsettha that none of the brāhmaṇas and their learned ancestors up to the seventh generation had ever seen Brahmā face to face, but claimed that they could show the straight path to salvation or union with Brahmā.

The Buddha shows how the path of salvation and the religious language based on the concept 'God' are equally meaningless, because no meaning can be attached to the concept of God.[299] The foolish brāhmaṇas are described as a set of blind men, none of whom could see the path. Their meaningless and insensible talk about the correct path to reach

298. *Visuddhimagga*, 511. Ñāṇamoli (tr.), *The Path of Purification*, p. 584, fn.23.

299. Dr. G. Dharmasiri, *op. cit.*, p. 228 (7.16).

Brahmā is compared by the Buddha to the talk of (1) a man who is making a staircase at the junction of four roads to mount up into an imagined mansion which he neither knows nor sees; (2) a man who while standing on the bank of the overflowing Aciravatī river, invokes and praises the further bank of the river to come over to his side; and (3) a man who desires a beautiful lady about whom he does not know anything and whom he has never seen.

The Conception of God is Unintelligible

The Buddha says that one has to clearly specify before one talks about and defines perfect things like 'God,' because all things have only relative characters. He illustrates this as follows. Though the Emerald jewel is supposed to be a perfect and a precious object, when it comes to the point of lustre, the fire-fly can be better than the Emerald jewel. Similarly, from the point of lustre, an oil-lamp is more excellent than a fire-fly; a great blaze of fire is more excellent than an oil-lamp etc.[300] Hence, the Buddhe affirms that for right reflection the concepts employed must be essentially intelligible.[301] But one does not know in what sense God is perfect, and in relation to what or whom.

The Conception of God is Inexplicable

In the dialogue between the Buddha and Udayi in *Cūla-Sakuludāyi Sutta* (*MN*, IXXIX) when the Buddha enquired about his teacher's doctrine, Udayi repeatedly said that 'God' is inexplicable. "This is a splendour greater and loftier than which there is none. That is the Highest splendour." How can one be certain that such an inexplicable thing exists?

REFUTATION OF GOD AS SUSTAINER AND DESTROYER

The Buddha repudiated the theist's notion that the world and

300. *MN*, II, pp. 33-34; (q.v.) G. Dharmasiri, *op. cit.*, pp. 232-33, and p. 233, fn.24 (7.21).

301. *MN*, II, p. 175; *MLS*, II, p. 364.

its beings are sustained as destroyer by the will and omnipotence of God.

The Buddhist theory of genesis in *Aggañña Sutta* (*DN*, XXVIII) pointed out the misconception that the brāhmaṇas did not spring up from Brahmā and that caste was a man-made institution. According to this *Sutta* certain beings who died from the *ābhassara* world through the exhaustion of merit or life-spans were reborn as beings on this earth by "apparitional birth." They were self-radiant, primarily sustained by joy as their food, endowed with spiritual bodies and immeasurable life. As time went on, the earth appeared on the surface of the priemeval ocean. The first human beings lived on savoury of earth (*rasāpaṭhavī* or the nutritive essence *oja* which is produced on the underside of world represented as layer-cake), honeymass, creeper and marvellous rice — which were gradually produced one after another on earth's surface spontaneously. They became solidified in course of time, correspondingly lost their luminence. Then vegetation evolved from a lower order to a higher order.

When the beings took rice as their regular food, sexual distinctions appeared in them. Thus, the institution of marriage and consequently the population growth lead to the formation of a society.[302] Such a cosmology has no place for God.

Just as beings are not sustained by the will of Creator God, the dissolution of the world system is also not due to God's omnipotence, but is a natural occurrence. It is stated in the Pāli canon[303] that the Buddha by virtue of his unbound and unfathomable insight witnessed some of the phenomena of destruction of the world system.

---

302. See, Mrs. Rhys Davids' tr. of the passage in *Aggañña Sutta.* (q.v.) B.M. Barua, *A History of Pre-Buddhistic Indian Philosophy*, pp. 217-19.

303. *AN*, v. 103.

To the question, why does the world perish? it is set forth in the *Viśuddhimagga*,[304] that by reason of the immoral roots, the world perishes. When lust, hate and delusion are superabundant the world perishes respectively by water, fire and wind. Thus, as a sign of moral deterioration, with the decrease of the life-span of human beings, the age of destruction begins. During the first intermeditate period of the "Age of Destruction" the animate world (*sattaloka*) gradually disappears. Then the receptacle-world (*bhājanaloka*) will be destroyed by a set of sixty-four great periods which consists seven destructions of fire, one by water and seven destructions by fire repeatedly in regular succession and the sixty-fourth being the destruction by wind.

The destructions by fire, water and wind are powerful one more than the other and hence their spheres of destruction increase until all *deva* spheres up to world of radiance (*ābhassara Brahmaloka*) are destroyed.[305] But Buddhaghoṣa differs in regard to the three limits of destruction. He contends that the three limits of destruction of fire, water and air are respectively the realms up to *ābhassara, subhakinha* and *vehepphala* heavens,[306] in which the case, the possibility of the birth of some beings in *ābhassara* at the end of dissolution can be questioned. But this is only a difference in detail. The conclusion is that God is not needed for world-destruction.

REFUTATION OF GOD AS BENEVOLENT

The central thesis of the Buddha that the world is full of evil and suffering, goes against the assumption of a "benevolent God." The Buddhist argument from Evil defies the theist's conception of a Benevolent God, by raising the question if the

304. Pe Maung Tin (tr.), *The Path of Purity*, vol. II, p. 488.
305. L. De La Valle Poussin, "Ages of the World (Buddhist)," *ERE*, vol. I, p. 188b.
306. Pe Maung Tin (tr.), *The Path of Purity*, Part II, trs. pp. 480-81.

world was created by a benevolent God, is the evil in it, inexplicable.

> If God (Brahmā) is Lord of the whole world and Creator of the multitude of beings, then
>
> (a) Why has he ordained misfortune in the world without making the world happy? or
>
> (b) For what purpose has he made the world full of injustice, deceit, falsehood and conceit? or
>
> (c) The Lord of creation is evil in that he ordained injustice when there could have been justice.[307]

In the *Bhuridatta Jātaka* also, the argument from evil is advanced to disprove the conception of a benevolent God.

> *He who has eyes can see the sickening sight;*
> *Why does not Brahmā set his creatures right?*
> *If his wide power no limits can restrain,*
> *Why is his hand so rarely spread to bless?*
> *Why are his creatures all condemned to pain?*
> *Why does he not to all give happiness?*
> *Why do fraud, lies, and ignorance prevail?*
> *Why triumphs falsehood, — truth and justice fail?*
> *I count your Brahmā one th' unjust among*
> *who made a world in which to shelter wrong.*[308]

Therefore if he is to be rightly called a benevolent God, he could have made the world otherwise or he must be essentially held responsible for creating such an evil form of existence. In

---

307. *sace hi so issaro sabbaloke Brahmā bahubhūtapi pajāṇam,*
(i) *kim sabbaloke vadabi alakkhiṁ sabbalokam na sukhī akāsi*
(ii) *māyāmusāvajjamadena c'āpi lokaṁ adhammena kimatth' akāsi...*
(iii) *adhammiyo bhūtapatī... dhamme sati yo vidahi adhammaṁ*
— *J.*, vol. VI.208.

308. *Bhuridatta-Jātaka* (*J.*, vol. VI, no. 543); See also, Narada Thera, "The Buddha on the so-called God-Creator," *The Mahā Bodhi*, vol. 50, no. 2, (February 1942), pp. 49-50.

the *Aṅguttara Nikāya*,[309] Buddha refuted God as benevolent by saying that as people become covetous, full of hate and hold wrong views, and if all this is due to the God's act of creation, God cannot be benevolent. In *Devadaha Sutta* (*MN*, CI), Buddha turns the theists' argument against them and argued that "if theists are suffering psychologically, then according to their own theories, it must be because God has withhold his grace from them, whereas in his own case (if theism were true) he must have been created by a good god."[310] In the *Aggañña Sutta* (*DN*, XXVII) the evolution of evil is graphically described by the Buddha without any recourse to the supernatural Creator God.

Doctrinal Points which are Inconsistent and Incompatible with the Conception of Creator God or the Absolute

DOCTRINE OF ANICCĀ (IMPERMANENCE)

The fundamental doctrine of impermanence repudiates the God of the theists and the eternal matter of Sāṅkhyas. There is no ultimate reality other than separate, instantaneous bits of existence.

Theravāda Buddhism conceived the world as not a thing but only as a vast series of evanescent changes. Matter which constitutes all the worlds of sense and form is causally conditioned (*sappaceyaṁ*), impermanent and subject to decay (*aniccam eva jarābhūtaṁ*). There is no static energy in the evolving universe of Buddhism. Though certain forces appear to be creative in the evolutionary process, yet they merely appear because of the necessity of disappearing elsewhere. In other words conditionality and impermanence are the rulers

---

309. See, *A.N. Tikānipāta*, no. 62; (q.v.) Nyāṇaponika Thera (ed.), *Buddhism and the God-Idea*, p. 20.

310. *bhadakena issarena nimmito* (*MN*, II.227); See, *Devadaha Sutta* (*MN*, CI).

of the cosmos, physically and psychically,[311] but not the Creator God.

DOCTRINE OF ANATTĀ (NOT-SELF OR UNSUBSTANTIALITY)

The doctrine of *anattā* negates the existence of Creator God or anything enduring and unchanging.[312] Without any unchanging principle of identity *saṁsāra* is the endless continuation of the causal process. For instance, Buddhaghoṣa points out that the denial of God's existence is the logical implication of "doerlessness" (*anattatā*). The world is without a 'doer,' a 'soul,' or a 'person.'

DOCTRINE OF PAṬICCASAMUPPĀDA (DEPENDENT ORIGINATION)

By means of the doctrine of *paṭiccasamuppāda*, the Buddha established that the world was not a creation of God, its origin was not accidental, it did not issue out of everlasting Nature, and it was not also predetermined as in *ājīvakism*.[313] Based on the dependent origination and cessation, the Buddha refuted an absolute beginning, an absolute existence and an absolute ending. Buddhaghoṣa, also links the argument of the Creator God to the dependent origination, by affirming that

> The wheel of becoming is without known beginning, lacking both maker (Kārako) such as Brahmā . . . and percipient (Vadako), for each consequent proceeds by reason of its antecedent.[314]

---

311. H.G.A. Van Zeyst, "Agnosticism," *Ency Bsm*, vol. I, Fasc. 2, pp. 275b-276a.

312. Dr. C.A. Hewavitarne, "Buddhism and its appeal to the West," *The Mahā Bodhi*, vol. XXI, nos. 2-3, (February and March 1913), p. 59; Dolly Factor, *The Doctrine of the Buddha*, pp. 62-63; J. Barthelemy Saint-Hilaire, *The Buddha and His Religion*, p. 164.

313. Dr. Devaprasad Bhattacarya, "Buddhist Views on Causation: An Advaitic Study," *Prabuddha Bharata*, vol, no. LXXII, (July 1967), p. 304.

314. See, Ñāṇamoli (tr.), *The Path of Purification*, Chap. XVII, 273 and 282, tr. pp. 666, 668.

DOCTRINE OF KAMMA

The suffering of the world is not intelligible on the hypothesis of God absolute, but on that of *kamma*. The formula that "The diversity of the world comes from the act"[315] summarizes all the necessary cosmological information.[316] Hence, the Buddhists denied both that the world was created by God and also that it developed due to the innate independent power of things. *Kamma* is inexorable and self-operating. By identifying *kamma* with the Law of causality (*kārya-kāraṇa-bhāva*), *kamma* was made absolutely independent of all outside agencies, and all things and phenomena were made subservient to it.[317]

DOCTRINE OF NIBBĀNA

From the Theravāda Buddhist doctrinal standpoint, *nibbāna* cannot be identified with the Upaniṣadic *Brahman* or with any form of God-idea, as it is neither the origin, nor the immanent Ground-Essence of the world. In his detailed study of the concept, Rune Johansson maintains that in the proper doctrinal context of Early Buddhism, *nibbāna* is not an ontological existent in any form, nor an "entity or a Reality"[318] nor a "dimension of existence."[319] G. Dharmasiri holds that it is not even a form of "Immortality."[320]

THE CYCLIC THEORY OF EVOLUTION

The Buddhist conception of a cyclic theory of universe does not have a place for any creator God who serves as the first

315. *karmajaṁ lokavaichitryam*, see, *Abhidharma-Kosa*, iv. st. 1.

316. L. De La Valle Poussin, "Cosmogony and Cosmology (Buddhist)," *ERE*, vol. IV, p. 130a.

317. H. Bhattacharya, "Karma," *The Mahā Bodhi*, vol. XXXIII, no. 2 (February 1925), p. 85.

318. E.A. Rune Johansson, *The Psychology of Nirvāṇa*, p. 111.

319. *Ibid.*, p 113.

320. G. Dharmasiri, *op. cit.*, pp. 189--91.

cause or as an external agent to supervise its operations. The principle of indestructibility of matter through its theory of residual energy explains the unceasing renewal of world systems (universes) and similarly the activity of each world system is due to that of the totality of the actions of the beings who belong to the preceding world-system. The Buddha expounds that the present world system is one of such infinite cyclic series whose beginning can neither be determined nor its past extremity can be known, because the succession of great world-periods do not exist in time, but the latter as a progression of events exists in them.[321] Therefore, the Buddha considered that *saṁsāra* (round of existence) is an endless continuation of causal process, which is inconceivable for it has no starting point[322] and none can reach its end.[323] The incalculable and immeasurable length of the Buddhist conception of world cycles also contributes to the idea of incomprehensible nature of the duration of the time-span of even the minor division of the world cycle. Prof. Poussin has shown that the Buddhist time-span of the world-period is incalculable, incomprehensible and indefinite.[324] Thus, the Buddhist conception of *saṁsāra* is infinite, incalculable and indefinite.

The *Cūla-Māluṅkya Sutta* (*MN*, XIIII) states that the object of Buddha's teaching is not to explain cosmological truths such as whether the world is eternal or not eternal, for the knowledge of these do not help us to extirpate the evils and suffering in the world. Another reason for not answering the

---

321. Francis Story, *Gods and the Universe in Buddhist Perspective*, pp. 40-41.

322. *SN*, II. 178.

323. *yatha nu kho bhante na jāyati, na miyati... sakkā nu kho bhante gamanena lokassa antaṁ ñātuṁ vā daṭṭhuṁ vā pāpuṇituṁ vā ti* — See, *SN*, I.61; *SN*, IV.93; *AN*, II.47; *AN*, IV.429.

324. L. De La Valle Poussin, "Ages of the World," *ERE*, vol. I, pp. 188a-b.

questions relating to the origin of the world is that "anything beyond the process of cause-effect cannot be known, since knowledge itself forms part of this process."[325]

It would be fallacious if we conclude from the *Cūla-Māluṅkya Sutta* that Buddha had no knowledge about the origin of universe, because he did not answer whether he knew or did not know that the world is eternal or not, for one of the conventional formulas which describe the Buddha's attainments shows that he has the complete knowledge of the entire universe.[326]

The Chief Purpose of Buddha's Teaching

Theravāda Buddhism is an ethico-philosophical discipline designed for attaining self-redemption from suffering.[327] The sole purpose of the teaching of the Buddha is self-salvation by the elimination of suffering and one's spiritual progress. It does not aim either to inculcate a belief in a Creator God or a belief in the *deva*s of the twenty-six heavens. That is why the whole interest was directed from God and gods to suffering (*dukkha*).[328] Buddha did not teach that one should seek for God even in the most appropriate places in the Pāli canon, when he narrated the things that a noble man should search for (*ariya pariyesanas*). He taught only that one should try to

---

325. H.G.A. Van Zeyst, "Agnosticism" *Ency Bsm*, vol. I, Fasc. 2, pp. 275a-75b.

326. *itipi so bhagavā arahaṁ sammāsambuddho vijjā-caraṇa-sampanno sugato lokavidū. . . buddho bhagavā. so imaṁ lokaṁ sadevakaṁ samārakaṁ sabrahmakaṁ sassamaṇa-brāhmaṇim pajaṁ sadevamanussaṁ sayaṁ abhiññā sacchikatvā pavedeti*

327. Shri Jamuna Prasad, "Can there be Religion Without God?," *The Indian Philosophical Congress*, 1951, p. 110.

328. R.L. Soni, "God and Buddhism," *The Mahā Bodhi*, vol. 43, no. 3 (March 1935) pp. 109-10; see, also Paul Dahlke, *Buddhist Essays*, p. 108.

be free from the vicious cycle of *saṁsāra* by getting rid of decay, death, disease and passions.[329]

The Buddha was mostly silent on metaphysical questions like God and Supernatural:

(1) Firstly, because they are ethically unimportant.

(2) Secondly, they are irrelevant to the major problem of suffering. For example, at the end of *Cūla Māluṅkya Sutta* (*MN*, XLIII) in a parable the man who often questions on the nature of the ultimate is compared to a seriously wounded man shot by an arrow, who refuses to allow the physician to treat him unless and until he gets answers to a host of irrelevant questions about the man who shot the arrow, the nature of the weapon, etc.

(3) Thirdly, metaphysical issues are unprofitable and ineffectual on the path to comprehend truth and to put an end to the evil of suffering. For instance, Buddha asks wanderer Sunakkhatta:

> . . . If then, Sunakkhatta, it matters not to that object whether the beginning of things be revealed or whether it be not, of what use to you would it be to have the beginning of thing revealed?[330]

---

329. Sri R. Siddhartha, *op. cit.*, p. 203.

330. *DN*, III, p. 45.

2

The Buddha in Theravāda Literature

Meaning of the word 'Buddha'

THE word *buddha* occurs in *Śatapatha Brāhmaṇa*[1] in the compound form of *prati-buddha* which denotes a person who has attained perfect knowledge of the Self. Hence in Theravāda Buddhist usage, the word 'Buddha' appears to have linguistic resemblance to its pre-Buddhistic origin.

The word 'Buddha' is the past participle noun derived from *bujjhati* which is an appellative one.[2] According to some *Khuddaka Nikāya* works,[3] the word which signifies final liberation is used to describe collectively the enlightened and blessed ones together with their obtainment of omniscient knowledge.

According to Buddhaghoṣa's commentary on *Minor Readings*,[4] 'Buddha' is a term which distinguishes those who have attained the supreme liberation and who have unobstructed knowledge of all ideas, from the ordinary creatures or it is the descriptive term that denotes the

---

1. *Śat. Brāh.*, XIV.7.12.17. This was first pointed out by Prof. A. Weber.
2. A.C. Taylor (ed.), *Paṭisambhidāmagga*, I, p. 174.
3. See, *Paṭisambhidā*, I. 174; *Mahā Niddesa*, 457f.
4. Ñāṇamoli (tr.), *The Illustrator of Ultimate Meaning* (Paramatthajotikā, Part I), p. 6.

attainment of the four noble truths which are the means of ominiscient knowledge. He points out[5] that the significance of the word lies in that it is not a proper name given by one's parents, relatives, companions, monks, divines or deities.

In his commentary on *Dhammasaṅgānī* Buddhaghoṣa defines the root word of 'Budh' formed out of 'Bujjhati' as "to rise from the slumber of the continuum of the lower nature. . . ."[6] He expounds[7] the meaning of the word 'Buddha' as the discoverer (*bujjhatā*) of Truths and the Enlightener (*bodhetā*) of the generation.

Whereas scholars[8] like Childers, Rhys Davids and Stede also derive the word Buddha from *bujjhati* rendering it respectively as "known, Expanded" and "wise, understood," etc., Malalasekera following Buddhaghoṣa[9] contends[10] that as against "sleeping or drunk" (*supito* or *matto*) the word (*buddho*) means "to be wakeful or awakened" and it is a generic name given to those who have attained the enlightenment or realised the truth.

The Exalted Personality of the Buddha

The Theravādins conceive the Buddha Gautama as elevated right from his *bodhisatta* career in his previous births down to the *parinibbāna* of the Buddha in his last and final birth as a human being. The term *bodhisatta* is generally confined to him in his previous births up to his enlightenment and further extended to similar beings in preparation. According to

5. *Ibid.*, pp. 7-8.
6. Maung Tin, *Expositor* (tr. of Aṭṭhasālinī), p. 294; Commentary on Dhammasangāni, 217.
7. *The Illustrator of Ultimate Meaning*, p. 6.
8. Childers, *DPL*, p. 96a; T.W. Rhys. Davids & Stede, *PTSs Dictionary*, p. 488b.
9. *Supra*, 6.
10. Malalasekera, "Buddha," *Ency Bsm*, vol. III, Fasc. 3, p. 357a.

Buddhavaṁsa[11] a *bodhisatta* must fulfil certain conditions, viz., that he must be a human being and a male; he must possess the ability to become an *arhant* and as a homeless one he must have made his vow before a previous Buddha.

The *Jātaka* describes how one becomes a *bodhisatta* by practising the thirty perfections (*pārami*) and made the five great gifts (*panca mahā pariccāya*) and thus reaches the pinnacle of three-fold conduct (*cariyā*). The *bodhisatta* or Buddha-in-making is one who has fulfilled all the conditions necessary for the attainment of *bodhi* (*bodhi-sambhāra*) at the time of his last birth, by accumulating immeasurable merit (*puñña-sambhāra*) and knowledge (*ñāṇa-sambhāra*) during a great number of his past lives. Therefore in the Pāli canon he is recognized as a "rare type of man appearing at a certain stage in time and space,"[12] for he is a product of a long evolution of virtue and merit.

The magnificent personality of the Buddha as pointed out by Chizen Akanuma[13] was due to his spirituality which flowed over his physical and mental frame by imparting "to his features and movements an inexplicable air of dignity, loving-kindness and irresistibility." The Pāli canon shows how the majestic personality of the Buddha and the splendour of his person captivated the minds and hearts of people of all occupations, and more too persons like Upaka, Vacchagotta, Vakkali, Magandiya, Jenta and Uttara. The Buddha's voice

11. R. Morris (ed.), *Buddhavaṁsa*, ii., p. 59; See also, Albert La Roche, "The Person of the Buddha," *The British Buddhist* (hereafter abbreviated as *BB*), vol. 7, no. 2 & 3, (November-December, 1932), pp. 84-100: This writer still more elaborates different aspects of Buddha's personality such as His personal appearance, His speech, Authority, Love, Fortitude, Sobriety, etc.

12. Kariyawasam, "Bodhisattva," *Ency Bsm*, vol. III, Fasc. 2, p. 231a.

13. Chizen Akanuma, "The Buddha," *The Eastern Buddhist* (hereafter abbreviated as *EB*) (Japan), vol. 1, no. 1, (May 1921), pp. 55-57.

was gentle and full of grace. The *Majjhima Nikāya*[14] shows how the Buddha observed the highest sense of discipline and dignity when he was on his alms rounds and at the time of preaching. Further the Buddha's intellect was a normal human intellect developed to its highest potency. He was a born arguer and a rhetorician. He attained highest stage of perfection in morality, contemplation, wisdom and freedom. The commentary on the *Dhammapada* states that the people of different dispositions were attracted towards different aspects of his personality. For instance, some were pleased by his appearance; others by his voice and words; others by his austerities; and still others found him incomparable in goodness.[15] Wisdom (*paññā*) and great compassion (*mahā karuṇā*) are his two special attributes, because of which he achieved precedence over all other beings.

The Supernormal Knowledge of the Buddha

The wisdom of the Buddha is constituted by the different phases of the knowledge and Enlightenment attained by him. As regards the content of his enlightenment, the Buddha called it *bodhi* (derived from the root *budh*), which means "to understand," distinguishing it from Veda (derived from the root *vid* (i.e., to know)) obtainable only by super-natural revelation. The terms *bodhi* and *sambodhi* are respectively defined as "Supreme Knowledge" and "Perfect Enlightenment"[16] which together comprises Buddhahood. Thus, the state of perfect enlightenment (*buddhatta* or *ñāna*) realized by Gautama Śākyamuni corresponds to the logos, nous or sophia of the Greeks.[17]

---

14. V. Treckner, *et al.* (ed.), *Majjhima Nikāya*, II, p. 139.
15. H. Smith, *et al.* (ed.), *Dhammapda Aṭṭhakathā*, III, p. 113f.
16. *PTS Dictionary*, pp. 491a and 694a.
17. Kariyawasam, "Buddha-Nature," *Ency Bsm*, vol. III, Fasc. 3, p. 437a.

Buddhaghoṣa mentions[18] six aspects or components of the Buddha's enlightenment. He is Enlightened (1) by his omniscience, (2) by seeing all, (3) without being led by others, (4) because of burgeoning (*visavitā*), (5) having exhausted the taints and attained immunity from defilement, (6) because he has travelled (*gata*) by the only path to the goal. Thus, in his opinion Gautama alone achieved the peerless and complete enlightenment (*samma-sambodhi*)[19] by abolishing non-discovery (*abuddhi*) and having obtained discovery (*buddhi*).

THE OMNISCIENCE OF THE BUDDHA

As distinguished from the Jaina conception of omniscience, the Buddha's omniscience is only a qualitative penetration into a man's character or into the basic nature of the world,[20] rather than a total quantitative inclusion of all existent facts, of all times embodied in the omniscience claimed by Nigantha Nātaputta.[21] The omniscience of the Buddha was interpreted[22] as a power within him by which he could so direct his attention to anything anywhere and bring it within the net of his knowledge (*ñāṇa-jāla*), the range of his vision. It is further added in the commentaries[23] on *Mahāniddesa* and *Suttanipāta*

18. Ñāṇamoli (tr.), *The Illustrator of Ultimate Meaning* (Paramatthajotika, Part I), pp. 7-8.
19. *PTS Dictionary*, p. 696a.
20. See, *Kaṇṇakatthala Sutta* (*MN*, XC).
21. See, *Tevijja-vacchagotta Sutta* (*MN*, LXXI); *MN*, II.31: *carato ca tiṭṭhato ca sutassa ca, jāgarassa ca, satataṁ nānadassanaṁ paccupatthitaṁ* (i.e., omniscience was constantly present in him (Nigaṭha Nātaputta) when he was walking, standing, sleeping, or in the waking state). The Buddha explained the impossibility of having such knowledge in the *Vacchagotta Sutta* (*MN*, I.482ff), *Sandaka Sutta* (*MN*, I.519ff) and also in *Kaṇṇakatthalaka Sutta* (*MN*, II.126ff).
22. *Majjhima Nikāya*, I, p. 482; *Dhammapada Aṭṭhakathā*, I, p. 26; *Dhp A*, II. p. 37; E. Hardy (ed.), *Vimānavatthu Aṭṭhakathā*, p. 63.
23. Buddhadatta (ed.), *Mahāniddesa Aṭṭhakathā* (Saddhammapajjotikā), vol. II, p. 316f; H. Smith (ed.), *Suttanipāta Aṭṭhakathā* (Paramatthajotika, II), vol. I, p. 18.

that the Buddha "could know anything only should he so desire." The *Milindapañha* explained nature of the Buddha's omniscience which depended on reflection by comparing it with a rich man's abundant wealth and property and valuable stores of food stuffs which are ready to be served to a traveller who goes to the former at any hour. The text also compared "the omniscience of the Buddha in the absence of his reflexion" with a tree laden with fruit which had not fallen to the ground.[24] On another occasion also Nāgasena reiterated the attainment of omniscience by the Buddha,[25] when king Milinda doubted whether Buddha's initial hesitation in preaching the doctrine implied his being not omniscient.

The omniscience of the Buddha embraces no less than forty-six items. According to Buddhaghoṣa[26] it envelops not only the ten kinds of knowledge involved in the ten intellectual powers, but also everything beyond them. Enumerating the characteristics of the omniscience of the Buddha, the *Paṭisambhidā* asserts that the Buddha knows everything in regard to all the activities of the entire world of gods and men.[27] It is further emphatically and unequivocally stated that Buddha's omniscience consists in knowing everything in the past, present and future,[28] and also in knowing everything

24. T.W. Rhys Davids (tr.), *The Questions of King Milinda* (SBE, vol. XXXV), Part I, pp. 160-62.

25. *Ibid.*, Part II, pp. 35-36.

26. J.H. Woods, *et al.* (ed.), *Majjhima Nikāya Aṭṭhakathā* (Papañcasūdanī), II. p. 31; Hardy (ed.), *Nettippakaraṇa*, p. 235.

27. *yavatā sadevakassaa lokassa . . . diṭṭham sutaṁ mutaṁ viññataṁ pattaṁ pariyesitaṁ anuvicaritaṁ manasā sabbaṁ jānātī ti*
See, Alec Robertson, "The Omniscience of the Buddha," *The Mahā-Bodhi*, vol. 78, no. 1 (January 70), p. 21.

28. See, Discourse on Knowledge (Naṇakathā) in *Paṭisambidāmagga. atītaṁ anagataṁ . . . paccuppannaṁ sabbaṁjānāti ti* . . . (q.v.) Alec Robertson, "The Omniscience of the Buddha," *The Mahā-Bodhi*, vol. 78, no. 1, (January 70), p. 21.

conditioned and unconditioned without remainder.[29] The *Nettippakaraṇaṁ* adds[30] that his knowing and seeing are unrestricted and unobstructed. The commentary on *Paṭisambhidā* further adds that Buddha's omniscience pertains to the five fields of knowledge (*ñeyyamaṇḍala*s) which include everything, mundane and supramundane.[31]

Some *Sutta*s of *Dīgha* and *Majjhima Nikāya*s and the commentaries on *Udāna* and *Paṭisambhidā*[32] emphasize that the Buddha's omniscience cannot be obstructed by anybody or everything.

The *Puggalapaññatti* and *Kathāvatthu*, the two important *Abhidhamma* works, maintain that "Buddha is the only omniscient being" and that he is all-knowing and all-seeing (*sabbaññū* and *sabbadassāvi*). The purpose of attaining such omniscience is an altruistic one according to *Ariya pariyesanā sutta* (*MN*, XXVI), which states that its object is not merely to seek *nibbāna*, but to propound, preach and promulgate the *dhamma* (doctrine).

FIVE EYES (PAÑCA-CAKKHŪNI)

One of the super excellences peculiar to the Buddha is the special attribute of "Five Eyes." According to the *Mahāniddesa* and the *Paṭisambhidā*,[33] these five eyes are:

(i) ***The Physical Eye or Eye of Flesh* (*mamsa cakkhu*)**, which enables the Buddha to see up to the distance of a league.

---

29. *sabbaṁ sankhataṁ asaṅkhataṁ anavasesaṁ jānāti tī, — ibid.*
30. Ñāṇamoli (tr.) *The Guide* (Netti-ppakaraṇaṁ), p. 31.
31. Alec Robertson, *op. cit.*, pp. 21-22.
32. See, *Pāsādikasutta* (*DN*, XXIX) and *Cūla-Saccaka-sutta* (*MN*, XXXV); F.L. Woodward (ed.), *Udāna Aṭṭhakathā* (Paramatthadīpanī), p. 144; C.V. Joshi (ed.), *Paṭisambhidāmagga Aṭṭhakathā* (Saddhamappakāsinī) II, p. 249ff.
33. Poussin and Thomas (ed.), *Mahāniddesa*, I-II, pp. 355-60; Taylor (ed.), *Paṭisambhidāmagga*, I, p. 133.

(ii) ***The Divine Eye (dibba-cakkhu)*** which enables him to see the disappearance and reappearance of beings. This is the faculty of clairvoyance by which the Buddha can see everything in all the worlds. The Buddha's locating the five *bhikkhus* in the deer park at Benaras and his power to perceive the forms of *devas* of ten world systems presented before his *parinibbāna* may be cited as two examples[34] of his exercising his heavenly eye.

(iii) ***The Eye of Wisdom (paññā-cakkhu)*** attained by him as the discoverer of the path.

(iv) ***The Buddha Eye (Buddha-cakkhu)*** which enables him to know the nature, thoughts and abilities of beings. In early Pāli canonical texts *buddha-cakkhu* denotes a special knowledge possessed by the Buddha alone. It is the Buddha's vision by which he sees beings whose minds are little and much defiled, beings whose faculties (such as "faith") are blunt and sharp, beings of good and evil dispositions, beings who can be convinced easily and with difficulty. According to the *Niddesa,* Buddha recognizes by his Buddha eye people of diverse natures, viz., greedy and hateful, dull and ruminating, faithful and intelligent.[35]

(v) ***The All-seeing Eye (Samanta-cakkhu)***: It is the eye of omniscience (*sabbaññuta ñāṇa*) which is infinitely extended, and there is nothing that can be unseen by this vision.[36]

---

34. T.W. Rhys Davids & H. Oldenberg (tr.), *Vinaya Texts,* Part I, p. 90; T.W. Rhys Davids & C.A.F. Rhys Davids (tr.), *Dialogues of the Buddha,* Part II, pp. 151-53.

35. (q.v.) Karunaratna, "Buddha-cakkhu," *Ency Bsm,* vol. III, Fasc. 3, pp. 388a; 388b-389a.

36. See, *Niddesa,* I. 355.

The *samanta-cakkhu* of the Buddha also constitutes fourteen items of Buddha-knowledge, of which the first eight (viz., the four Noble Truths and the four kinds of analytical knowledge) are also shared by *arhants*. But the later six kinds of special knowledge mentioned below are possessed only by the Buddha:

(i) Knowledge of the higher and lower states of the spiritual faculties of beings (*indriyaparopariyatta-ñāṇa*),

(ii) Knowledge of views and inclinations of beings (*āsayānusaya ñāṇa*),

(iii) Knowledge of the Twin Miracle (*yamakapāṭihīra ñāṇa*),[37]

(iv) Knowledge of the attainment of great compassion (*mahākaruṇāsamāpatti-ñāṇa*),

(v) Omniscience (*sabbaññuta-ñāṇa*), and

(vi) Knowledge which is unobstructed (*anāvaraṇa-ñāṇa*).

The commentary on *Majjhima Nikāya*[38] adds that the Buddha *ñāṇa* is one of the four illimitables.

SPECIAL KNOWLEDGE

The Buddha is also accredited with the ten kinds of knowledge derived from his knowledge of dependent origination, knowledge of unobstructed knowing and seeing and infinite vision, three-fold knowledge and six-fold psychic knowledge; knowledge of heavens and hells; and knowledge of mental and spiritual attainments of others.

Ten Kinds of Knowledge

According to the *Visuddhimagga*, the Buddha by his attainment

37. The "Yamaka-pāṭihāriya" is the miracle of the double appearance performed by the Buddha in Sāvatthī to refute the heretical teachers. It is specially demonstrated by the Buddha as producing the phenomena of opposite character in pairs, i.e., streaming forth of fire and water. *PTS Dictionary*, p. 551a; see also, *Infra*, 134.

38. J.H. Woods, *et al.* (ed.), *Majjhima Nikāya Aṭṭhakathā*, III, p. 419.

of perfect knowledge of depedent origination, comprehends the law of cause and effect in the true sense of these terms.[39] In *Ñāṇa Vibhaṅga* (Chap. XVI) of the *Abhidhamma Piṭaka,* the Buddha is said to have been endowed with ten kinds of knowledge, by means of which he acquired the leading position. These are as follows:

The Buddha comprehends as it really is:

(i) Cause and absence of cause as they are,

(ii) By way of cause, by way of root, the resultant of past, future and present actions that are performed,

(iii) The way leading to all,

(iv) The world that has many elements,

(v) The different dispositions of beings,

(vi) The improvement, the deterioration of the controlling faculties of other beings,

(vii) The corruption, the purification as well as the emergence from *jhāna,* release, concentration and attainment,

(viii) Remembrance of previous existences,

(ix) The passing away and rebirth of beings, and

(x) The destruction of the defilements.

Endowed with such exhaustive knowledge of causality the Buddha knows fully the operations of *kamma* of beings.[40] It is mentioned in the latter *sutta* that the complex operations of *kamma* are fully comprehensible only by the vision and understanding of a Buddha. For example, the Buddha by his supreme knowledge describes the clairvoyant visions of Mahā

---

39. Pe Maung Tin (tr.), *The Path of Purity,* Part II, pp. 230-31.

40. See, *Mahāsīhanāda* and *Mahākammavibhaṅga Suttas* (*MN,* XII; *MN,* CXXXVI).

Buddha's power but due to their own merit does not appear plausible in view of the literal accounts of the Pāli canon wherein it is expressly stated that only by the Buddha's glance they were healed and not before. Moreover, it is also said Suppiya was astonished at the wonderful and mighty power of the *tathāgata*. Patācāra (who lost all her relations), Vāsiṭṭhī (whose husband died), queen Ubbarī (who lost her daughter) and Kisa-Gotamī (who lost of her son), all of whom became mad with grief and anguish, regained not only presence of mind and sanity, but also understood the truth of impermanence, developed their insight and gained *arhant*-ship, due to the Buddha's power and his teaching.[126]

It is stated in *Vinaya*[127] that the Buddha by the mere movement of his lips, caused five hundred pieces of firewood to split at once, and by his power of manifestation created five hundered vessels with burning fire in a cold winter night by which the Gatilas warmed themselves. Similarly, when on the way to Kuśinara he was thirsty and on another occasion in the village Thuna of the Mallas, by his mighty miraculous power the Buddha transformed foul and turbid water into drinking water.[128]

The commentary on *Theragāthā* points out the omnipotence of Śākyamuni Buddha, who blessed childless parents with a child.[129]

BUDDHA'S SPECIAL POWERS

The Buddha, it is stated, had also the monopoly of certain other special powers:

---

126. *Psalms of the Sisters*, Sec. XLVII, tr., pp. 68-71; LI tr., p. 79; XXXIII tr., p. 39; LXIII tr., pp. 106-07.
127. *Vinaya Texts*, Part I, tr., pp. 130-31.
128. *Dialogues of the Buddha*, Part II, tr., p. 140; *The Udāna*, tr., pp. 108-09.
129. *Psalms of the Brethren*, tr., pp. 231-32. Psalms CCXXVI.

(1) He possessed the eighteen unique qualities (*āveṇika-dhamma*)[130] and the sixteen *anuttariyas*.[131]

(2) Of the three sorts of miracles, or marvels ascribed to the Buddha, viz., the marvel of magic (*iddhi-pāṭihāriya*), the marvel of mind-reading (*ādesanā-pāṭihāriya*), and the marvel of instruction (*anusāsanī-pāṭihāriya*), the third, the marvel of instruction (*anusāsanī-pāṭihāriya*), was the most excellent.[132] In that the Buddha excelled all others. By this special power he converted all. It is stated in the commentary of the *Suttanipāta*[133] that some beings could be converted only by a Buddha and they are known as "Buddha-veneyyā."

(3) The Buddha only had the power to perform the Double and the Three-fold Miracles. He performed the first at the foot of Gaudambaka tree by emitting fire from the upper part of his body and water from the lower part; emitting fire and water from different pores of his skin, and also ejecting six kinds of rays which illuminate all the ten thousand world-cycles.[134] He performed the second when he created a jewelled-walk in the sky and simultaneously exhibited the three-fold miracle: efficient will, thought-reading and instruction.[135]

---

130. See, *Ency. Bsm.*, vol. II, Fasc. 3, p. 450b; also see PTS Dictionary (S.V. Buddha), p. 490a.
131. See, Malalasekera, "Buddha," *Ency Bsm*, vol. III, Fasc. 3, p. 364b.
132. Woodward (tr.), *The Book of the Gradual Sayings* (*AN*), vol. I, pp. 155-56.
133. *Suttanipāta Aṭṭhakathā* (Paramatthajotikā II), I, p. 331.
134. See, *Paṭisambhidā*, i.125; *Milindapañha*, ii.247; Sumaṅgalavilāsinī, i.57, etc., See, Law, *A History of Pāli Literature*, Part II, pp. 415-16.
135. Law (tr.), *The Minor Anthologies of the Pāli Canon: Part III: Buddhavaṁsa*, pp. 1-2.

(4) According to the commentary on the *Buddhavaṁsa*,[136] the Buddha is immune from four dangers:

(a) He can never meet with any misfortune,

(b) Nobody can bring about his death,

(c) The marks which characterize him as a superman cannot be erased or affected in any way, and

(d) Because of his special power (*iddhipāda*), if he wishes he could live the full span of his life.[137]

But it is to be emphasized that the Buddha dedicated all his miraculous powers only for the benefit of all beings[138] in general and for the welfare of the members of his order in particular.

The Functions of the Buddha

The unique mission of all Sammāsambuddhas is to proclaim the saving truth to all beings. For this reason the Buddha is known as Satthāro (the Teacher or Master).[139] He is the founder of the order who converted and gladdened his followers by his discourses. The attainment of *arhant*-ship was the constant aim and chief objective of his instruction.[140] Perfectly enlightened he is the guide and teacher of gods and men, who teaches all the supreme means of *dhamma*, which is full of meaning and excellent in language and which is beneficial from

136. Horner (ed.), *Buddhavaṁsa Aṭṭhakathā* (Madhurattavilāsinī), p. 299.

137. Hare (tr.), *The Book of the Gradual Sayings* (*AN*), vol. IV, p. 206; T.W. Rhys Davids, *et al.* (ed.), *Dīgha Nikāya Aṭṭhakathā*, II, pp. 554-55; Woodward (ed.), *Samyuttanikāya Aṭṭhakathā*, III, pp. 251-52.

138. Mathuralal Sharma, "Magical Beliefs and Superstitions in Buddhism," *The Journal of the Bihar and Orissa Research Society* (*JBORS*), vol. I (1956), pp. 287 and 296.

139. See, *PTS Dictionary*, p. 489a.

140. *Dīghanikāya Aṭṭhakathā*, II, p. 732.

beginning to the end.[141] *Dharma* is renewed by the succession of Buddhas.

The Supremacy of the Buddha

Gautama Buddha is superior to all other human beings, gods, holy persons and previous Buddhas.

BUDDHA'S SUPREMACY, OVER ALL OTHER HUMAN BEINGS

The superiority of the Buddha lies in his having found the path to perfect enlightenment (*sambodhi*) which was either not discovered or incompletely discovered by his non-Buddhist contemporaries.

According to the *Aṅguttara Nikāya*[142] he claims that he is the foremost among all creatures which are without legs or with two legs, etc., and none of them are equal to him. The *Suttanipāta*[143] informs that he distinguished himself from all classes of society and said that since he has realized *anattā* (non-self) it is improper to ask his lineage:

> I am not a Brahmin, rajah's son, or merchant; nor am I any what; I fare in the world a sage, . . . self completely gone out it is inept to ask me of my lineage. . .[144]

The *Puggalapaññatti*[145] makes it clear that the Buddha is not to be included with any of the rest of the forty-nine human types.

---

141. Law (tr.), *Designation of Human Types* (Puggalapaññatti), pp. 78-79.

142. (q.v.) See, *AN*, ii.34; Ñāṇamoli (tr.), *The Minor Readings* (Khuddakapāṭha), p. 193.

143. *The Suttanipātha* (vv. 455-56).

144. See, J.K. Fozdar, *The God of Buddha*, p. 14; The Idea in this passage is further elaborated at *AN*, II.37-39 and Dhammapada verses 58-59.

145. *Designation of Human Types* (Puggalapaññatti), tr., pp. 4-8.

In the *Kathāvatthu*[146] the Theravādins are stated as maintaining that though he was born and grew up in the world, like a lotus he had overcome it, since he is undefiled by any sort of corruption.

BUDDHA'S SUPREMACY OVER DEITIES

While the Buddha is not a god (*deva*) in the Hindu or Buddhist sense, or a Creator God in the Judaeo-Christian sense of the term, he is superior to all the gods of higher and lower status.

In a famous *Aṅguttara Nikāya* passage, the Buddha distinguishing himself from *devas*, *gandharvas*, *yakṣas* and *manuṣyas*, self-asserts he is the Buddha and nobody else: "I am not indeed a *deva*, nor a *gandharva*, nor a *yakṣa* nor a *manuṣya*. Know ye that I am the Buddha"[147]. He transcended all the *deva* states in his previous births as a *bodhisatta* by living the lives of both the *devas* of higher and lower status. According to the canon, he affirmed that he was born seven times as Mahā Brahmā, the highest god,[148] and thirty-six times as Sakka,[149] the next highest god. He was also variously born in lower status[150] such as a Garuḍa king, as a Tree-sprite/spirit,

146. *Points of Controversy* (tr. of Kathāvatthu), tr., pp. 323-24; see also, *SN*, III. 140.

147. *na kho ahaṁ devo bhavissāmi, no kho ahaṁ gandhabbo bhavissāmi. . . yakkho. . . manusso. . . buddho ti maṁ dharchi. .*
See, Morris *et al.* (ed.), *Aṅguttara Nikāya*, II, pp. 38-39.

148. *The Guide* (Nettippakaraṇaṁ), pp. 237-38; also see, Woodward (tr.), *The Itivuttka* (The Minor Anthopologies of the Pāli canon, Part II), pp. 125-27.

149. Chalmers (tr.), *The Jātaka*, vol. I, p. 104; Rouse (tr.), *The Jātaka*, vol. IV, p. 449.

150. *Jātaka*, vol. III, nos. 360 and 399; *Jātaka*, vol. V, no. 518; *Jātaka*, vol. I, nos. 105, 109, 113, 139; *Jātaka*, vol. II, nos. 187, 190, 209, 217, 227, 283, 294-95, 298; *Jātaka*, vol. III, no. 400; *Jātaka*, vol. IV, no. 475; *Jātaka*, vol. I, nos. 146; *J*. 147.

as a wood-deity; as a Sea-sprite and as a spirit of the air. Thus the Buddha had gone through and risen above all the divine states in his previous existences.

BUDDHA'S SUPREMACY OVER ALL OTHER HOLY PERSONS

Buddha as Distinguished from a Paccekabuddha

(1) A Buddha is the discoverer as well as the preacher of the path whereas a *paccekabuddha* (solitary Buddha) is only the discoverer of the path.[151]

(2) A *paccekabuddha* has neither the intention nor the capacity to preach the truth, because to use Parrinder's language "he is said to have penetrated the flavour of enlightenment, but not the flavour of Dhamma."[152] Moreover, he lacks the skill of adopting different expedients (*upāyakausalya*) in teaching.

(3) Though both are enlightened, a perfectly enlightened one (*sammāsambuddha*) as the omniscient teacher of the way of deliverance is distinguished from a *paccekabuddha* whose realization of enlightenment is like "a dream seen by a deaf-mute."[153]

(4) A Buddha is further distinguished from *pacceka-buddhas* by his possession of omniscience, omnipotence and great compassion.[154]

(5) A Buddha has also precedence over *paccekabuddhas* in respect of his higher spiritual attainments, other than magical power (*iddhis*), attainments (*samāpattis*) and analytical knowledge (*paṭisambhidhās*).

---

151. Morris (ed.), *Puggalapaññatti*, pp. 14ff.

152. Parrinder, *Avatar and Incarnation*, p. 158.

153. Angaraj Chaudhary, "Concept of Pacceka Buddha," *The Mahā-Bodhi* (October-December 1975), p. 428.

154. Poussin, "Pratyekabuddha," *ERE*, vol. X, p. 153a; see also, Puggala-paññati, pp. 23, 110.

(6) Like a Buddha[155] *paccekabuddhas* do not possess the fruits of full Buddhahood. The latter's perfection is delimited because they think that they are self-sufficient, and it is enough if they alone have access to ultimate truth.

(7) By having practised *pārami* for the minimum duration of four incalculables (*asaṅkheyya*) and one hundred thousand *kappas*, a Buddha excels *paccekabuddhas* who practice it for only two *asaṅkheyya* and hundred thousand world-periods (*kappas*).[156]

(8) In contrast to Buddha, *paccekabuddhas* have not attained mastery over the fruitions (*phala* or path-results).

(9) In the discernment of their previous existences, while that of a Buddha is like "a disc of the autumnal Sun adorned with thousand rays," that of *paccekabuddhas* is like that of moonlight; or, the former is like a "high way for carts" and the later like "a walkers' high way."[157]

The Buddha is quoted as having asserted[158] that even an unthinkable number of *paccekabuddhas*, fully packing the entire Jambūdīpa would not be equal to a part of a single *sammāsambuddha*, because of the Greatness of the latter's qualities.

Buddha as Distinguished from an Arhant

(1) Whereas a Buddha is a discoverer, preacher and promulgator of the path which leads to *nibbāna*, *arhants*

---

155. According to *Puggalapaññati* commentary, just as all the powers of a king will come simultaneously when a prince is anointed, in the same way when a *bodhisatta* has become *arhant*, he is endowed with all the powers of an omniscient Buddha which are nothing but the fruits of perfection (*Pug A.*, 14, 189).

156. See, *SN*, II, p. 154.

157. *The Path of Purity*, Part II, pp. 477-78.

158. *Khuddakapaṭha*, tr., p. 193.

are merely its followers.[159]

(2) A Buddha is the Teacher (*satthā*) whereas *arhants* are disciples (*sāvaka*)[160] who are therefore described as *buddhānubuddhā* (i.e., those who have attained enlightenment after the Fully Enlightened one).[161]

(3) Unlike *arhants*, a Buddha is the guide and protector of others as he shows the way to liberation and hence is regarded as the first and foremost of Triple refuges (*tisaraṇa*).

(4) A Buddha has not only fulfilled himself by realizing the supreme saving truth like *arhants*, but also fulfils others by imparting the doctrine to them.[162]

(5) A Buddha is superior to all *arhants* for none of them is endowed with all the attributes possessed by the former.[163] A Buddha has primacy over *arhants* as the superman endowed with the marks of a superman (*mahāpuruṣa*), and as an extraordinary person (*uttari manussa*) for a number of events in his life are accompanied by miracles.

(6) Of the ten intellectual powers of a Buddha, except in "the knowledge of the total eradication of passions" (*āsavakkhayañāṇa*) the *arhants* are weak in all the others, whereas a Buddha is perfect in all.[164] Further, the attribute of Fourfold self-confidence is monopoly of a Buddha and is not shared by *arhants*.

---

159. Trenckner, *et al.* (ed.), *Majjhima Nikāya*, II, p. 8; Feer & Mrs. Rhys Davids (ed.), *Saṁyutta Nikāya*, III, pp. 65-66.

160. *Dīgha Nkāya*, I, p. 49.

161. Oldenberg (ed.), *Theragāthā*, p. 111.

162. *Designation of Human Types*, tr., p. 39.

163. *MN*, III, p. 8.

164. J. Minayeff (ed.), *Kathāvatthuppakaraṇa Aṭṭhakathā*, I, p. iii, also see, *Saṁyuttanikāya Aṭṭhakathā*, III, p. 263.

(7) Unlike an *arhant*, a Buddha has a two-fold relation to the universe. He knows the entire universe as a field of his knowledge and also exercises authority and influence over a certain range of world systems.

(8) A Buddha's ideal of supreme and perfect enlightenment (*anuttara samyak-sambodhi*) distinguishes him in a marked degree from the mere *nibbānic* ideal of an *arhant*.

(9) Whereas Buddhahood is the ideal of Transcendental Reality which has omniscience,[165] omnipotence and omnipresence; the ideal of *arhant*-hood is perfection of conduct and meditation, for an *arhant* merely emancipates himself from attachment, hatred and delusion.[166]

(10) Lastly, the notion of plurality of Buddhas and the succession of Buddhas distinguishes him from an *arhant*.

Buddha as distinguished from the members of the Order in General

(1) A Buddha differs from the members of the Order as one who rediscovered the *dhamma*[167] by his own efforts.

(2) Moreover he is the one who shows the way to others by proclaiming it anew to all.[168]

(3) The future attainment of Buddhahood of a Buddha is foreseen and announced by the preceding Buddhas while he is still a *bodhisatta*. Nothing like that happens to others including *arhants* and *paccekabuddhas*, who had never been *bodhisattas*.

(4) Only a Buddha alone is the conqueror, perfectly

---

165. See, *Kathāvatthu Commentary*, p. 67.
166. *Designation of Human Types*, tr., pp. 21, 27 and 97 and 104.
167. Morris (ed.), *Puggalapaññatti*, p. 29.
168. Trenckner, *et al*. (ed.), *Majjhima Nikāya*, III, p. 15.

enlightened, all-knowing and all-seeing, Lord of *dhamma* and its fountainhead of *dhamma*.[169]

(5) Only he is capable of revealing and showing the path, as its knower, expert and the specialist.[170]

(6) He surpasses in power other personages of spiritual eminence by means of his "Higher virtue, Higher concentration and Higher wisdom" (*adhisīla, adhicitta* and *adhipaññā*).[171]

(7) Endowed with the eighteen characteristics of a *sammā-sambuddha* and having attained the ten-fold power and unlimited mastery in his power to think and omniscience he surpasses the other six types of minds;[172] the worldlings (*puthujjana*), the stream-winner (*sotāpaññā*), the once-returner (*sakadāgāmi*), the non-returner (*anāgāmi*), the *arhant*, and the *paccekabuddha*.

(8) Further he has unlimited knowledge regarding the causation of all things, as well as seven other matters, the disciples know them only to a limited extent.[173]

(9) Finally, the Buddha excels his disciples in his clairvoyant powers.[174]

Gautama Buddha's Supremacy over other Buddhas

The Gautama Buddha is regarded as supreme owing his birth

---

169. See, *Kathāvatthu*, 2, 10; 18.I; 18, 4.

170. Feer & Mrs. Rhys Davids (ed.), *Saṁyutta Nikāya*, I, p. 191:

anuppannassa maggassa uppādetā, asañjātassa maggassa sañjānetā ǀ
anakkhātassa maggassa akkhātā, maggññū maggavidū, maggakovido ǁ

171. See, the explanation of the world "Bhagavā" in Niddesa: Poussin & Thomas (ed.), *Mahāniddesa*, I-II, pp. 142-43; W. Stede (ed.), *Cullaniddesa*, I-III, pp. 215-16.

172. *The Questions of King Milinda* (SBE vol. XXV), Part I, pp. 154-60.

173. *Points of Controversy*, tr., p. 139.

174. See, *SN*, V. 302.

in an aeon (i.e., Bhaddha *kappa*) where in five Buddhas are rarely born.[175] Gautama Buddha is further distinguished from other two kinds of Buddhas: (1) those who possess excessive Faith (*saddhādhika*), and (2) those who possess excessive energy (*viriyādhika*). By excelling in *paññā* and having attained Buddhahood in a minimum period of four *asaṅkheyyas*, he surpassed these two kinds of Buddhas who have to necessarily strive respectively for periods of eight and sixteen *asaṅkheyyas*. He is also superior to them having made his mental resolve (*manopanidhi*) in the presence of 125,000 Buddhas for seven *asaṅkheyyas*, and his verbal resolve (*vaci-paṇidhi*) in the presence of 387,000 Buddhas for nine *asaṅkheyyas*, in connection with his great aspiration to attain Buddhahood during his *bodhisatta* career.[176]

The Pre-eminence and the Divinity of the Buddha

BUDDHA'S SELF-ASSERTION ABOUT HIS PRE-EMINENCE

According to *Nidānakathā*,[177] during his *bodhisatta* career itself, the future Buddha Gautama in his two preceding births as Mahosadha and Vessantara, as soon as he was born, rose up and after walking seven steps proclaimed that he was the chief of the world. In his last birth as Gautama too he made a similar proclamation: "In the world I am the best, the highest and the noblest. This is my last birth, there is no further birth now."[178]

Soon after his supreme enlightenment he affirmed again

175. Horner (ed.), *Buddhavaṁsa Aṭṭhakathā*, p. 191f.

176. Nārada, "The Bodhisatta Ideal," *Buddhism in England*, vol. 2, no. 10, (April 1928), p. 216.

177. See, T.W. Rhys. Davids (tr.), *Buddhist Birth Stories* (*Jātaka Tales*), The Commentarial Introduction entitled Nidāna Kathā, p. 155.

178. T.W. Rhys Davids & Carpenter (ed.), *Dīgha Nikāya*, p. 15:
aggo'ham asmi lokassa jettho'ham asmi lokassa
settho'ham asmi lokassa ayam antimā jāti, natthi'dani punabbhavo

that he was peerless and matchless.[179] According to the *Lakkhaṇa Sutta* (*DN*, XXX), the Buddha narrating the benefits of the superman's marks, stated that he was revered by all the four divisions of the order (Saṅgha), human and non-human; that he was the best, foremost and supreme of all beings, endowed with unsurpassable wisdom and numberless virtues; that he got loyalty from all beings as they conform to his wishes, and that he had the power to overcome all his foes, subhuman, human and non-human including the *devas*.[180] The *Sela Sutta* (*MN*, XCII), shows him informing the brāhmaṇa Sela that he was the All Enlightened, Chief Healer, Perfect and Peerless, etc.[181] On another occasion, speaking to a *deva* the Buddha asserts that of all the shining things, the light of a Buddha is incomparably brighter than even the Sun, Moon and Fire.[182] In another place,[183] Buddha similarly affirmed that he was ever bright with splendour by day and night surpassing the brightness of the sun and moon who are respectively bright during day and night only, as well as the brightness of the warrior and the brāhmaṇa who are respectively bright in their armour and meditation only. Likewise the *Aṅguttara Nikāya*,[184] records his claim that "in the whole world of *devas*, *māra*s and Brahmā and mankind, he was a conqueror, unconquered, all-seeing and omnipotent."

---

179. See J. Kashyap (ed.), *Vinaya* I, p. 8; *The Mahāvagga*, 1.6.11. p. 11: *ahaṁ hi arahā loke ahaṁ satthā anuttaro, eko'mhi sammāsambuddho. . . na me achariyo, atthi sadiso me na vijjati*
See also, *Vinaya Texts*, Part I, tr., p. 91.

180. *Dialogues of the Buddha*, Part III, see *DN*, III.148-75.

181. Chalmers (tr.), *Further Dialogues of the Buddha* (*MN*), vol. II, p. 82.

182. *The Book of the Kindered Sayings* (*SN*), Part I, tr., pp. 22-23.

183. Mrs. Rhys Davids (tr.), *Dhammapada*, verse. 387; see also Max Müller (tr.), *Dhammapada*, p. 89.

184. *The Book of the Gradual Sayings* (*AN*), vol. II, tr., p. 25.

BUDDHA REGARDED AS PRE-EMINENT BY OTHERS

The Buddha is regarded as pre-eminent among all other beings in seven matters,[185] viz., in his body, living, wisdom, virtue, practice, mystery and deliverance. So, only one Buddha can appear at a time in the world. By virtue of his uniqueness there is neither a need, nor a possibility for two Buddhas to arise simultaneously, as Sāriputta and Deva Sakka admit.[186] Nāgasena explains the reasons for this:[187]

(1) This world system (*sahalokadhātu*) can only sustain the virtue and the special qualities of a single Buddha only at a time. If there were a second Buddha, the world would tremble, twist and disappear due to the excessive weight of their goodness, like a tiny boat meant for one, sinking under the weight of two passengers.

(2) If there were two perfect Buddhas at the same moment, disputes would arise, among their disciples, who would be saying 'your' and 'our' Buddha.

(3) If there were two perfect Buddhas simultaneously the scriptural statements that the Buddha is foremost, exalted, the highest of all, matchless, supreme and without rival would be proved false.

(4) All things that are mighty in the universe, are unique, like the earth, the sea, space, Māra, and Mahā Brahmā. Similarly, the *tathāgata*, is also almighty and unique in the world.

The pre-eminence of the Buddha is brought out in the clear and conscious parallelism between the universal world-

---

185. Malalasekera, "Buddha," *Ency Bsm*, vol. III, Fasc. 3, pp. 396b-370a.

186. See *DN*, II. p. 108; *DN*, III.114.

187. *The Questions of King Milinda*, Part II, tr., pp. 47-51.

ruler and the *tathāgata*. They almost appear to be of equal status in different roles. Theravāda tradition saw Gautama's Buddhahood as an alternative to his being a *cakravartin*. Both the Buddha and the *cakravartin* are born for the profit, happiness and welfare of many people, both of them are extraordinary men and the deaths of both are regretted by many people and both are worthy of having relic-shrines. The universal ruler is the temporal counterpart of the spiritual universal teacher, resembling each other in every way, but also in their unique role as universal benefactors.

According to the *Puggalapaññatti*,[188] the Buddha is superior to the teachers who uphold two doctrines of eternalism and annihilationism. The *Milindapañha*[189] says that even after his *parinibbāna*, the Buddha is incomparable, firstly, because of the existence of his mighty disciples and secondly because, of the doctrine or *dhamma* left by him. Later canonical texts like *Khuddakapāṭha* and *Suttanipāta* assert his incomparableness. In the former work it is stated[190] that the Buddha-jewel is invaluable in all the worlds and the wheel jewel, the gem jewel, or the Kāśī cloth of great value are not its equals. In *Ratana Sutta* of the later work,[191] it is said that even the whole earthly and heavenly health is not equal in value to him.

BUDDHA'S PRE-EMINENT PLACE IN THE ORDER

It is found that the Buddha claimed to be the "King of the Norm"[192] who has no superior. He is exalted as the perfect type of all the virtues taught by him, and as the supreme field of merit. Gifts offered to him both during his life as well as

---

188. *Designation of Human Types* (Puggala-paññatti), pp. 53-54.
189. *The Questions of King Milinda* (*SBE*, vol. XXXV), Part I, pp. 109-10.
190. *The Monior Readings* (Khuddakapāṭha), tr., pp. 186-87, 189 and 196.
191. V. Fausböll (tr.), *The Suttanipāta*, p. 37.
192. *Psalms of the Brethren*, tr., p. 312.

after his *parinibbāna* are thought of as supremely merit producing.[193] He serves as the perfect model and pattern but also as an object of meditation for all time. Hence, according to the Vinaya rules, to speak against such a perfectly enlightened one is regarded as one of the ten cases which results in the expulsion from the religious order. Different kinds of ecclesiastical disciplinary actions (*ukkhepanīya kamma, tajjanīya kamma, nissaya kamma, paṭisāraṇīya kamma* and *pabbājanīya kamma*) have to be taken against a monk, who speaks ill of the Buddha.[194]

THE BUDDHA'S EPITHETS

The Buddha is described in the Pāli texts by varied and numerous epithets which show the profound veneration in which he was held. Some indicate his intellectual and ethical eminence; some symbolize his marvellous power; some others signify his relation to the Truth or *dhamma*; and still others are based on his yeoman service to the mankind.

We find two important general formulas used in the Pāli texts to refer to the historical Buddha Śākyamuni. The first which contains ten epithets as mentioned in the *Dīgha Nikāya*[195] is as follows:

> Bhagavā (Lord), arahaṁ (the perfect one), Sammāsambuddho (perfectly enlighted one), Vijjā-caraṇa-sampanna (endowed with knowledge and conduct), Sugata (well-gone), lokavidū (the knower of the entire world), anuttaro purisa dhamma-sārathi (the supreme Charioteer of men to be tamed); Satthā deva manussānam (the teacher of gods and men), Buddho (the Enlightened one).

---

193. See, *Milindapañha* (*SBE*, vol. XXXV), p. 144.

194. C.S. Upasak, *Dictionary of Early Buddhist Monastic Terms*, pp. 38, 103, 123, 131 and 139.

195. *Dīgha Nikāya*, I, p. 49, etc.

Another formula which provides the highest and most comprehensive characteristics of the Buddha is found in other parts of the canon:[196] the *Majjhima* and *Saṁyutta Nikāyas*; the *Paṭisambhidā* and *Mahāniddesa* of *Khuddaka Nikāya*.

The Pāli and Sanskrit Buddhist lexicons,[197] the *Abhidhānappadīpikā* and the *Mahāvyutpatti* give each a list of thirty-nine and eighty epithets of the Buddha.

The epithets of Buddha Gautama include those given by the seven hundred Satullapa group of *deva*s who praised him as "Lion, unrivalled, patient, burden-bearer, matchless one, a creature so self-controlled,"[198] and also those found in brāhmaṇa Pingiyāyin's acclaimation as "Aṅgīrasa, illuminant, midday Sun, all radiant."[199]

In later Pāli books[200] such as *Suttanipāta*, *Vimānavattu* and *Apadāna*, laudatory epithets of the Buddha like "Loka-nātha" (Lord of the world), "Loka-nāyaka" (Leader of the world) are found.

The two books of *Theragāthā* and *Therigāthā* abound in Buddha-Epithets used by the elder *bhikkhu*s and nuns, while paying homage after achieving spiritual eminence. To give some instances, the Buddha is eulogized by *theras*[201] thus:

> by *Bākula* as "The utterly awake";
>
> by *Senaka* as "The Great Light, who hath won the highest, Guide of all, unrivalled seer, Mighty magician, hero glorious, Far-shining splendour, etc.";

---

196. See, *PTS Dictionary*, p. 489b.
197. B.C. Jain (ed.), *Pāli Kosa Sangaho*, Part I, p. 3; R. Sakaki (ed.), *Mahāvyutpatti*, vol. I, pp. 1-6.
198. *The Book of the Kindered Sayings* (*SN*), Part I, tr., pp. 38-39.
199. *The Book of the Gradual Sayings* (*AN*), vol. III, tr., pp. 174-75.
200. See, *PTS Dictionary*, pp. 587b-588a.
201. *Psalms of the Brethren*, tr., pp. 161, 181, 217, 220, 235, 293-94, 311, 395-411.

by *Migajala*, as "offspring of the Sun's race;"

by *Jenta* as "Leader Supreme, the peerless chief among drivers of mankind, shining like the Sun in his glory, best and chief among all creatures;"

by *Sopāka* as "the Man among men and the highest of all beings";

by *Adhimutta* as "The Master infinite, the entire world's physician";

by Sela as "a Bull drawing the Chariot of the world's empire, Lord of the earth from end to end four square, chief of Jambūdīpa, Sovereign lord of lords, etc."; or Sovereign Lord of the whole world or entire earth;

by *Vangīsa* as "Space, ocean, the Lion, the Elephant, the peerless Master of the caravan, Mysterious spirit, Great storm-cloud in the summer sky, Light bringer, Aṅgīrasa, most mighty seer, Seventh of mighty *ṛṣis* and greater than the gods."

The nuns too lauded the Buddha[202] as "Peerless among the sons of men, chief of the Awakened," etc.

The commentary on the *Saṁyutta Nikāya*[203] states that the appellation *guru* (Teacher) can denote only the Buddha, who is the Teacher of gods and men.

Of all the epithets attributed to the Buddha, 'Bhagavā' and 'Tathāgata' have special spiritual significance. The first is the same as the term 'Bhagavat' (the Lord) used by pre-Buddhistic and contemporary religious sects either for their special deity, or for their Teacher as in the case of Jainas. But the meaning of 'Bhagavā' is not identical with the meaning which Bhagavat has for theistic sects. The word 'Bhagavā' is used for him because he is a partaker (*bhagi*) of the ten powers of a *tathāgata*, namely the four confidences, the four analytical

---

202. *Psalms of the Sisters*, tr., pp. 97 & 105.

203. *A History of Pāli Literature*, Part II, p. 439.

insights, the six super-knowledges, etc. In the *Visuddhimagga*, Buddhaghoṣa contends[204] that the epithet is used since he is blessed with six states, viz., lordship, state, fame, glory, desire and endeavour. The appellation *tathāgata* denotes one who has attained the truth or realized the culmination of his own *dhamma*.

Buddha as Superman

The Buddha is stated to have possessed the great marks of a Superman right from his birth. According to the *Dīgha* and *Majjhima Nikāya* accounts,[205] when he was presented as an infant to the soothsayers for their prognostications, they discovered in him thirty-two major and eighty minor physical characteristics of a superman. According to the *Sutta*s of Pāli canon, in his later life the Superman's marks of the Buddha were also seen and recognized by a number of brāhmaṇa scholars and their pupils who were experts in traditional lore on the subject of the signs of a Great Being (*mahāpuruṣa*).[206] Thus, Gautama was born as a superman according to the Pāli tradition. This was because of his abundant merit in his previous existences, due to the noble aspirations and objectives with which he then cultivated the *pāramitās*. The commentary on *Cariyāpiṭaka* testifies to this.[207] According to the *Lakkhaṇa Sutta* (*DN*, XXX), the Buddha himself explained the origin of the superman's marks on his body (e.g., thousand-spoked wheels on the soles, bodily proportions, turban like head and hairy mole between the eyebrows, etc.) as the results of his accumulation of past merit; and he also narrated the various

204. *The Path of Purity*, Part II, tr., pp. 234-44.

205. *Dīgha Nikāya*, II, pp. 17-19; *Majjhima Nikāya*, II, pp. 136f.

206. *Dialogues of the Buddha*, Part I, pp. 130-34; *Further Dialogues of the Buddha*, vol. II, p. 71; *Cankī-Sutta* (*MN*, XCV); *The Book of the Gradual Sayings* (*AN*), vol. II, tr., p. 43; *The Suttanipāta*, tr., p. 101.

207. Nārada, "The Bodhisatta Ideal," *Buddhism in England* (hereafter abbreviated as *BE*), vol. 2, no. 10 (April 1928), p. 218.

benefits of possessing such marks. But the presence of such physical marks alone does not make a superman. In *Saṁyutta Nikāya* of the Pāli canon, the Buddha defined as 'Superman' as one, "who is skilled in the seven points (i.e., the full knowledge of arising, ceasing, the way of ceasing, the satisfaction and misery in it and the escape from it) with reference to the body feeling, perception and consciousness;" and as one who is the investigator of the three ways (i.e., the investigation of things by way of the elements, sense-spheres and causal happening).[208] Moreover, according to him, the superman is one "whose mind is emancipated."[209] Further, in *Majjhima Nikāya*, while addressing Sāriputta, the Buddha warned that those who deny his being a superman, and erroneously regard him as merely another wise man (who had devised his own system of salvation through a method of trial-and-error) will be consigned to Niraya hell for this sin.[210]

The Divinity of the Buddha

The Pāli texts show that during his own lifetime, the Buddha was considered to be divine by his disciples.[211] This tendency is known from the *Bhayabherava* and *Ariyaparivesana Sutta*s (*MN*, IV; XXVI) and his divinity is unequivocally asserted in the *Mahāpadāna Sutta* (*DN*, XIV) and *Acchariyabbhuta dhamma Sutta* (*MN*, CXXIII). Among the three kinds of *deva*s the Buddha comes under the category of 'Viśuddhideva' who is superior to the others. Therefore, in the later Pāli works[212] like *Cullaniddesa, Suttanipāta, Jātaka, Vimānavatthu* and *Milindapañha* he is described as *deva-atideva* (variously translated into English

---

208. *The Book of the Kindered Sayings* (*SN*), Part III, tr., pp. 54-57.
209. *The Book of the Kindered Sayings* (*SN*), Part V, tr., pp. 137-38.
210. See, *MN*, I.71-72.
211. Geden, "Images and Idols (Buddhist)," *ERE*, vol. VII, p. 119b.
212. *PTS Dictionary*, pp. 329b-330a.

as a Pre-eminent God, God above gods, Divine beyond divinities, or a Super Deva). In the *Theragāthā* and the commentaries on *Peṭavatthu* and *Dhammasaṅgāni* he is stated to be *deva-deva* (the God of gods). In *Puggalapaññatti* he is described as the *tathāgata* who lives "at peace, enjoying bliss, with a self become God-like" (*brahmabhūtena attanā*).[213] It may be also mentioned that his proper name Gautama is little used after his enlightenment, for he had become Bhagavā, the *tathāgata*.

The Transcendence of the Buddha

The origins of transcendental (*lokuttara*) conception of the Buddha can be traced as far back as the accounts regarding Gautama's descent as *bodhisatta* on the earth. According to Poussin[214] the Theravāda Pāli canon has admitted all the three *lokottaravāda* doctrines regarding Buddha's birth, viz., (i) of the *bodhisatta* (future Buddha's) descent into the maternal womb in the form of an elephant, (ii) of the miracles of uterine life, and (iii) of the birth through his mother's side.

Therefore N. Dutt rightly remarks[215] that although the Theravādins do not regard Buddha as *lokuttara*, they attribute almost all the powers and qualities of a *lokottara* Buddha to him. It is held in the *Jātakanidāna*[216] that the future Buddha when he was requested by the *devas* in *tuṣita* heaven to descend on earth he made his own choice of the place and time of his birth and his parents. According to Theravāda tradition, a Buddha is born only in this world-system (*cakkavāḷa*),[217] out of

---

213. *Designation of Human Types* (Puggalapaññatti), Chap. IV, p. 78.

214. Poussin, "Bodhisattva," *ERE*, vol. II, p. 741b.

215. Dutt, *Buddhist Sects in India*, p. 87.

216. Fausböll (ed.), *Jātaka* (with Commentary), I, p. 53.

217. *Dīgha Nikāya Aṭṭhakathā* (Sumaṅgalavilāsinī), III, p. 897; Walleser and Kopp (ed.), *Aṅguttara Nikāya Aṭṭhakathā*, II (Manorathapūrani), p. 9.

the ten thousand *cakkavāḷa*s which constitute his birth domain (*jātikkheta*). The suitable age for a Buddha to be born is when the life span of human being is not less than one hundred years and not more than ten thousand years. Further a Buddha arises in the world of human beings only at the end of the total disappearance of Buddha *dhamma* preached by the previous Buddha. One thousand years before a Buddha's birth his descent will be announced by pure-abode deities (*suddhāvāsa devas of rūpa-brahmaloka*).[218] The Pāli canonical texts, *Dīgha*, *Majjhima* and *Aṅguttara Nikāya*s which deal in detail with the conception, the uterine life and the birth of *bodhisatta* have stated that his birth is *aupapāduka* (i.e., he becomes incarnate by his own wish and without regard to the ordinary laws of conception). The *Milindapañha* which further supported the conception describes the *bodhisatta*'s birth as "parthenogenetic."[219] To deny the existence of such beings is a great heresy according to the *Dīgha Nikāya*.[220]

It is stated in *Mahāpadāna Sutta* (*DN*, II) and *Acchariyabbhuta dhamma Sutta* (*MN*, III), that the *bodhisatta* descended from *tuṣita* heaven and quite mindful and conscious, entered his mother's womb, when she was observing celibacy. After ten months, he issued forth from his mother not only quite undefiled and unstainted, but came off stretching his hands and legs just like a man descending a ladder.[221] The *Sampasādnīya Sutta* and *Sangīti Sutta*s (*DN*, XXVIII, XXXIII) add that he was born with every mental faculty alert. The Buddha is said to have performed these acts purposefully and

218. *The Minor Readings* (Khuddakapāṭha), tr., p. 131; See, the announcement of the Buddha (Buddhakolāhala) in *Khuddaka-pāṭha*, Commy. 121; (PTS, 1915); Cf. *Jātaka*, vol. I. 27; see, *PTS Dictionary*, p. 489b.

219. See, Trenckner (ed.), *Milindapañha*, p. 123.

220. See, *DN*, I.55.

221. Fausböll (ed.), *Jātaka with Commy*, I, p. 53.

delibrately. All these four suttas record accounts of several miracles which took place at the conception and birth of Buddha. For instance at the time of his conception a wonderful radiance manifested throughout the world and the ten thousand world-systems trembled.

The entire life of Gautama Buddha was according to a fixed pattern which was conforming with minor variations to the life history of other Buddhas. His parents, and the whole scheme of his life which included his son, his attendant, his chief disciples and the tree of enlightenment were all determined before hand. In view of these special circumstances he was born and his birth was never regarded as an accidental occurrence.[222]

In the later canonical texts like *Milindapañha* and *Theragāthā*, the transcendental or supramundane conception of the Buddha is more pronouncedly stated. When Milinda questioned how the Buddha was endowed with the marks of a Superman, as neither of his parents were, Nāgasena asserted that just as a hundred-petelled-lotus would not resemble the water or mud of the lake in colour, smell, or taste, similarly the Buddha, had characteristics which his parents did not have.[223] Similarly, Udāyin compared the Buddha who was born in the world lived in it sinless and perfect, to a lotus in a lake which grows in it undefiled, fragrant and beautiful.[224] In the commentary on the *Dīgha Nikāya*, the *lokuttaratā* of the future Buddha is brought out in such passages as: "the *bodhisatta* walked on earth, but the onlookers felt he was travelling through the air; he was naked, but the onlookers felt he was gaily adorned; he was an infant, but looked sixteen years old; and after his roar he reverted to infancy."[225] This is about the newly born

---

222. Malalasekera, "Buddha," *Ency Bsm*, vol. III, Fasc. 3, p. 371a.
223. *The Questions of King Milinda, SBE*, vol. XXXV, Part I, pp. 116-17.
224. *Psalms of the Brethren*, tr., p. 290.
225. *Dīgha Nikāya Aṭṭhakathā* (Sumaṅgalavilāsinī) II, p. 442.

Gautama! In the *Jātaka Nidāna* it is recorded that the "future Buddha's hair and beard remained the same length since he cut them off on the day of his renunciation; they never grew afterwards."[226] During the nights of his enlightenment and his *parinibbāna*, the skin of the Buddha became exceedingly bright.[227] The commentary on the *Buddhavaṁsa* stated that "during the seven weeks that followed his attainment of Buddhahood, he did not have to attend to his bodily requirements such as answering the calls of nature."[228] The supernormality of the Buddha's voice is asserted in the commentaries on the *Dīgha* and *Majjhima Nikāya*s thus: It "possesses eight qualities, i.e., it is frank, clear, melodious, pleasant, full, carrying, deep and resonant; it does not travel beyond his audience."[229] The Buddha himself told Ānanda that whenever he used to enter in any kind of eight assemblies, viz., of nobles, brāhmaṇas, householders and wanderers, angel hosts of the guardian kings, of the great thirty-three, of the Māras and of the Brahmās, he used to appear in their own colour and his voice and language too changed according to the nature of the assembly.[230]

Some more supramundane features regarding the Buddha's personality and life, mentioned in the commentarial and in a lesser degree in the canonical literature may be given. The commentary on the *Dhammapada* asserted that "in walking he always starts with the right foot, his steps are neither too long nor too short, only his lower limbs move; when he gazes

---

226. *Jātaka* (with Commy.) I, p. 64.
227. See, *DN*, II, p. 134.
228. *Buddhavaṁsa Aṭṭhakathā* (Mathuratthavilāsinī), p. 290.
229. *Dīgha Nikāya Aṭṭhakathā*, II, pp. 452f; *Majjhima Nikāya Aṭṭhakathā*, I-V, pp. 382f.
230. *Dialogues of the Buddha*, Part II, p. 117; See also, Morris *et al.* (ed.), *Aṅguttara Nikāya*, IV, p. 308.

on anything, he turns right sound to do so like an elephant (*nāgavilokana*) — when entering a house he never bends his body, the entrance is unobstructed."[231] It is stated in the commentary on the *Dīgha Nikāya* that

> while, namely the Lord of the world is entering for alms, gentle winds clear the ground before him; the clouds let fall drops of water to lay the dust in his pathway, and then become a canopy over him; other winds bring flowers and scatter them in his path; elevations of ground depress themselves, and depressions elevate themselves; wherever he places his foot, the ground is even and pleasant to walk upon, lotus flowers receive his tread. No sooner he set his right foot within the city-gate, then the rays of six different colours which issue from his body race hither and thither over the palaces and pagodas, and deck them as it were, with the Yellow sheen of gold, or with the colours of painting. The elephants, the horses, the birds, and other animals give forth melodious sounds; likewise the tomtoms, lutes, and other musical instruments, and even the ornaments worn by the people give forth sound. By these tokens the people would know, the Blessed one has now entered for alms.[232]

It is further said that the Buddha possessed the halo of a fathom's length, which could spread further at his will,[233] and that whenever he was present no other light could shine.[234] His body was not, it is recorded, subject to decay; it seems during his whole lifetime there appeared only a solitary wrinkle between his shoulders (of the size of a hair) which too was noticed only by Ānanda.[235] Thus, old age and decay did not affect his body for, as the *Papañcasūdani* said, it was

231. *Dhammapada Aṭṭhakathā*, II, p. 136.
232. Warren, *Buddhism in Translations*, p. 92.
233. *Buddhavaṁsa Aṭṭhakathā* (Mathuratthavilāsinī), p. 131.
234. *Suttanipāta Aṭṭhakathā* (Paramatthajotikā, II) II, p. 525.
235. Woodward (ed.), *Saṁyutta Nikāya Aṭṭhakathā* (Sāratthappakāsini), III, pp. 244-45.

immeasurable in comparison with all other bodies.[236] On the day of his *parinibbāna* the Buddha's robes of gold cloth lost their splendour. In the *Mahāparinibbāna Sutta* it is stated that until Mahākassapa came and paid his last homage, the Buddha's funeral pyre did not lit, but thereafter instantly it caught fire of its own accord. When Kassapa went to the coffin to pay his respects, the Buddha's legs stretched themselves out of the coffin.[237] To conclude, all this shows that according to the Pāli texts the Buddha was not a mere human being.

Theravāda and Docetism

On the one hand, in works like the *Kathāvatthu* and its commentary the view that while the Buddha abided in the *tuṣita* heaven, only a created form of his and taught the doctrine in this world to Ānanda, is rejected by the Theravādins.[238] On the other hand they maintain in works like the commentary on *Dhammasaṅgāni* that the Buddha possessed two bodies. Whenever he descended on earth, he left a phantom body in the *tāvatiṁsa* heaven, which preached *abhidhamma* to the *devas*, while he taught here; and so his body here was not a mere form-body.[239]

BUDDHOLOGY

The beginnings of Buddhological speculations can be traced as far back as the *abhidhamma* of the Pāli canon.[240] In the *Puggalapaññatti*, the nature of the Buddha's personality is described as "the little seed that grows a bulk and lays on every side a thousand arms." This work conceived the Buddha as not confined to any category of being earthly or celestial, for he had conquered all imperfections and became the fully

236. Woods, *et al.* (ed.), *Majjhima Nikāya Aṭṭhakathā*, III, p. 419.

237. See, *DN*, II.164; *Dialogues of the Buddha*, Part II, pp. 186-87.

238. See, *Kathāvatthu, and Commentary*, XVII, 1 & XVIII, 2.

239. Muller (ed.), *Dhammasaṅganī Aṭṭhakathā* (Aṭṭhasālinī), pp. 15ff.

240. Karunaratna, "Buddhology," *Ency Bsm*, vol. III, Fasc. 3, p. 490b

Enlightened One.

Theravāda Buddhology maintains that

(i) All the Buddhas are united and are one because of Buddha-nature which is ever existing;

(ii) This Buddha-nature is identical with *dhamma*-nature;

(iii) This *dhamma*-nature in its transcendental aspect is the ultimate reality of *nibbāna;*

(iv) By virtue of his realization of such transcendental reality, the Buddha is identified with the *tathāgata;*

(v) The *tathāgata* in turn is re-identified with Absolute Truth, which is nothing but the omnipresent Buddha-nature. Thus the Buddha is universal and immortal.

UNITY IN THE PLURALITY OF BUDDHAS

If there did not exist some underlying Reality, how could there be a *tathāgata* or Buddha to show the path of *nibbāna* by proclaiming the truth of *dhamma*? Hence the Theravādins assumed that a transcendental Buddha-nature existed as the basis of all Buddhas including the historical Buddha Gautama, who is only its incarnated form. The Buddha-nature remains as ever-existent, irrespective of other worldly occurrences. As an integral part of phenomenal operations, it manifests periodically through a *tathāgata* at sometime or other.[241] Thus, from the number of seven Buddhas mentioned in early Buddhist texts like *Vinaya, Dīgha* and *Saṁyutta Nikāyas*, the number increased from time to time to twenty-five in the *Buddhavaṁsa*, to twenty-seven in the *Jātakanidāna*, and even up to more than thirty-five in the *Apadāna*.[242] Moreover, the *Cakkavatti Sīhanāda Sutta* (*DN*, XXVI) and Buddhaghoṣa's *Aṭṭhasālini* provide particulars of Metteyya, the future Buddha.

---

241. Kariyawasam, "Buddha-Nature," *Ency Bsm*, vol. III, Fasc. 3, p. 437b.

242. M.E. Lilley (ed.), *Apadāna*, I, p. 5.

From the above accounts it may be argued that the Theravādins came to believe in a plurality of Buddhas who are types or ideals, more or less similar in their descent, lives teachings and mission. Another marked similarity among all the Buddhas is that they have the same four fixed spots and the thirty facts (*dhammatā*).[243]

It would also appear that once a particular *bodhisatta* attains Buddhahood by complete realization of Buddha-nature, he becomes identified with all his predecessors by undifferentiating himself with the *tathāgata*. So, the words Buddha, and *tathāgata* are used as appellatives to the Enlightened ones of all times without distinction. This identity of all Buddhas is lucidly expressed in *Milindapañha*,[244] which states that all the Buddhas are exactly the same as regards Buddha *dhamma*s. It seems to follow from this that their Buddha-nature is unique and non-dual, for in spite of their apparent plurality they are identical with *dhamma*. Theravāda conceived the Buddha-nature to be one and unique because of the oneness of the content of enlightenment and oneness of *dhamma* realized by the Buddhas of all times. Poussin opines[245] that the unity of the Buddha-nature through all manifestations and forms of existence was made possible by the doctrine of transfer of merit found in some of the later Pāli texts.

THE IDENTITY OF BUDDHA AND DHAMMA

In Theravāda, *dhamma* is inseparably linked with Buddha. *Dhamma* is described as a good old rule (*esa dhammo sanantano*) which had been in existence since eternity.[246] It is immanent

---

243. For details see: Malalasekera, "Buddha," *Ency Bsm*, vol. III, Fasc. 3, pp. 360b-361a.

244. *Milindapañha*, p. 285.

245. Poussin, *The Way of Nirvāṇa*, p. 33.

246. Law, "Buddhist Conception of Dhamma," *Journal of the Dept. of Letters* (hereafter abbreviated as *JDL*), vol. XXVIII (Cal. Univ. Press, 1935), p. 14.

orderliness of cause and effect (*dhammaniyamatā*) and is only perceived by the *tathāgatas*,[247] but ever present as the law of necessity in the presence as well as the absence of the *tathāgatas*.[248] Hence, the primacy of authority of *dhamma* over Buddha, is suggested[249] because the former lasts for ever. No Buddha passes away till the teaching or doctrine (*sāsana*) which constitutes *dhamma* is firmly established.[250] After a Buddha's *parinibbāna dhamma* is gradually lost beginning with *abhidhamma* and ending with Vinaya.[251] But his teaching completely disappears only when all the bodily relics of a Buddha disappears (*dhātu parinibbāna*). Then another Buddha appears in the world, rediscovers and teaches it.

The Buddha as an embodiment or personification of *dhamma* is variously delineated[252] as "Lord of Dhamma (Dhamma-sāmi or Dhammesvara), Self-born in Dhamma (Dhamma Sayambu), Friend of Dhamma (Dhammabandhu), Master of Dhamma (Dhammasāmin), king of Dhamma (Dhammarāja) and also as having a body according to the norm (Dhammakāya) and having become the Dhamma (Dhammabhūta)." Further, in Theravāda the Buddha is not only the embodiment of immaculate *dhamma*, but also the

---

247. *PTS Dictionary*, p. 335b.

248. *uppādā va tathāgatānam anuppādā vā tathāgatānaṁ thitā va sā dhātu dhammthitatā dhammaniyāmatā idappaccayatā* — *SN*, vol. II,25

249. See also: George D. Bond, "Two Theravada Traditions of the Meaning of 'the word of the Buddha,'" *The Mahā-Bodhi*, October-December, 1975, p. 402.

250. *DN*, III, p. 122.

251. Buddhadatta (ed.), *Vibhaṅga Aṭṭhakathā* (Sammohavinodinī), p. 432.

252. L.M. Joshi "The Concept of Dhamma in Buddhism," *The Mahā-Bodhi*, vol. 75, no. 11 (October-November, 1967) p. 346.

bestower of Immortality[253] and protector of *dhamma* which have their root, light and basis in the Buddha. He himself declared to Vakkali, "Whoever does see the Dhamma sees me and whoever does see me, sees the Dhamma."[254] In *Milindapañha* Nāgasena is found affirming that when the material form of the Buddha had dissolved, his *dhamma* body remains.[255]

The *dhamma*-nature is synonymous with Buddha-nature,[256] for the *dhamma* preached by the Buddha is the total revelation of Buddha-nature. Every Buddha realizes and preaches the same *dhamma* uniformly and hence the unity of *dhamma* provides a basis for the doctrine of the unity of Buddhas. The essence of the teaching of Buddhas is known as "entity-*dhammatā*."

THE IDENTITY OF BUDDHA AND NIBBĀNA

Dhamma in its transcendental aspect is *nibbāna*, the ultimate realized by the Buddha. The Buddha asserted "that the terms dhammakāya, brahmakāya, dhammabhūta and brahmabhūta are synonyms for Tathāgata."[257] *Nibbāna* is conceived by Theravādins as the only uncompounded (*asaṅkhata*). It is not mere nothingness or non-existence[258] or utter annihilation, for in the *Vinaya* it is said that soon after his enlightenment the Buddha declared that knowledge and light arose in him,

---

253. . . . *dhammabhūto brahmabhūto* . . . *amatassa dāta dhammasāmi tathāgato.* (q.v.) Dutt, *Early Monastic Buddhism*, p. 296.

254. *SN*, III, p. 119f:

yo kho dhammam passati so maṁ passati ।
yo maṁ passati so dhammam passati ॥

255. *dhammakāyena pana kho mahārāja sakkā bhagavā ni dessetum dhammo hi mahārāja bhagavata desito.*

256. *Milindapañha*, p. 276.

257. Kariyawasam, *op. cit.*, p. 439a.

258. Andre Bareau, "Absolute as the Unconditioned," *Ency Bsm*, vol. I, Fasc. 1, p. 149a.

replacing ignorance and darkness. *Nibbāna* is depicted as positive state in a number of the Pāli canonical texts. It is variously characterized as "Higher bliss than the acquisition of perfect health" (*MN*); as "nectar like, quiescent, immutable" (*SN*); as "Supreme safety attained through Yoga, and relief from all kinds of sorrows" (*AN*); as "unborn, uncreated and uncompounded" (*Itivuttaka* and *Udāna*); as "Life Eternal," etc. (*Dhammapada*);[259] as "the immortal state devoid of suffering" (*Vimānavatthu*); as "the True, the Supreme, the Abstruse" (*Nettippakaraṇam*);[260] as "the Eternal, the Tranquil, the Everlasting place" (*Suttanipāta*); and as the unconditioned (*Dhammasaṅgāni*).[261]

A more positivistic conception of *nibbāna* is found in the *Theragāthā* and the *Therigāthā*, which are dated back to about *circa* 80 BC. It is described, "bliss" in *Theragāthā*[262] and by some *theris*, either as mental illumination or a state of happiness (a feeling of cool, calm, content, peace and safety), or as a state of will. Some of them described it variously as the Highest Good, Supreme opportunity, as a regulated life, a communion with the Best, etc.[263]

In the *Milindapañha*, upon the king's inquiry about its form, figure, duration, place and realization, Nāgasena asserted that by no metaphor, explanation, reason or argument, the form, figure, duration or measure of *nibbāna* can be made clear, even though it is an existent condition. Although the quest of *nibbāna*

259. S.B. Dasgupta, "Positive Conception of Nirvāṇa," *World Buddhism* (abbreviated as *WB*), vol. XXIII, no. 5 (December 1974), Ceylon, pp. 121-22.

260. See, Kalipada Mitra, "Nibbānam," *JBORS*, vol. X, Part 1 & 2, (December 1924), p. 338.

261. V.P. Varma, "Nirvāṇa in Early Buddhist Philosophy," *The Mahā-Bodhi*, vol. 68, no. 7 (July 1960), pp. 220-21.

262. *Psalms of the Brethren*, tr., p. 161.

263. *Psalms of the Sisters*, tr., pp. xxxvii-xxxviii (Introduction).

involves the affliction of one's body and mind but after achieving it, one enjoys the bliss of *nibbāna* unalloyed with pain. With the help of a number of metaphors, *nibbāna* is described as "untainted, an embrosia, support of life, source of all beings, unborn, undecayed, infinite, full of lustre, exalted, immovable, unproducible, peaceful, blissful and all-encompassing, etc."[264]

If such is *nibbāna*, the Buddha who attained it must have become identical with it.

THE BUDDHA AND TATHĀGATA

Gautama Buddha claimed to belong to the lineage of *tathāgata*s of Buddhas.[265] It is significant that the very first title assumed by the Buddha in the canon was not a *sammāsambuddha*, but *tathāgata*. This appellation is a self-designation used by him referring to himself in the third person, on the occasion of his arrival in Isipatana, when he advised those who greeted him not to address him as "Gautama" or "Friend," but only as "Tathāgata" (*MN*, XXVI). Again before his *parinibbāna*, he referred to himself as *tathāgata* more frequently than elsewhere.

The Buddha is identified with *tathāgata* not only because he reveals the transcendental truth, but also personally represents it, and hence is rightly characterized as, "personal perfection united with universal truths."[266] R. Chalmers defined the word *tathāgata* as "who has come out at the real truth."[267] It also connotes one who has gone (*gata*) from the realm of attachment to the other beyond it, the realm of reality.

---

264. *The Questions of King Milinda*, Part II, tr., pp. 181-85 and 188-95.
265. See, *Jātaka*, I, p. 90: "... ours is the lineage of the Buddhas (*amhākaṁ pana buddhavaṁso*)."
266. Anesaki, "Ethics and Morality (Buddhist)," *ERE*, vol. V, p. 448a.
267. Chalmers, "Tathāgata," *The Journal of the Royal Asiatic Society of Great Britain and Ireland*, hereafter abbreviated as *JRAS* (*GB & IR*), (1898), p. 113.

THE BUDDHA AND ABSOLUTE TRUTH

The commentary on the *Dīgha Nikāya*,[268] while listing eight reasons for the Buddha being called as *tathāgata*, holds that, thereby, he is also identified with truth:

(1) He is endowed with the sign *tathā* (Truth) by realizing the true characteristics of *tathālakkhaṇam*;

(2) He is supremely enlightened in *tathā-dhamma* (Truth) by realizing the four sublime Noble Truths and the law of dependent origination;

(3) He has seen *tathā* (Truth) in all its forms;

(4) He preaches *tathā* (Truth) from the time of his enlightenment till his *parinibbāna*; and

(5) He does *tathā* (Truthfully), for his actions of body, mind and speech correspond or accord with Truth.

Thus, the Buddha identified with *tathāgata* is "the concrete realization of Truth which cannot be reduced to any precise formula, philosophy or metaphysic."[269]

The Buddha as Immeasurable, Unthinkable and Infinite

The transcendentality of Buddha-nature which is shared by all Buddhas, universalizes a Buddha by identifying him with the Absolute.[270] Buddha or *tathāgata* is thus the Absolute in an apparently personal form.[271] As such, the Buddha is stated to be inestimable in respect of the different categories, viz., virtue, concentration, understanding, deliverance, behaviour, dignity, seeking welfare, compassion and supernormal success.

---

268. See, *Sumaṅgalavilāsinī*, Part I, pp. 59-68; (q.v.) *A History of Pāli Literature*, vol. II, pp. 411-13.

269. W.M. Theodore De Bary, *et al.* (ed.), *The Buddhist Tradition in India, China, and Japan*, p. xvii.

270. Kariyawasam, *op. cit.*, p. 438a.

271. Conze, *Buddhist Thought in India*, p. 159.

Similarly, it is impossible to answer whether the Buddha is form, or possesses form, or is in form or vice versa. It cannot be answered also whether the Buddha is apart from (or without) form, feeling, perception, determinations or consciousness, or with them. Because of the above reasons, the major one remain unanswerable.[272] In the *Aṅguttara Nikāya* and *Apadāna*[273] it is taught that one would be distraught and come to grief if he tries to understand the range of Buddhas which is one of the four unthinkables. The transcendental nature of the Buddha is further revealed in his affirmation that the Buddha is Infinite,[274] in contrast to the finite creeping things.

The individuality of Gautama is completely submerged at the very moment of his enlightenment. The real state of the Buddha who perfected himself in the four *jhāna*s is therefore inexpressible, for the Buddha is beyond the three dimensions of time and the categories of logic. It is beyond the range of human speech to assert anything about him.

In two Suttas of *Majjhima Nikāya*,[275] the Buddha declared that even the highest *deva*s cannot ascertain and trace out a *tathāgata*, whose mind is emancipated. Though the bodily functions of a Buddha or *arhant* persist as real for others, he is no longer alive in the ordinary sense. Even in his present life a *tathāgata* is inscrutable (*ananuvejjo*), not to speak of his

---

272. *The Guide* (Nettippakaraṇaṁ), tr., pp. 231 and 233.

273. *The Book of the Gradual Sayings* (*AN*), vol. II, tr., pp. 89-90; See, *Therāpadāna*, I. 1.82.

274. *Vinaya Texts*, Part III, tr., p. 77.

275. See, *MN*, XXII (Alagaddūpama Sutta) and *MN*, I.140:
evam vimuttacittam kho bhikkave bhikkhum sa-indo-devā sa-brahmā sa-pajāpatikā anavesaṁ nādhigacchanti. idaṁ nissitam tathāgatassa viññānaṁ ti.
(O monk, *devas* with Indra, Brahmā, and Pajāpati, are not capable of conceiving the nature of the mind of the emancipated monk that here lies the consciousness of the *tathāgata*.)

posthumous existence. Similar is the purport of the conversation of Sāriputta and Yamaka on this matter.[276]

In the *Avyākata Saṁyutta*,[277] on the inquiry of king Pasenadi about *tathāgata*'s existence after death, not only Khemā, but Anuruddha, Sāriputta and Moggallāna, are reported to have said unanimously that the Buddha had not answered that question and so it was impossible to define the *tathāgata*, because he was boundless and unfathomable as the vast ocean. This is the reason why nothing is stated about the Buddha after his *parinibbāna* either in affirmative or negative.

There is another noteworthy fact in this connection. According to the commentary on the *Dīgha Nikāya*[278] there are three *parinibbāna*s in the case of a Buddha:

(a) Extinction of passions (*kilesa-parinibbāna*),
(b) Extinction of aggregates (*khaṇḍa-parinibbāna*), and
(c) Extinction of bodily relics (*dhātu-parinibbāna*).

Of these, whereas the first two take place under the Tree of Enlightenment and at his *parinibbāna*, the third will occur long afterwards. This seems to indicate that Buddha still lives spiritually in his relics, although he does not exist in his *skandha*-body.

---

276. See, *SN*, III.10.

277. *Saṁyuttanikāya*, Part IV, pp. 374-403.

278. *Dīgha Nikāya Aṭṭhakathā* (Sumaṅgalavilāsinī), III, p. 899b.

3

Saddhā and Bhatti in Theravāda Buddhism

Part A - Saddhā

The Meaning and Scope of Saddhā

THE Pāli word *saddhā* which is rendered into English as " 'Belief, Trust and Faith' has its parallels in Vedic *śraddhā* (to believe), Latin 'cred-(d) o' (cp. 'creed'), old Irish, 'Cretim' (to believe) and German 'Kred + dhe' (literally to put one's heart on, to believe, to have faith."[1] The word *saddhā* based on different prefixes of the word[2] connotes different shades of meaning, viz., credulous, trust, belief, faith, confidence, etc., which are its distinguishing features in Theravāda Buddhist usage.

Saddhā is of paramount importance because it is the preliminary requisite of the whole spiritual endeavour to attain *nibbāna* and also governs all spiritual growth. As the primary factor of the five spiritual faculties, it conditions the development of the rest of the four, viz., Mindfulness (*sati*), Concentration (*samādhi*), Energy (*viriya*) and Understanding (*paññā*). It is the root of the correct view (*samma diṭṭhi*) in Buddhist theory of salvation, because without *saddhā* there is no inner urge or inclination for the realization of *nibbāna*.

This indispensable character of *saddhā* which is the first

1. See, *PTS Dictionary*, p. 674b.
2. *Infra*, 18.

step for higher exertion is revealed in the *Vinaya*, the earliest part of the Pāli canon itself, when the Buddha having acceeded to the request of Brahmā Sahāmpati proclaimed it as the basic requirement, which is the *sine qua non* for salvation:

> Wide opened is the door of the Immortal to all who have ears to hear; let them send forth faith to meet it.[3]

Saddhā is invaluable, as it is an infallibly effective instrument (means) in drawing a worldling towards the Buddha and his doctrine. Its further development roots out the doubt, perplexity or scepticism with regard to the teacher and his *dhamma* or doctrine for it functions as the seed[4] which increases purity of virtue, purity of mind, purity of views, purity of knowledge of the right way, purity of practice and purity of wisdom.

In view of its enormous importance *saddhā* is characterized in the *Dīgha Nikāya*[5] as first among the seven treasures, seven virtuous qualities, seven powers; it is one of the five spiritual faculties and the five factors of spiritual wrestling. In the *Majjhima Nikāya*,[6] *saddhā* is described as one of the five factors of endeavour and it has also the characteristic to purify one's qualities to reach the goal. In the *Saṁyutta Nikāya*,[7] *saddhā* is expounded as the best wealth in this world and also as the controlling faculty of faith (*saddhindriya*), it is identical with the power of faith (*saddhābala*).

---

3. Rhys Davids & Oldenberg (tr.), *Vinaya Texts*, Part I, tr., p. 88.
4. See, *Suttanipāta*, Verses 77, 209, 235; also *J.I.*, 242, 281.
5. See, *DN*, III.251; *Dialogues of the Buddha*, Part III, pp. 235-36; *Dasuttara Sutta* (*DN*, XXXIV).
6. See, *MN*, VIII; *MN*, I.320.
7. *The Book of the Kindered Sayings* (*SN*), Part I, p. 59; *The Book of the Kindered Sayings* (*SN*), Part V, p. 194.

In the *Aṅguttara Nikāya* passages,[8] *saddhā* is enunciated as one of the three attainments and three growths; as one of the delightful and desirable four conditions which is hard to win in the world and as one of the four controlling powers; as one of the five powers of a learner; as one of the five powers and five growths; as one of the five perfectings and five treasures; it is further stated to be one of the seven powers, seven treasures and seven grounds for praise; and as one of the ten growths.

In the *Milindapañha*,[9] a later Pāli canonical work, *saddhā* is described as the basis of all good qualities and also further characterized as the basis of edifice of righteousness. In the *Nettippakaraṇaṁ*[10] the cognitive aspect of *saddhā* whose characteristics are trust and inclination is emphasized. *Saddhā* is used in this work in the sense of trust and belief; while undisturbedness and clarification are shown as its characteristics and respective manifestations. The faculty of faith is defined in the above work, as any act of trusting in the faculties of mindfulness, concentration, energy and understanding.

According to the *Peṭakopadesa*,[11] *saddhā* is one of the four factors which imbue cognizance. It is further stated that it has both the characteristics of confidence and faith. As confidence

---

8. *The Book of the Gradual Sayings* (*AN*), vol. I, tr., p. 266; *The Book of the Gradual Sayings* (*AN*), vol. II, pp. 74, 144-45; *The Book of the Gradual Sayings* (AN) Vol. III, pp. 1-2, 6, 36, 44; *The Book of the Gradual Sayings* (*AN*), vol. IV, pp. 2, 3, 22; *The Book of the Gradual Sayings* (*AN*), vol. V, p. 93.

9. *The Questions of King Milinda* (SBE vol. XXXV) Part I, p. 52; Part II, pp. 211-12.

10. *okappana lakkhaṇā saddhā adhimutti-paccupaṭṭhānā*; (q.v.) Jayatilleke, *Early Buddhist Theory of Knowledge*, p. 388; *The Guide* (*Nettippakaraṇaṁ*), tr., pp. 30, 33.

11. *The Pitaka-Disclosure* (*Peṭakopadesa*), tr., pp. 234, 232 & 235.

it is the placidity of the heart and as faith it is the undisturbed intention. It is also stated that non-remorse is the characteristic of it, whose manifestation is "placing faith" and whose footing is stream-entry; it is also mental good conduct.

In the *Dhammasangaṇi*[12] of the *Abhidhamma Piṭaka*, it is stated that faculty of faith is one of the fifty seven states which accompany a good thought in this world and one of the seven powers. In the *Vibhaṅga*,[13] *saddhā* is defined as confidence, trust and implicit faith and is explained both as a faculty as well as power. It is variously referred as one of the fourteen controlling faculties in the element of form; as one of the eleven controlling faculties in the plane of formless element and also as one of the twenty-two controlling faculties. In the *Puggala-paññatti*[14] *saddhā* is described as one of the twenty-two functions.

In the *Dhātukathā*,[15] the faculty of faith is categorized under the twenty-two faculties and is mentioned as a mental factor present at fifty-nine beautiful consciousness and is also regarded as one of the five faculties and strengths. Further *saddhā* both as a faculty and power is included in the classification of fourteen faculties. In an elaborate way it is said to have been associated, partially associated and dissociated with combinations of diffferent numbers of aggregates, bases and elements. In the commentary of the *Kathāvatthu*,[16] *saddhā* is stated to be different from the controlling power of faith.

TYPES OF SADDHĀ

In the early Theravāda conception, *saddhā* appears to have

12. *Dhamma-Sangani*, tr., p. 3.
13. *The Book of Analysis*, tr., pp. 162, 519-21, 159.
14. *Designation of Human Types*, pp. 3-4.
15. *Discourse on Elements* (*Dhātu-kathā*), tr., pp. 33, 35, 67, 85-87, 112-13, 120, 130, 132-35, 145-46.
16. *The Debates of Commentary*, tr., p. 83.

restricted to four objects,[17] viz.,

(1) Belief in the doctrine of *karma* and rebirth (i.e., *kamma* and *punaruppatti* or *punabbhava*);

(2) Belief in the three characteristics of existence, i.e., that all is suffering, impermanent and devoid of self and doctrine of dependent origination.

(3) Belief in the Three-Refuges.

(4) Belief in the results of actions and *nibbāna* as the final attainment.

In Theravāda epistemology there are two main species of *saddhā*, i.e., *saddhā* as faculty (*saddhindriya*) and *saddhā* as power (*saddhā bala*), which play significant roles. In the *Kīṭāgiri Sutta* (*MN*, LXX)[18] and in the *Abhidhamma* books like *Puggala-paññatti*, two levels of *saddhā* are distinguished namely,

(i) Mundane Faith (*lokika saddhā*) which is the lower level of faith, and

(ii) Supramundane faith (*lokuttara saddhā*) which is a higher level of faith.

It is evident from the early as well as later Pāli canonical texts[19] that there are five distinct conceptions of *saddhā*, viz.,

(i) the faith of the ordinary worldling (*andhaputthujjana*) who is devoid of faith (*asaddhā*);

(ii) the faith of an inquirer before he receives instructions or an average person's blind faith which is based on heresy or time-honoured tradition (*okappana saddhā*);

---

17. Conze (ed.), *Buddhist Texts*, p. 170.

18. See, *Further Dialogues of the Buddha*, vol. I, pp. 336-38; *MN*, I.477-79.

19. See, (s.v.) *Asaddhā, Okappanā, Okappati, Okappeti, Ākāravant, Aveccappasāda*, and *Adhigamana* in *PTS Dictionary*, pp. 90b, 163a, 93b, 86a, 28b.

(iii) the faith of an inquirer who undergoes the primary course of training or the rational faith of an average person (*kalyāṇa-putthujjana*), who although possessing faith is not fully freed from doubt (*ākāravati saddhā*);

(iv) the faith of a stream-winner (*sotāpanna*), who is free from one of the three fetters, i.e., doubt (*vicikicca*), known as unshakable faith (*aveccappasāda*) and;

(v) the faith of the Āryans (*ariyapuggala*), who have not yet reached the goal, known as realized faith based on experience and not information (*adhigamana saddhā*).

Of the above five types of *saddhā* in his commentary on *Mahāparinibbāna Sutta*,[20] doctrinal importance is limited by Buddhaghoṣa to four. Of these, three are common, viz., *okappana saddhā, aveccappasāda* and *adhigamana saddhā*. The fourth is known as *agamana saddhā* which means the *bodhisatta*'s great resolution to become a Buddha.

AVECCAPPASĀDA

Of these four types of *saddhā, aveccappasāda* is faith in Buddha and other two Jewels.[21] There are two characteristics of this aspect of *saddhā*, i.e.,

(i) The characteristic of placidity, and

(ii) The characteristic of belief which is its resultant condition.

In its aspect of *aveccappasāda, saddhā* is an antidote to doubt (*vicikiccā*) about the greatness of Buddha and other two jewels, etc. It is observed[22] that the word *pasīdati* is rendered into English as "to have faith, believe, be converted" when it is particularly connected with the passages that refer to Buddha

20. See, Children, *DPL*, pp. 409-10.

21. *Ibid.*, p. 410a; p. 86 a: (s.v. *Avecca*).

22. E.L. Gyomroi, "Note on the Interpretation of 'Pasīdati,'" *University of Ceylon Review*, April 1943, p. 76.

and his doctrine, while the words *pasādo, cittapasādo*, etc., are always used in the faith or rejoicing in the Buddha, viz., the joy or peace of mind which is resulted from such belief in him. In this context, the word *pasīdati* denotes "a mental attitude which unites deep feeling, intellectual appreciation and satisfaction, clarification of thought and attraction towards the teacher."[23]

In its highest, i.e., supermundane aspect *saddhā* is *aveccappasāda* (unshakable faith in the Triple Gem), which when accomplished, helps a person to overcome two other mental factors (*samyojana*), viz., sceptical doubt (*vicikicchā*) and clinging-to-rites-and-rituals (*sīlabbata-parāmāsa*).

In a *Dīgha Nikāya* passage,[24] Sāriputta is stated to be a possessor of *aveccappasāda* which is explained as the disciple's total confidence in the Buddha which is devoid of even the least selfish attachment to or affection for the latter. In the *Vatthūpama Sutta* (*MN*, VII) *aveccappasāda* is regarded as the basic factor for the attainment of *nibbāna*. It is enunciated in the *sutta* that after removing the mental impurities such as hypocrisy, deceitfulness, etc., the adept is required to develop unflinching faith in the Three Jewels. Here *saddhā* in Three Jewels which are also Three Refuges is emphasized as an essential element for spiritual progress at the second stage. The growing mental satisfaction resulting from the increasing faith or *saddhā* in Buddha and other Jewels, corresponding to the level or degree of the removal of mental impurities, producing joy and deep pleasure (*pīti*) ultimately leads to mental concentration (*samādhi*). *Saddhā* as *aveccappasāda* in this *sutta* which skips over the process of the third and fourth *jhāna*s is a new and shorter method that suits any person who need not be a monk or nun, because this process eliminates

23. E.L. Gyomroi, "Note on the Interpretation of 'Pasīdati,'" *University of Ceylon Review*, April 1943, p. 82.

24. See, *DN*, III.102.

the usual hard task of attaining the perfection of four *jhānas* by means of comprehension of three characteristics of existence, four noble truths, etc. In this *sutta*, the special emphasis on this aspect of *saddhā*, i.e., *saddhā* in the Buddha and other Jewels also exempts the adept from the observance of *sīlas* (i.e., the *pātimokkha* rules prescribed in the *Vinaya* such as observances with regard to the rules of food).

Two works, i.e., *Nettippakaraṇaṁ* and *Milindapañha*,[25] assert that *saddhā* in the sense of *pasāda* has the characteristic mark of tranquillization (*sampasadana*) which subsides the mental disturbances in proportion to the intensity of faith, resolution or trust. This function of *saddhā* which settles and clears the mind of breaking through the hindrances and destroying evil dispositions is compared in *Milindapañha* to a king's water-clearing gem, which clears muddy water by making it transparent and serene. Besides this, the *Milindapañha* adds the second characteristic of *saddhā*, i.e., the characteristic of aspiration (*sampakkhandhana*) which functions as the aspiration to leap up into higher things which have yet to be realized or attained. This function of faith is compared to a brave man's setting an example to others by leaping from one side of the overflowing brook to the other.

According to the *peṭakopadesa*,[26] *saddhā* has three levels, i.e., blunt, medium and outstanding.

SADDHĀ — ITS SCOPE AND LIMITATIONS

Of all the above types of *saddhā* primary importance is given to logical faith (*ākāravatī saddhā*),[27] which is explained as based on reason and rooted in understanding (*paññāvaya saddhā*). Pointing out the limitations of *saddhā*, according to a *Majjhima*

25. *The Guide*, tr., pp. 47, 47, fn. 162/1; *The Questions of King Milinda*, Part I, pp. 54-56.

26. *The Pitaka-Disclosure*, tr., 241.

27. See, *MN*, I.401.

Nikāya dialogue,[28] the Buddha explains that *saddhā* is merely one of the five states of consciousness and hence by possessing it alone it is not possible to judge what is true and false. Elsewhere, the Buddha exhorts[29] that *saddhā* has its own alternative outcome, because a false thing which is empty in itself may give rise to abundant faith and similarly a real and veritable thing may fail to inspire or evoke faith.

In the *Saṁyutta Nikāya, saddhā* in the Buddha is compared to a person's confidence in a teacher or a good physician. Whereas *saddhā* rooted in understanding (*paññāvaya saddhā*) is given a primary place, mere confidence or faith is given only a secondary status.[30]

In the *Aṅguttara Nikāya,* in view of the delimited role and meaning of *saddhā* it is stated that there is no necessity of cultivating *saddhā* for those who are devoid of doubt and wavering but only for those who have not realized the *nibbāna* by insight.[31] The householders were advised to develop *saddhā* and *paññā,* only after their practice of *dāna* and *sīla*. One of the duties prescribed for laity is that an *ariya sāvaka* is to develop firm faith in the Buddha and other jewels.[32] It is stated[33] that *saddhā* itself is insufficient for final release or attainment of *nibbāna,* unless it is accompanied by virtue, learning, etc.

The Buddha repeatedly discouraged excessive emotional faith which becomes a serious obstacle to the progress on the path of deliverance, since it obstructs one's spiritual progress

---

28. Chalmers (tr.), *Further Dialogues of the Buddha,* vol. II, tr., p. 96.
29. *Ibid.,* p. 97; *MN,* II.170.
30. *saddhā dutiyā purisassa hoti, paññā c'enaṁ pasāsati* — *SN,* I, p. 38.
31. *The Book of the Kindered Sayings* (*SN*), Part V, tr., pp. 196-97.
32. See, *AN,* II, p. 212; *AN,* IV.271.
33. See, *AN,* V, p. 10f (PTS edn.).

by disturbing the development of a balanced character.[34] Therefore, he warned the *bhikkhus* who aspire for *nibbāna* that mere *saddhā* in the teacher is insufficient for complete ethical progress. For instance the *Kīṭāgiri Sutta* (*MN*, IXX) of the *Suttapiṭaka* and the *Puggala-paññatti*[35] of the *Abhidhamma* refer to two types of persons, i.e.,

(i) Those who are conforming by faith (*saddhānusāri*), and

(ii) Those who are emancipated or released by faith (*saddhāvimutta*).

According to *Majjhima Nikāya Sutta,* referred above, the *saddhānusāri* are those who have intense faith or confidence, in the Buddha and attachment to him and adhere to the *tathāgata*'s teaching although they have not destroyed the influxes or intoxicants (*āsavās*). The *saddhāvimutta* are those whose faith and attachment in the Buddha is deeply rooted and established although they too destroy only some of the intoxicants. Both these above types of persons have still to strive further diligently since they have yet to attain the last release.

The limitation of *saddhā* is revealed in regard to the *saddhāvimutta* who is relatively in an advantageous position compared to the *saddhānusāri*, for the former's defilements have been destroyed.[36] But from the Theravāda epistemological standpoint, like *cetovimutti* (deliverance of mind) *saddhāvimutti* too is an intermediate release (or a partial emancipation) which is not the final or complete attainment, but that which leads a person for further progress. Thus, it is obvious from the *sutta* that both the above types of spiritual attainments are inferior to *arhant*-ship or ultimate perfection.

---

34. *Infra*. 36.

35. *Designation of Human Types*, pp. 7, 15-16.

36. See, *Majjhima Nikāya Aṭṭhakathā*, I, p. 188f.

In the *Puggala-paññatti*,[37] a *saddhānusārin* is defined as the possessor of believing faculty which proceeds to realize the fruition stage of a stream-attainer by means of cultivation of the Noble Path preceded by faith. On the other hand, a *saddhā-vimutta* is distinguished from the former as one who is emancipated by faith by establishing himself in the fruition, and by understanding the Noble Truths and who only through insight and practice perceives the *dhamma*.

According to Theravādins the limitation of *saddhā* is also due to the fact that even in the above two types of person, *saddhā* does not wholly exclude the other four faculties, but is only predominant over them. Similar is the case with regard to those who are emancipated through wisdom (*paññā-vimutta*).

The *Visuddhimagga*[38] draws our attention to the harmonious relation of faith and knowledge in its exposition of "Regulation of the controlling faculties." It enunciated that unless all the five faculties are balanced, they are unable to perform their functions and cannot assist the individual to cultivate skill in ecstasy. For instance, if the *saddhindriya* (faculty of faith) is strong and others are weak, the rest of the faculties, viz., that of energy, mindfulness, concentration and understanding cannot perform their respective functions of upholding, establishing, unscattering and seeing. Further a person who is strong in faith and weak in understanding will place his faith in good-for-nothing people and believe in a wrong object. Similarly he who is strong in understanding and weak in faith leans towards dishonesty. Only a person in whom both faith and understanding are equally balanced can believe in the right object. Thus, when all the five faculties, viz., faith, energy, mindfulness, concentration and understanding, are regulated and equalized, one will be led to ecstasy.

---

37. *Designation of Human Types*, tr., pp. 22-23.

38. *The Path of Purity*, Part II, pp. 150-51.

FAITH IN THE BUDDHA AS THE SATTHĀ

We find that Buddha had been the object of *saddhā* primarly in his *satthā* or *ācāriya*'s role. In the *Saṅgīti Sutta* (*DN*, XXXIII)[39] *saddhā* (confidence) in the Buddha as the supreme teacher and in his enlightenment is stated as one of the five factors of spiritual wrestling. The Buddha warned his disciples not to direct their faith (*saddhā*) towards an inefficient or unenlightened teacher (who is compared to a foolish cowherd), because it will bring them woe and suffering for a long time.[40] In contrast to the above in another *sutta*,[41] the Buddha expounded the qualifications of a perfect teacher in whom alone they should deposit their faith, because it is conducive to long standing welfare and happiness.

The Buddha also instructed that even the initial faith of the pupils by which they select their teacher/s should be based on a thorough moral scrutiny. It is known as "rational faith" (*ākāravatī saddhā*) as distinguished from the uncritical faith of the brahmaṇas' characterized as "dogmatic, baseless and blind faith" (*amūlikā saddhā*).[42] The Buddha enunciated that only after a faithful follower finds out on examination that he (the Buddha) is of pure conduct and behaviour and the enlightened teacher, he may have faith in him[43] (the Buddha). Thus, after the preliminary inquiries and tests the disciple selects his teacher by placing *saddhā*, and after listening to the doctrine with faith and trust in the teacher,[44] realizes the truth of some of his teachings.

As an *ācāriya*, the Buddha is the religious guardian of his

---

39. *DN*, III. 237; *Dial. of the Buddha*, Part III, tr., pp. 226-27.
40. *Cūlagopālaka Sutta* (*MN*, XXXIV).
41. See, *Cūlasīhanāda Sutta* (*MN*, XI); *MN*, I.64-67, 226.
42. See, *Caṅkī Sutta* (*MN*, XCV); *MN*, II.170.
43. *Vīmaṁsaka Sutta* (*MN*, XLVII).
44. See, *MN*, I.480; *Further Dialogues of the Buddha*, vol. I, tr., p. 338.

pupils/disciples and the latter are assisted and protected by the former during their lives. According to Pāli commentaries on the *Vinaya*, *Majjhima Nikāya* and *Apadāna*, the term *ācāriya* means one who trains his pupil in good conduct and ethical behaviour as well as in transcendental virtues. It is stated in the commentary on the *Dhammapada* that an *ācāriya* teaches the doctrine leading to emancipation. According to the *Visuddhimagga*, supremacy of an *ācāriya* lies in his being a "spiritual teacher" who is regarded as superior to that of the Upajjhāya in the specific context of a disciple's progress in cultivating mental concentration as prescribed by Buddhism, and for this reason the entire Buddhist monastic life centres round him.[45]

Furthermore the attitude of an *ācāriya* towards his disciple is similar to that of a father towards his son.[46] The Buddha's intimacy with his pupils is evident from the *Khuddaka Nikāya* works. The *Itivuttaka* says that the Buddha declared that the monks are his "own true sons, born of his mouth, born of dhamma and are his spiritual heirs."[47] In the *Theragāthā* the Buddha is compared to the father of all.[48] As an *ācāriya*, the Buddha's care of his disciples is metaphorically described in the *Kumbhakāra Jātaka*[49] as follows. He guards his disciples twice a day and twice a night, just as a joy bird guards her egg, or a yalk-cow her tail, or a mother her beloved son, or a one-eyed man his eye, so that in the very instant he checks them if they entertain evil thoughts. In the commentary of the

---

45. Jayawickrama, "'Ācāriya' in Pāli Buddhism," *Ency. Bsm.*, vol. I, Fasc. 2, pp. 164a-165a.
46. *ācāriyo, bhikkhave, antevāsikamhi puttacittaṁ upatthapessati* — (s.v.) 'Ācāriya' in *Dictionary of Early Buddhist Monastic Terms*, p. 26.
47. *Itivuttaka*, tr., p. 185.
48. See, *Theragāthā*, St. 1237: *"sabbe bhagavato puttā palāpo ettha na vijjati."*
49. *The Jātaka*, vol. III, tr., p. 228.

Dhammapada[50] also the Buddha is stated to have addressed his disciples as his sons.

Not only as *satthā*, the Buddha as *tathāgata* also is regarded as the object of *saddhā* in the early Pāli canon,[51] for the order (*saṅgha*) was depended on him even though he did not claim its leadership.[52] In a good number of *suttas*[53] of the *Majjhima Nikāya*, *saddhā* (faith) in the Buddha or *tathāgata* is variously described as one of the five tilled fallows of the heart which is conducive to a disciple's ardour, zeal, perseverance and exertion; as one of the seven virtuous qualities of an adept; as sound faith based on direct knowledge; and as foremost of the five qualities of the path-enterer.

In the *Khuddaka Nikāya* works,[54] viz., the *Itivuttaka*, *Suttanipāta* and *Theragāthā*, the Buddha is stated to be one of the three best objects of faith and hence attachment to and unwavering confidence in the Buddha is advocated, as he is the only knowable and real object of faith.

In the Pāli *Abhidhamma* works[55] such as the *Dhammasaṅgāni* and *Vibhaṅga*, it is stated that one claims himself as a follower of Buddha by faith.

---

50. See, *Dhammapada Commy*, I.21, 430, etc. (q.v.), C.A.F. Rhys Davids, 'Love (Buddhist),' *ERE*, vol. VIII, p. 160b.

51. See, *MN*, XXII; *MN*, XXXIV.

52. See, *DN*, II.100; *Dialogues of the Buddha*, II.107.

53. See, *NM*, I.102, 356; Chalmers (tr.), *Further Dialogues of the Buddha*, vol. I, tr., pp. 73, 256; *MN*, (XXXXVII); vol. II, tr., p. 49; *MN*, II.95.

54. See, *Itivuttaka: As It Was Said*, tr., pp. 178-79; *The Suttanipāta*, tr., p. 103; *Theragāthā*, 507: *yassa saddhā tathāgate acalā supatiṭṭhitā*; *Theragāthā*, 828 & 29: *abhiññeyyaṁ abhiññātaṁ, bhāvetabbañ ca bhāvitaṁ, . . . vinayassu mayī kankhaṁ adhimuccassu brāhmaṇa dullabhaṁ dassanaṁ hoti sambuddhānam abhinhaso.*

55. *yā saddhā saddhanā okappanā abhippasādo saddhā saddhindriyam saddhābalaṁ idaṁ vuccati saddhindriyam* — *Dhammasangāni*, 12, 15; *Vibhaṅga*, p. 123; See Mrs. Rhys Davids, *A Buddhist Manual of Psychological Ethics*.

The early Pāli *Nikāya* texts[56] show that *saddhā* or faith in the Buddha also includes a pupil or disciple's acknowledgement of the Buddha's enlightenment, and his perfect knowledge or wisdom, wherein too he should place his faith. *Saddhā* in the Buddha is explained in the Pāli canon[57] as not merely faith in the Buddha, but also in his teaching or doctrine because the latter inculcates faith in the former.

FAITH IN BUDDHA AS COMPASSIONATE PROTECTOR

The Buddha is an object of faith because due to his great compassion, he protects and helps all beings in general and the members of his order in particular. It can be inferred from the *Sīgalovada Sutta* (*DN*, XXXI) that as a teacher, he has compassion on his pupils in five ways. He is reported to have the great compassion and also responsibility in guiding the order (*saṅgha*).[58] For example, he led the monks away from the mental defilements and worldly pleasures;[59] helped the progress of monks' meditation as suited their interests and abilities as in the case of Moggallāna;[60] released the nuns from ill and sorrow;[61] and he took concern for each living being.[62]

---

56. See, *DN*, II.93; *Dialogues of the Buddha*, Part II, p. 99; *jānāti bhagavā nāhaṁ jānāmi ti* — *MN*, I.480; *The Book of the Kindered Sayings* (*SN*), Part V, tr., p. 172; . . . *ariyasāvako saddho hoti, saddhāti tathāgatassa bodhim*. . . — *SN*, V.196; *saddhati Tathāgatassa bodhim* — *MN*, 53; *AN*, III.2.

57. See, *DN*, vol. I, p. 171; (q.v.) Joshi, "True Buddhism," *The Mahā Bodhi*, vol. 74, no. 1-2; (January-February 1966), p. 8; *Further Dialogues of the Buddha*, vol. I, tr., p. 227; *MN*, I.319-20; *Dhammasangāni*, tr., p. 12.

58. See, *MN*, I.457-58.

59. See, *MN*, II.460ff; Horner (tr.), *The Middle Length Sayings*, II.131.

60. See, *SN*, IV.263.

61. C.A.F. Rhys Davids, "Desire (Buddhist)" *ERE*, vol. IV, p. 668a.

62. See, *SN*, IV.314ff.

The Buddha in truth is born in the world out of his mercy for the good and welfare of all beings including gods and men.[63] Referring to a *Saṁyutta Nikāya* passage Buddhghoṣa comments[64] in his *Visuddhimagga* that beings are free from the cycle of existence on account of the Buddha who is a good friend endowed with all qualities.

According to the *Nettippakaraṇa*,[65] the well-wishing nature, compassion and super-normal success of the Buddha are inestimable and hence positively unanswerable. The *Kathāvatthu*,[66] rejects the argument of the Uttarāpathakas that as the passionless Buddha felt no compassion, the epithet 'compassionate' (*kāruṇika*) cannot be an attribute of him, for to be compassionate is to have a form of attachment (*rāga*). This work declared that the Buddha was full of pity and kind to the world and compassionate, because he attained universal pity.[67] According to the Theravādins the rejected view implies that the Buddha lacks love sympathetic joy and equanimity too, and so is untrue. The commentary[68] elucidating the Theravādin argument adds that "pity" also belongs to the same category of the four *brahmavihāras*; so it must be accepted that the Buddha is compassionate. According to Theravādins the misconception of their opponent is due to that the latter took 'pity' in the sense of a state blended with affection or passion, which springs out of attachment.

Saddhā in the Ti-Saraṇa (Three Refuges)

As already noted earlier[69] the four objects of Theravāda

63. See, *AN*, I.13, I; *The Questions of King MIlinda*, Part II, tr., p. 56.

64. See, *SN*, I. 88; *The Path of Purity*, Part II, p. 114.

65. *The Guide*, tr., pp. 231-32.

66. *Points of Controversy or Subjects of Discourse*, tr., pp. 325-26.

67. See, *Patisambhida Magga*, I.126f.

68. *The Debates Commentary*, tr., pp. 212-13.

69. See, *Supra*, 17.

conception of *saddhā* is unflinching faith in the Three Refuges, i.e., Buddha, Dhamma and Saṅgha. *Saddhā* which is expressed by resorting to them is a preliminary requisite for a non-Buddhist to become a Buddhist.

THE ORIGIN OF "TI-SARAṆA" AND ITS MEANING

In the Theravāda resorting to the three refuges is a *sine qua non* for both the monks as well as the laity. The significance of resorting to the three refuges is as old as *Vinaya*, because in the early Buddhist monastic order, the *pabbajjā* and *upasampadā* ordinations were performed by resorting to the *ti-saraṇa*. Even in early Pāli canonical texts[70] where *saraṇa* is interpreted as *kammapaṭisaraṇā* (beings who have *kamma* for their refuge) the word *kamma* is used in the sense of *kusala-dhamma*s whose object is the Buddha and other jewels which are refuges.

The *Paramatthajotikā*[71] also accords with the above view by stating that the formula of Three Refuges (*saraṇattayaṁ*) were pronounced by the Buddha himself and not just by his disciples, seers or deities. The formula of *ti-saraṇa* was pronounced by the Buddha after *yasa* attained his *arhant*-ship (in *Vinaya*) and when the sixty one *arhant*s began to preach the *dhamma*. This formula was initiated as the pathway of full admission for gods and men to become laity or monks. Later it was recorded in the Minor Readings of the *Khuddaka Nikāya* for the purpose of recitation.

The word *saraṇa* which means refuge or protection and the phrase *saraṇam gacchati* are mentioned in the early as well as later Pāli canonical texts[72] like the *Vinaya, Dīgha, Aṅguttara Nikāyas*, and *Suttanipāta, Dhammapada, Itivuttaka, Jātaka*.

---

70. *Vinaya*, 87-88; *MN*, III.203; *AN*, III.186; See Saddhātissa, "The Three Refuges," *The Maha Bodhi*, June & July 1965, p. 168.
71. See, *The Illustrator of Ultimate Meaning* (*Paramaṭṭhajotikā*, Part I), p. 5.
72. See, *PTS Dictionary*, p. 697b.

Further, the word *saraṇa* in the specific sense of shelter and protection in the three refuges[73] and *saraṇāgamana* in the sense of taking refuge in the three *saraṇas*[74] are used in the Pāli canon.

It is stated in the *Dīgha Nikāya* commentary[75] that the word *saraṇa* means "seeking protection from suffering" and by resorting to the three refuges is meant to conduct oneself according to them by keeping them as the goals and respecting them. In the commentary on the *Khuddakapāṭha*,[76] *saraṇāgati* is defined as the birth of a religious impulse or the tendency to accept an object as the ultimate, by serene faith in which a person's sins are destroyed. Both the commentaries on the *Dīgha Nikāya* and *Khuddakapāṭha* assert that *saraṇāgamana* (going for refuge) is "not a mere formal recital of faith in the three refuges, but an expression of self-devotion to an object and communion."[77]

THE MEANING OF THE WORD "BUDDHA" IN "TI-SARAṆA"

In its ultimate nature, the word Buddha among the *ti-saraṇa* does not mean merely Buddha Gautama, but a personification of world-transcending enlightenment. For instance, according to the *Ariya-pariyesana* (*MN*, XXVI) and *Vimaṁsaka sutta*s (*MN*, XlVII) Refuge in the Buddha means refuge not in a particular Buddha, but in the principle of Buddhahood or enlightenment. Hence, it is expounded in the *Abhidharma Kośa* that a person should take refuge in the Buddhatva (Buddhahood) but not

73. See, *DN*, I.145; *AN*, I.56; *Jātaka*, I.28.

74. *Vinaya*, III.24; *SN*, IV.270.

75. See, *Sumaṅgalavilāsini*, pt. I, pp. 230-31.

76. *Paramaṭṭhajotikā* (*PTS*), p. 16; See Law, "Three Refuges (Trisaraṇa) in Buddhism," *The Mahā Bodhi*, vol. 61, no. 5 & 6, May-June, 1953, pp. 155-57.

77. *tappasādataggarukkatāhi vihata-kileso tappasāyatākārappavatto cittuppādo saraṇāgamanaṁ*
— See *Sumaṅgala-vilāsini*, I, p. 231; Cp. *Paramaṭṭha-jotikā*, I, p. 16; (q.v.) Law, *Concepts of Buddhism*, p. 1.

Buddha, the person.[78] This is also because that there is no enduring self or person in Thervāda epistemology and therefore not the Buddha's person or physical body but his *dhamma* body is to be taken as the object of refuge.[79] According to later Pāli canonical and commentarial works,[80] the Buddha who is the first among the *ti-saraṇa* is *sammāsambuddha* (perfectly enlightened) and *bhagavā* (the Blessed one).

THE PLACE OF THE BUDDHA IN THE TI-SARAṆA

The object of going for refuge in the Buddha is that he combats the creature's fear[81] and prevents him from harm by promoting his good. According to the *Khuddakapāṭha Commentary*, the object of going for refuge in the Buddha is the conscious recognition that "he is the highest value, the eliminator of abyss, the provider of welfare."[82]

The arising of the two jewels which are refuges, i.e., *dhamma* and *saṅgha* is preceded by the Buddha whose measure and province are incalculable. The rationale of the display of the specific order of the *ti-saraṇa* is explained in the commentary on *Khuddakapāṭha*[83] as follows. The Buddha precedes other refuges as the foremost of all creatures and the promoter of their welfare. He is followed by the *dhamma* because it owes its existence to him as it is discovered and taught by him for the universal welfare. The *saṅgha* follows next, for it is not only the bearer and server of the *dhamma* but also which practised it for the attainment of welfare. The interrelationship

78. See Krishnan, "The Kaya Doctrine in Buddhism," *The Mahā-Bodhi*, vol. 60, No. 8, August 1952, p. 282.
79. See, Conze, *Buddhist Thought in India*, p. 171.
80. See, *Mahāniddesa*, pp. 142-43; *Paramaṭṭha-Jotikā*, pp. I, 107-09.
81. See, (s.v.) "Sarati" in *PTS Dictionary*, p. 698a; Ñāṇamoli, "Three Refuges," BPS, Ceylon, 2nd Imp. 1972, p. 6.
82. *Paramaṭṭha Jotikā*, tr., p. 12.
83. *The Illustrator of Ultimate Meaning*, p. 13.

and inseparable nature of the *ti-saraṇa* is described in the above work in twenty-two similies.[84] For example, the Buddha, *dhamma* and *saṅgha* have been compared to the moon, its effulgence, and the world inspired by it; the extractor of the darts (arrows) of sorrow, means for removing them and the people who are freed from them; good pilot, ship and the persons who have reached the further shore of it; blossomed lotus flower, its honey and the swarm of bees that make use of it.

The Buddha is considered as a unique refuge because during his lifetime[85] he did not appoint anyone as his successor or as the leader of the *saṅgha*, and the *saṅgha* after his *parinibbāna* also did not do so; and the unity of the order is maintained by his *dhamma* (doctrine) which is regarded as the alternative refuge.[86] Some of the *Majjhima Nikāya* passages also show that none else but the Buddha can serve as the refuge even after his *parinibbāna*. The new entrants are advised by the Buddha's disciples to seek refuge only in the Buddha and in no one else.[87]

In later canonical and commentarial works,[88] taking refuge in the Buddha and other jewels is regarded as one of the categories of virtue and taking refuge in the three jewels is a

---

84. *The Illustrator of Ultimate Meaning*, pp. 14-16.

85. See, *MN*, III.9: *natthi. . .ekabhikkhu pi tena bhagavatā. . . ṭhapito ayam vo mam accayena paṭisaraṇaṁ bhavissātī ti.*

86. See, *Gopaka-Moggallāna Sutta* (*MN*, CVIII); *Further Dialogues of the Buddha*, vol. II, tr., pp. 160-62; *MN*, III. 9-12.

87. For example, at *MN*, II, 83, 90; Ven. Kāccana instructs Avantiputta, king of Madhura to take refuge in Lord Buddha in whom he himself sought refuge (*mā kho maṁ tvaṁ, mahārāja, saraṇam agamāsi. tan eva tvaṁ bhagavantaṁ saraṇaṁ gacchayam aham saraṇaṁ gato*); Similarly at *MN*, II.162-63, Udena preached to the brāhmaṇa Goṭamukha to take refuge only in the Buddha.

88. See, *The Questions of Kind Milinda*, Part II, tr., pp. 214-15; *Sumaṅgalavilāsinī*, I, p. 231.

mundane refuge (*loukika saraṇa*) in contrast to supermundane refuge whose object is the *nirvāṇic* attainment.

According to Buddhaghoṣa, there are four modes of *saraṇāgamana*[89] (ways of taking refuge) in the Buddha and other two refuges:

I. Refuge taken in the form of self-dedication to the Buddha and other jewels by surrendering oneself to them (*atta-sanniyyātanā*). This surrender of self is expressed in two forms.

   (i) "I surrender myself to the Buddha. . ."

   (ii) "To the exalted one I am giving myself . . . my life! Until my life ends, I am taking refuge in the Buddha! The Buddha is my refuge, my shelter and my protection."

II. Acceptance of the Buddha and other two jewels as one's guiding Ideal or guiding principle (*tapparāyanatā*). For example, Tapassu and Bhalluka (*Vin.*, I.4), *Bhayabherava Suttas* (*MN*, IV) and in *Suttanipāta* (*Sn.*, V.192: Ālavaka's assertion) refuge is sought in Buddha as one's guiding Ideal: "Starting from today I adopt the Buddha for my guiding principle. . . ."

---

89. See, Ñāṇamoli, *The Three Refuges*, (BPS, Ceylon), 1972, pp. 8-10; for Pāli passage referred below under four modes of *saranāgamana*, See Nyanaponika Thera, *The Threefold Refuge* (BPS, Ceylon), 1965, pp. 4-6.

I. (i) *ajja ādiṁ katvā ahaṁ attānaṁ Buddhassa niyyāte ni. . .*

(ii) *bhagavato attānaṁ pariccajāmi. . . jīvitañca pariccajāmi. paricatto yeva me attā, pariccattaṁ yeva me jīvitaṁ. jīvita pariyantikaṁ buddhaṁ saraṇaṁ gacchāmi. buddho me saraṇaṁ leṇaṁ tānan'ti.*

II. *ajja ādiṁ katvā ahaṁ Buddhaparāyano. . . iti mam dhāretha.*

III. *ajja ādiṁ katvā ahaṁ Buddhassa antevāsiko*

IV. *ajja ādiṁ katvā ahaṁ abhivādana-paccuṭṭhāna-anjalikamma-samīcikammaṁ buddhādīnnaṁ yeva tinnaṁ vatthūnaṁ karomi*

III. Acceptance of discipleship or assuming oneself as a pupil of Buddha, etc. (*sissabhāvūpāgamana*), An example of this is Mahākassapa's acceptance of discipleship (*SN*, II.220).

IV. Refuge taken by different means such as acts of veneration, i.e., veneration of three jewels, reverential salutation and homage to the Buddha, etc. (*paṇipāta*). This is illustrated in Brahmāyu's mode of refuge taking (*MN*, II.140) and various modes of expression of reverence by *kalāmas* (*AN*, III.65).

"From today onward I shall give respectful greeting, devoted attendance, the *añjali*-salutation and homage only to the Buddha," etc.

According to the *Dīgha Nikāya* commentary,[90] while observing this fourth mode, a devout follower must believe that the object of worship, i.e., Buddha, etc., is the highest of its kind (*aggadakkhineyya*). Besides the above four modes of refuge taking, the *Khuddakapāṭha* commentary mentions two other modes of taking refuge.[91] Thus, resorting to *ti-saraṇa* by the various modes of refuge taking not only admits a non-Buddhist into the order but it helps to the growth of *saddhā* in the Buddha and other jewels.

ADVANTAGES OF TAKING REFUGE IN THE BUDDHA

In the early canonical texts[92] it is stated that refuge taking in the Buddha and other jewels is a true sacrifice which is meritorious and productive of good results, such as heavenly

---

90. See, *DN*, *Commy.*, I, p. 231.

91. *The Illustrator of Ultimate Meaning*, tr., p. 9; See *Vinaya*, I.15; *Visuddhimagga*, Chap. III.

92. See, *Kūtadanta Sutta* (*DN*, V), *Mahā-Samaya Sutta* (*DN*, XX; *DN*, II. 255; *Dial. of the Buddha*, Part II, p. 285; *The Book of the Kindered Sayings* (*SN*), Part II, pp. 48-49; *SN*, V, tr., p. 342; *The Book of the Gradual Sayings* (*AN*), vol. III, tr., p. 233.

rebirth, attainment of *sotāpanna* and keeps a monk on the path of success. In the later Pāli canon[93] refuge-taking in the Buddha is described as the best and safe refuge by means of which a person understands the four noble truths; delivers from all suffering and subjects himself only to *deva* rebirth but not to rebirth in any states of suffering.

Means of Cultivation of Saddhā

Saddhā which is stated as one of the eight qualities to be possessed by a perfect monk[94] is founded on understanding (*paññā*), but not on belief or heresy, tradition or authority, miracle or divinity. According to the *Vibhāṅga*,[95] *saddhā* (faith) which results in "decision" is aroused by feeling.

CULTIVATION OF SADDHĀ BY MEANS OF BUDDHĀNUSSATI

Buddhānussati (Buddha-recollection) seems to have been intended to create *aveccapasāda* (i.e., *pasāda saddhā* in the Buddha) by means of the knowledge of the special qualities of the Buddha. The purpose of meditation on these good qualities (of the Buddha) is "to bring about a mental state of peaceful devotion."[96] It can be inferred from a *Saṁyutta Nikāya* passage[97] that the chief object of Buddha-recollection is to realize the *dhamma-kāya* of the Buddha, with which he is identified, but not to develop affection and attachment to his physical body (*rūpa kāya*). The *Therigāthā* informs that two *therīs*, i.e., Jentā and Mahāpajāpati Gotamī, declared that they realized Buddha's *dhammakāya* which is stated to have been the fruit of *arhat*-hood.

---

93. See, Mrs. Rhys Davids (tr.), *Dhammapada*, Vs. 190 & 92; *J.*, vol. I, no. 1; *The Jātaka*, vol. I, p. 3.

94. *The Book of the Gradual Sayings* (*AN*), vol. IV, tr., p. 211.

95. *The Book of Analysis*, tr., pp. 221& 294; *Vibhaṅga*, 292, 296.

96. H.G.A. Van Zeyst, "Buddhānussati," *Ency Bsm*, vol. III, Fasc. 3, p. 447a.

97. *SN*, III, p. 119f.

The Buddha-recollection is one of the earliest meditation topics which is mentioned in the early and later Pāli texts.[98] It is stated to be the first of the six "matters of recollection" and states of everminding.[99] According to the *Visuddhimagga*,[100] it is the first and foremost of the ten recollections of the forty subjects of meditation.

The Buddha had recommended this recollection as a gladdening (or elevating) subject, to which a meditator can divert his mind at the stage of strenuous practice of any subject of meditation such as the "contemplation of the body," when the meditator experiences bodily agitation, mental lassitude or distraction.[101]

To the question what is meant by Buddhānussati and how it should be practised? the *Dīgha* and *Saṁyutta Nikāyas* assert that it is mindfulness or recollection which has for its object the virtues of the Buddha. The *Nettippakaraṇa*[102] gives a list of synonyms for Buddha-recollection such as the recollection that the Blessed one is accomplished, fully enlightened, perfect in science and conduct, knower of the worlds, immeasurable and incalculable in qualities, etc. According to the *Peṭakopadesa*, it is "a state of undistorted recollection, (which) is a unity in diversity."[103] It is defined in this work as "the cognizance that has occurred with the teacher as its object," wherein the meditator pays attention to the qualities of the Buddha.

---

98. See, *DN*, III, p. 76; *MN*, I, p. 37; *SN*, V, p. 197; *AN*, III, p. 285; *SN*, p. 132.
99. See, *DN*, III. 250; *Dial of the Buddha*, Part III, p. 234; *The Book of the Gradual Sayings* (*AN*), vol. III, tr., p. 204.
100. *The Path of Purity*, Part II, p. 129.
101. See, *The Satipaṭṭhāna saṁyutta* (*SN*, XLVII); *Saṁyutta Nikāya* (PTS), pt. V., pp. 141-92, etc.
102. *The Guide (Nettippakaraṇaṁ)*, tr., p. 81.
103. *The Pitaka-Disclosure*, tr., pp. 139-40; pp. 230-31.

According to the commentarial works like the *Suttanipāta Aṭṭhakathā* and *Visuddhimagga*, while practising Buddhānussati, the disciple should meditate and thoroughly understand the meaning of each word of the formula which consists of nine special virtues of the Buddha, viz.,

> Lord, the perfect one, perfectly enlightened one, endowed with knowledge and conduct, well-gone, the knower of the entire world, the supreme charioteer of men to be tamed, the teacher of gods and men, the Enlightened and the Blessed one.[104]

The meditator should also recollect the reasons for the Buddha is possessing these special virtues. Thus in the practice of this recollection the disciple's attention is focused on the Buddha as state of perfection and embodiment of enlightenment.

BENEFITS DERIVED FROM THE PRACTICE OF BUDDHĀNUSSATI

Various benefits of Buddhānussati have been enumerated in different passages of the *Aṅguttara Nikāya*.[105] It is a means of attaining perfection in *dhamma* and keeps a person calm and at ease; it serves as a valuable aid to attain concentration of mind (*cittaṁ samādhiyati*) by giving rise to the four meditations and is the basis of liberating insight; it frees a person from lust, hatred and delusion and is thus efficacious in leading a person to mental purification.

According to the *Dhammapada* those who practice Buddha-recollection are "well-awake," and it is stated in its commentary that as a result of such recollection, some members

104. *bhagavā arahan sammā-sambuddho vijjā-caraṇa-sampanno sugato lakavidū anuttaro purisa-damma-sārathi satthā devamanussānam buddho bhagavā.*

105. See, *The Book of the Gradual Sayings* (*AN*), vol. III, p. 205; *Mahānāma Sutta* (*AN*, III, p. 285); *Aṅguttara Nikāya Commentary*, vol. III, p. 337; *AN*, The Sixes, nos. 10, 25; *The Threes*, no. 71.

of the order like Upakā renounced the householder's life and joined the Buddhist order.[106]

According to the *Visuddhimagga*,[107] the various benefits that accrue from the practice of *buddhānussati* are as follows. It leads to the arising of rapture, the wisdom factor, and sometimes also results in the transporting rapture. Further, its practitioner acquires true respect and reverence for the Buddha by cultivating abundant faith and establishing mindfulness in the latter. As a result of the contemplation of Buddha-virtues, the meditator's mind is exalted with gladness, becomes full of joy and produces satisfaction (*buddhālambanapīti*). By its practice, overcoming the fear and gaining ability to bear pain, the meditator obtains a sense of intimacy with the Buddha and his body becomes worthy of adoration like a temple as it is inhabited by the contemplation of virtues of the Buddha. By its practice and devotional meditation, the meditator's mind bends towards the Buddha-sphere and hence he endeavours to live as if it were in the presence of the Master (*satta sammukhibhūto*). Hence, the meditator feels a sense of shame and becomes afraid of being blamed for doing, speaking or thinking anything unworthy and coming into contact with sinful objects. As a consequence of the above, on the one hand, he shrinks from evil and, on the other hand, is inspired to zealously follow the great example of the Buddha by keeping himself "upright and free from slime." The meditator discards hindrances and strives to realize *arhant*-ship as in the case of Phussadeva the Elder, resident of Kaṭakandhakāra, who attained *arhant*-hood through increasing his insight by means of this kind of recollection.

In the *Vimuttimagga* of Upatissa Thera, which is probably composed in the first century AD long before Buddhaghoṣa's

106. See, *Dhammapada*, verse 296; *Upakājivaka Vatthu* in *Dhammapada Commentary*.

107. *The Path of Purity*, Pt. II, tr., pp. 154, 156-57, 166, 245, 262-63.

Visuddhimagga, it is stated[108] that by Buddha-recollection a person obtains thirteen benefits, viz., "fullness of confidence, abundance of mindfulness, completion of wisdom, reverence, plenty of merit, great joy, ability to endure hardship, fearlessness, steadfastness in the presence of evil, the state of living near the teacher, enjoyment of activity belonging to the ground of the Buddhas, the happiness of faring well and approaching the deathless state."

But contrary to the above Upatissa's *Vimuttimagga*, and Buddhaghoṣa's *Visuddhimagga* also assert that by means of *buddhānussati* a person cannot attain one-pointedness of mind (*ekaggatā*) and fixed mental absorption (*jhāna*), but can reach up to access concentration only.[109]

Advantages of Cultivation of Saddhā

In Theravāda absolute faith in Buddha is regarded as a meritorious action. A possessor of steadfast and an unshakable faith can claim as the own son of the Buddha whose body and essence is *dhamma*.[110] According to the *Alagaddupama Sutta* (*MN*, XXII), those who have faith in the Buddha are fortunate beings. *Saddhā* (faith) in and right conduct towards the Buddha is conducive to great merit, and best reward, for the Buddha is declared as the best among all kinds of beings.[111]

It is stated in the *Paṭṭhana* one of the *Abhidhamma* works, *saddhā* is one of the merit producing activities. It is explained in the *Cūlagopālaka Sutta* (*MN*, XXXIV) that those who have faith in the Buddha will obtain welfare and happiness for a

108. See, H.G.A. Van Zeyst, "Buddhānussati," *Ency Bsm*, vol. III, Fasc. 3, p. 448a.

109. See, *Ency Bsm*, vol. III, Fasc. 3, p. 448b.

110. See, *DN*, XXVIII.9.

111. See, *The Book of the Gradual Sayings* (*AN*), vol. I, tr., p. 133; *The Book of the Gradual Sayings*, vol. II, pp. 4, 38-39; *The Book of the Gradual Sayings* (*AN*), vol. III, tr., pp. 26-27.

long time. The other benefits for those who have perfect faith in the Buddha, according to other early Pāli texts,[112] include unwavering faith in his teaching; access to one of the four abodes of ease by purifying impure thoughts; keeping them away from taking wrong steps; confidence to learners; ability to practise righteousness and live in pure conduct by abandoning unrighteous and evil ways and progress in the spiritual path.

In the later Pāli canonical and commentarial works[113] *saddhā* in the Buddha is stated to be the best property, conducive to a purposeful life, and that it makes one righteous and good.

It is also evident from the Pāli canon[114] that by faith or trust in the Buddha a person is subjected to the happy rebirth among *deva*s and other good states.

Further, the faculty of faith is one of the five preponderant faculties which is conducive to wisdom, swift attainment of the concentration.[115] Unwavering faith in the teacher makes a person's mind incline to exertion, application, perseverance and striving, which collectively help to abandon the first mental obstruction.[116] According to the *Peṭakopadesa*,[117] by cultivating

112. *The Book of the Kindered Sayings* (*SN*), Part V, tr., p. 202; *The Book of the Gradual Sayings* (*AN*), vol. III, pp. 155, 4, 97; *The Book of the Gradual Sayings* (*AN*), vol. IV, tr., pp. 71-72, 233; *The Book of the Gradual Sayings* (*AN*), vol. V, tr., p. 85.

113. See, *The Suttanipāta*, p. 30; *The Pitaka-Disclosure* (Peṭakopadesa), tr., p. 90; *The Path of Purity*, Part II, p. 118.

114. See, *Alagaddūpama Sutta* (*MN*, XXII); *Cūḷa-Punnama-sutta* (*MN*, CX); Woodward (tr.), *The Book of the Kindered Sayings* (*SN*), vol. IV, tr., p. 186; *The Book of the Gradual Sayings* (*AN*), vol. III, pp. 26-27.

115. See, *The Book of the Kindered Sayings* (*SN*), Part V, tr., p. 206; *The Book of the Gradual Sayings* (*AN*), vol. II, tr., p. 155.

116. *The Book of the Gradual Sayings* (*AN*), vol. V, p. 15.

117. *The Piṭaka-Disclosure* (Peṭakopadesa), tr., pp. 232-33, 235-39.

saddhā, a person accepts statements or doctrinal teachings, and contemplates the three characteristics of existence even before verifying them. The faculty of faith functions as a footing for insight and understanding by rooting out faithfulness and ignorance. In the state of undisturbed intention, it helps a person to reach the stage of second meditation.

The *Nikāyas* maintain[118] that the unwavering and steadfast faith in the Buddha serves as an indirect means to attain the states of stream winner (*sotāpanna*) and non-returner (*anāgāmi*). It is also stated that corresponding to the completion and fulfilment of the controlling power of faith and other four powers in different degrees, a person attains different states of perfection, viz., *arhant*, non-returner, once-returner and stream-winner.[119]

Saddhā is regarded as the basis of the ethical process that finally leads to the highest truth, which is promoted by a number of factors linked with one another respectively in descending order, viz., by striving, cognition, energy, zeal, interest, study, knowledge, hearing, listening, and attention. Attention is ultimately fostered by *saddhā* (faith) without which a person does not incline at all to pay attention to the teacher and his doctrine.[120]

By development of *saddhā* as a faculty and strength, a person is led to tranquillity and full enlightenment.[121] The

118. See, *MN*. II.238; *DN*, XXXIII; *The Book of the Gradual Sayings* (*AN*), vol. III, p. 8; *MN*, I, pp. 480-81; *Further Dialogues of the Buddha*, vol. I, p. 339; *SN*, V, p. 219; Woodward (tr.), *Some Sayings of the Buddha*, pp. 204-05; *The Pitaka-Disclosure*, tr., p. 243.

119. *The Book of the Kindered Sayings*, Part V, tr., p. 180.

120. See, *MN*, II.171; *yasma cha kho śaddhā jāyati tasma upasankhamati tasama upasankhamanassa saddhā bahukārā ti* — *MN*, II.174-76; *Further Dialogues of the Buddha*, vol. II, pp. 99-100.

121. See, *Mahā-sakuludāyi sutta* (*MN*, LXXVII); *MN*, II. 12; *Further Dialogues of the Buddha*, vol. II, p. 7.

faculty of faith along with other faculties gives rise to five powers, which in turn lead to the seven Enlightenment factors, and these in turn finally result in the Eightfold path. All these factors collectively lead to Enlightenment.[122]

It is also expounded that faith serves as an indirect means to cross the flood of *saṁsāra*.[123] The *Saṁyutta Nikāya* states that the power of faith leads to the deathless, those who have not realized it by the faculty of insight.[124]

It is further expounded[125] that by means of the controlling faculty of faith a person attains *nibbāna* and an *upāsaka* who has firm faith and realizes the undesirability and essencelessness of worldly objects attains *nibbāna*.

In the *Aṅguttara Nikāya* passages[126] it is stated as follows. A possessor of *saddhā* in the long run attains *sambodhi*. By means of it a monk abides in the cankerless mind-emancipation. By faith in the *tathāgata*, a monk destroys his cankers and attains heart's release. Some of those who have unwavering faith in the Buddha will attain the goal in the present existence and some others in the existences to come.

A passage of the *Nikāya*[127] enumerates that a number of persons, viz., Tapussa, Bhallika, Sudatta, Anāthapiṇḍika, Citta,

---

122. *The Guide*, tr., p. 52.
123. *The Book of the Kindered Sayings* (*SN*), Part I, p. 276; *The Suttanipāta*, p. 30; See, *Commentary on Suttanipāta*, verse 77; (q.v.) Nyanatiloka, *Buddhist Dictionary*, p. 154; *The Questions of King Milinda*, Part II, p. 55.
124. *SN*, V.220ff; *The Book of Kindered Sayings*, vol. V, p. 196.
125. *The Book of the Kindred Sayings* (*SN*), Part V, p. 223; See also *SN*, V, pp. 376ff.
126. See, *AN*, V, p. 182; *AN*. *The Fours*, no. 34; *The Book of the Gradual Sayings* (*AN*), vol. IV, p. 50; *The Book of Gradual Sayings* (*AN*), vol. V, pp. 10-11, pp. 81-82.
127. *The Book of the Gradual sayings* (*AN*), vol. III, pp. 313-14.

Macchikāsaṇḍika, Hatthaka, Āḷavaka, Mahānāma Sakka, Uggavesālika, Uggatta, Sūra Ambaṭṭha, Jīvaka Komārabhacca, Nakulapitā, Tavakaṇṇika, Pūraṇa, Isidatta, Sandhāna, Vijaya, Vajjiyamahita, and Meṇḍaka, the lay disciples Vāseṭṭha, Ariṭṭha and Sāragga, have realized the deathless by means of possession of unwavering faith in the Buddha. In the *Suttanipāta*,[128] the Buddha exhorted Piṅgiya that just as the faithful of the past such as Vakkali, Bhadrāvudha and Alavagotama were delivered by faith, likewise he too shall be released by means of faith and shall attain the deathless.

According to the *Peṭakopadesa*[129] at any of its three levels (i.e., blunt, medium and outstanding) faith leads a person for "non-renewal of being." It is further said that accompanied and assisted by the faculties of energy and mindfulness faith as a power (*saddhābala*) reaches the goal.

Disadvantages of Lack of Saddhā

The word *assaddhiya* (disbelief) is used in the early Pāli canonical works like the *Saṁyutta* and *Aṅguttara Nikāya*s and two Pāli adjectival forms *assaddhā*[130] (without faith, unbelieving) and *avissāsaniya*[131] (untrustworthy) are mentioned in other canonical works, viz., the *Suttanipāta*, *Puggalapaññatti*, *Dhammasaṅgani* and *Jātaka*.

In the *Dīgha Nikāya*,[132] lack of faith and doubt are described respectively as one of the seven vicious qualities; seven kinds of latent bias and seven fetters. In the *Sangīti Sutta* (*DN*,

128. *yathā ahū vakkali muttasaddho, bhadrāvudho ālavi-gotamoka, evam eva tvam pi pamunkayassu saddham, gamissasi tvam piṅgiya makkudheyya pāram.* — See, *Suttanipāta*, 1142-44; *The Suttanipāta* (tr.) , pp. 212-13.

129. *The Piṭaka-Disclosure*, tr., pp. 241, 243.

130. See, *PTS Dictionary*, p. 90b.

131. *Ibid.*, p. 85b.

132. See, *DN*, III.251; *Dialogues of the Buddha*, Part III, pp. 235-37.

XXXIII)[133] doubt concerning the Buddha is stated as the foremost of the five spiritual barennesses.

Some of the *Majjhima Nikāya Suttas*[134] show that entertaining doubt and getting perplexed about the teacher (Buddha) is first of the five religious dobuts (*cetokhilas*), which is an obstacle to higher aspiration and a mental hindrance to moral and spiritual progress, and that a person who is devoid of faith is destined to rebirths in states of misery.

In *Saṁyutta* and *Aṅguttara Nikāyas*,[135] doubt and wavering are described as one of the five hindrances and lower fetters. The *Aṅguttara Nikāya* abounds in passages[136] which show the disadvantages of faithlessness. It causes vexation and trouble in the present life and leads to rebirth in the states of woe; casts the possessor into hell; does not lead to progress in discipline and displaces a monk from his respectful position; does not establish a monk in the *dhamma*; subjects a person to wavering in the world; makes a person to regard faith-talk as ill-talk; makes a monk afraid at heart; and declares a layman as an outcast. It is one of the five forms of mental bondage; an obstacle to realize the fruit of the non-returner and *arhant*-hood; a hurdle for one entering the noble path and realize the achievement of right view. It prevents a monk from becoming all proficient; and is one of the five mental obstructions for perseverance and progress.

---

133. See, *DN*, III.238; *Dialogues of the Buddha*, Part III, p. 227.
134. See, *Cetokhila Sutta* (*MN*, XV); *MN*, I.101; *Further Dialogues of the Buddha*, vol. II, pp. 168-69.
135. *The Book of the Kindered Sayings* (*SN*), Part V, p. 49; *The Book of the Gradual Sayings*, (*AN*), vol. IV, p. 301.
136. *The Book of the Gradual Sayings* (*AN*), vol. III, pp. 2-3, 108, 5-7, 124, 135, 151, 182-83, 297, 303-06; *The Book of the Gradual Sayings* (*AN*), vol. V, tr., pp. 12-13, 85.

According to the *Paṭisambhida Magga*[137] the faithless are those whose company should be abandoned. Non-confidence (faithlessness) is defined in the *Vibhaṅga* as disbelief in the Buddha or his teaching or his order.[138] According to it,[139] one in whom the controlling faculty of confidence is not developed is known as a possessor of weak controlling facutly. Further, doubt regarding the Teacher (Buddha) is one of the five mental spikes, five hindrances, etc. Elsewhere it is stated that doubt and wrong view are two among the seven latent tendencies, seven fetters, seven elements, eight and ten bases of corruption. In the *Puggala-paññatti*[140] the faithlessness one regarded as incapable of progress and in the commentary on the *Dhammasaṅgani*,[141] doubt and puzzle concerning the Buddha is explained as the doubt about his superman's marks and his omniscience.

DISADVANTAGES OF DISRESPECT, DISREGARD, IRREVERENCE AND HARMING THE BUDDHA

In the *Dīgha Nikāya*,[142] irreverence and insolence towards the Buddha is stated as the foremost of the six forms of irreverence, opposed to six forms of reverence.

In the *Vibhaṅga* the term "Disregard" is defined as ". . . being disgraceful, disrespect, non-deference, irreverence, being irreverent, state of being irreverent, unmannerliness, absence of esteem."[143] It is also stated that disrespect towards the

137. See, Devapriya Walisinha, "Patisambhidamagga," *The British Buddhist*, vol. III, no. 10, (July, 1929), pp. 9-10.

138. *The Book of Analysis* (*Vibhaṅga*), p. 481.

139. *Ibid.*, pp. 447, 474, 487-88, 494, 497, 502.

140. *Designation of Human Types*, p. 19.

141. See, *Aṭṭhasālinī*, pp. 354-55; *Manual of Buddhist Psychological Ethics*, p. 260, fn. 2.

142. *DN*, III.244; *Dialogues of the Buddha*, Part III, p. 231.

143. See, *Vibhaṅga*, 93; *The Book of Analysis*, tr., p. 481.

teacher (Buddha) is one of the six types of disrespect.[144]

The *Visuddhimagga* describes[114a] the Revilers of the Elect as those "who revile, accuse, and deride the Buddhas, silent Buddhas and Buddha's disciples, etc., intending to harm them by the worst sin or by ruining their character." Therefore, those who revile knowingly or unknowingly the Buddha and others by saying that they have no saintly character or have not attained the path of fruition, *jhāna* or emancipation, commit a grave action and are subjected to immediate retribution. But whoever reviles the Elect provided they seek forgiveness in person or through their own pupils are pardoned and their offences are condoned. For instance it is evident from *Jātakas*[145] how the revilers, i.e., Devadatta and Ciñcamāṇavika, were swallowed by the earth and fell into *avīcī* hell.

Harming the Buddha and its Retribution

According to the *Vinaya* and *Abhidhamma Piṭaka*s to harm the Buddha by shedding his blood is stated to be one of the five kinds of "Hindrances or impediments" in the attainment of "higher life" of "heaven" or "emancipation."[146] According to Theravādin *Vinaya*, a shedder of the Buddha's blood (*lohituppādaka*) is not eligible for ordination and will never be readmitted into the order as it is regarded as the most grievous type of offence known as *pārājika*. Such a person is also forbiddens from the *upasampadā* (higher ordination).[147] Further, *pabbajjā* should not be conferred on the murderer of an *arhant* or the Buddha and also the two ceremonies of Uposatha and

---

144. *Ibid.*, 945, tr., pp. 491-92,

144a, *Path of Purity*, Part II, pp. 492-94.

145. See, *Samudda-vāṇija-jātaka* (*J.*, vol. IV, no. 466), tr., p. 99; *Mahāpaduma Jātaka*, (*J.*, vol. IV, no. 472), tr., p. 117.

146. (s.v.) "Antarāyika," in *Dictionary of Early Buddhist Monastic Terms*, p. 16.

147. *Ibid.*, pp. 158, 47.

Pavāraṇā should not be performed in the presence of the shedder of Buddha's blood.[148]

It is reiterated in the *Vibhaṅga*[149] too that the two among the five immediate resultant actions are "to deprive an *arhant*'s life or to cause to shed *tathāgatha*'s blood."

Part B - Bhatti

Origins and Meaning of "Bhatti" in the Pāli Canon

The etymological roots of both the Sanskrit terms *bhakti* and its Pāli equivalent *bhatti* are idential as they are derived from the root *bhaj*.[150] Both Childers and Rhys Davids defined[151] the Pāli word *bhatti* as "Devotion, service" and also as "attachment and fondness."

Even though the word *bhatti* occurs as early as in the *Vinaya*, it does mean only "making lines, decoration, ornamentation."[152] The Pāli word *bhatti* is more frequently used in the *Khuddaka Nikāya* of later Pāli canon and in some books of *Abhidhamma Piṭaka*. For instance, we come across the word *bhatti* in the sense of "devotion" in the following psalm of *Theragāthā*.

> Him ye may call devoted and wise: Thus, he may be one that winneth distinction in knowledge of doctrines.[153]

---

148. (s.v.) "Antarāyika," in *Dictionary of Early Buddhist Monastic Terms*, pp. 138, 54, 148.

149. *The Book of Analysis*, tr., pp. 488-89.

150. See, s.v. "Bhakti" in Monier-Williams, *Sanskrit-English Dictionary* (New edn., Oxford, 1899); G.A. Grierson, "Bhakti Marga," *ERE*, vol. II, pp. 539a-b; Cp. Childers, *DPL*, p. 84b; *PTS Dictionary*, p. 497b.

151. See. Childers, *DPL*, p. 84b; *PTS Dictionary*, p. 497b.

152. *Vinaya*, II.113: Bhatti-kamma; See, *PTS Dictionary*, p. 497b.

153. *so bhattimā nāma ca hoti paṇḍito ñatvā ca dhammesu visesi assa* — Oldenberg (ed.), *Theragātha* (PTS, 1883), p. 41; *Psalms of the Brethren*, p. 204.

In Therigāthā *bhatti* means service or doing service.[154] In the *Jātaka* and *Abhidhamma* works like *Dhammasaṅgani* and *Puggalapaññatti*, it is used in the sense of devotion, attachment and fondness.[155]

There are two adjectival forms of the word *bhatti*:[156] (1) *Bhattavant*, and (2) *Bhattimant*. The former which is directly derived from *bhatta* meant one possessing reverence or worshippers, or worshipful or adored. The Buddha-epithet "Bhagava(-nt)" is interpreted as "Bhattava" which is rendered as worshipful or adored.[157] The other form "Bhattimant," derived from the root *bhatti* might have been translated primarily as "devoted," and the word is mentioned in the *Theragāthā* (V. 370). In the Pāli commentarial literature, such as in the commentaries on the *Jātaka*, *Theragāthā* and *Vimānavatthu*, the word is referred.[158]

Besides the usage of *bhatti*, the word *bhajati* which is direct derivation from the root *bhaj* is translated as "to divide partake . . . to associate with, keep companionship with, follow, resort to; to be attached to, to love." It is frequently used as a synonym of *sevati*.[159] The word *bhajati* is also used in other senses, e.g., "to cultivate and to choose" in the *Dhammapada*.[160]

---

154. See, *Therīgāthā*, 413.

155. See, *J.*, V.340; *J.*, VI.349; *Dhammasangani* (PTS, 1885), 1326; *Buddhist Manual of Psychological Ethics*, 345; *Puggala-paññatti* (PTS, 1883), 20.

156. See, *PTS Dictionary*, p. 497b.

157. See, *Dīgha Nikāya Aṭṭhakathā*, I.34; *Visuddhimagga*, 210 sq; 212; *bhaji-sevi-bahulaṇ karoti.*

158. See commentary on *Jātaka*, v. 340 (rendered as *sineha*); *Theragāthā Commentary*, on 370: *yathānusiṭṭhaṇ paṭipattiyā tattha bhattimā nāma; Vimānavatthu Commentary*, 353, 54.

159. See, *PTS Dictionary*, p. 496a.

160. See, Childers, *DPL*, p. 81a.

The word *bhajin*, the adjective form of *bhajati*, which means "loving, attached to, worshipping" is interpreted in the *Mahāniddesa* (142) in the sense of "Loved and worshipful."[161]

PĀLI TERMS USED IN THE CANON FOR CONSTITUENTS OF DEVOTION

Apart from these, other accessories of devotion and worship rendered towards the Buddha and other personages of spiritual eminence are expressed in the canon by means of a number of Pāli terms, viz., *purakkharoti* and *purakkhata*, *garukaraṇa*, *apacāyati* (revere, honour and esteem); *payirupāsati* and *namassati* (to attend on, honour, to venerate, pay homage to); *vandana* and *paṇāma* (salutation, paying homage and obeisance); *pema* and *pemanīya* (love, affection, kind, amiable);[162] *pūjā*, *accanā*, *patthanā*, *thava* and *thuti*,[163] their derivative and related forms.

Nature and Scope of "Bhatti"

In some *Majjhima Nikāya* passages[164] the words *pema* and *bhatti* are used in the sense of *saddhā*. When *bhatti* is used in the sense of *saddhā* it means "allegiance, or devotion," which an evil or good person directs towards their folk.

In some *Aṅguttara Nikāya* passages, the meanings of *bhatti* (devotion), *pema* (filial affection), and *pasāda* (mental appreciation) are interchanged with *saddhā*. For instance, it is stated that "here a person has very little faith, very little

---

161. See, *PTS Dictionary*, p. 496b.

162. *Ibid.*, pp. 496a, 246a, 51a, 418a, 347a, 601a, 403a-b; See, *DN*, I.50; III.284 sq; *MN*, I.101sq; *SN*, III.122; IV.72, 329; V.89, 379; *AN*, II.213; III. 326 sq; *SN*, 41; *Dhp*. 321; *J.*, IV.371 (Pemaka); *DA*, I.75, etc., *DN*, I.4; *DN*, II.20; *AN*, II.209 (Pamassara); *J.*, IV.470; *Pug*. 57; see *PTS Dictionary*, p. 472b.

163. See, *Infra*. 219, 228-29, 252-54.

164. See, *MN*, I.142, 444, 479; *MN*, III.21 & 23.

devotion, very little affection and very little appreciation."[165] Similarly, the meaning of *pema* overlaps with that of *pasāda*.[166]

In Buddhaghoṣa's commentaries on the *Dhammasaṅgani* and *Puggala-paññatti*, we find a special emphasis on the interrelationship of *saddhā* and *bhatti*, and their close identity. In *Aṭṭhasālinī*, *saddhā* is defined as trusting and taking refuge in the Buddha and other jewels, and as an act of belief by which a person enters into their qualities.[167] In *Puggala-paññatti Commentary*, it is stated that *saddhā* can be transformed into intense devotion (*bhatti*) by repeated religious practices with its invariable accompanying elements, viz., love (*pema*) and a sense of assurance coupled with serene delight (*pasāda*).[168] This commentary also defined Faith and Affection respectively as "continuous adoration" and "affection of faith; filial affection" while regarding *saddhā* and *pasāda* as identical.[169]

Objectives of Buddha-Bhakti

The Buddha had become the object of veneration and devotion, because no one else possess all the qualities possessed by him.[170] Some of the prominent attributes of the Buddha described in the Pāli canon[171] are that he is the highest and holiest of men;

165. *idha. . . ekacco puggalo ittarasaddho hoti, ittara bhatti ittarapemo ittara pasādo* — *AN*, III.165; See Jayatilleke, *Early Buddhist Theory of Knowledge*, p. 385.
166. *niviṭṭhasaddho niviṭṭhapemo. . . abhippasanno* — *AN*, III.326.
167. See, *Aṭṭhasālinī*, p. 145; *buddhādīni va ratanāni saddhati pattiyāyatī ti saddhā. . . buddhādīnaṁ guṇe ogāhati bhinditvā viya anupavisatī. . . pasīdati.*
168. *Puggala-paññatti Commentary*, p. 248: *punappnaṁ bhajanavasena saddhā va bhatti pemaṁ saddhāpemaṁ gehasitapemaṁ pi vaṭṭati pasādo saddhāpasādo va.*
169. See, Jayatilleke, *Early Buddhist Theory of Knowledge*, p. 386.
170. See, *Gopaka-Moggallāna Sutta* (*MN*, CVIII); *MN*, III.8.
171. See, *SN*, I.147; III.84: *loke anuttaro, lokassa aggo*; *Miln*. 70; See, *SN*, I.50, 132, 206, 301; *AN*, I.142; II.33; III. 65; *SN*, 157sq; *ādicca-bandhu*,

→

supremely wise, the conqueror of evil, the teacher of gods and men; kinsman of the Sun; universal monarch, lion, the king of animals; who is not subjected to rebirth, freed from sorrow, compassionate towards all beings, *buddha-vīra*, the refuge of all beings and unrivalled.

In two *suttas*[172] of *Majjhima* and *Aṅguttara Nikāya*, upon Buddha's inquiry king Pasenadi explained several reasons for his showing great reverence and affectionate obeisance to the Buddha. For example, in the above-referred *Aṅguttara Nikāya Sutta*, the king explained that he honoured the Buddha to show his gratitude and thankfulness. He paid affectionate obeisance to the Buddha because (i) The Buddha has arisen for the profit and happiness of many and established many in the noble path; (ii) He is endowed with Buddha virtues; (iii) He is unsurpassed field of merit; and (iv-vi) He is possessed with threefold higher knowledge.

The *Aṅguttara Nikāya*[173] also asserts that the Buddha is foremost of the ten persons who are worthy of worship, gifts and salutations with clasped hands, as they are unsurpassed fields of merit in the world. In a passage of this *Nikāya*,[174] it is categorically stated that to see the *tathāgata* is the sight above all sights; to go and hear his doctrine is the sound above all sounds; to have faith in him is the gain above all gains; to train in the discipline and doctrine preached by him is the

---

→ — *SN*, I.186; See, *AN*, I.176; III.150; See, *AN*, III.122; *antima-sariro*: *SN*, I.210; *vimutto* — *SN*, III.165; *AN*, IV.258; See, *MN*, II.100; *SN*, I.25, 51; *Theragāthā*, 47; See, *MN*, II.305; *DN*, *Commentary* I.233; *Milindapañha*, 95; *appaṭipuggala* — *SN*, I.134; also see *SN*, I.158; III. 86; *Therīgāthā*, 185, *J.*, I.40; *Milindapañha*, 239.

172. See, *Dhammacetiya Sutta* (*MN*, LXXXIX); *MN*, II.118-25 (PTS edn.); *The Book of the Gradual Sayings* (*AN*), vol. V, p. 46.

173. *The Book of the Gradual Sayings* (*AN*), vol. V, tr., p. 17.

174. *The Book of the Gradual Sayings* (*AN*), vol. III, pp. 229-32.

training above all training; to serve him is the service above all services and recollecting him is above all recollections.

We may infer from the *Theragāthā* that the Buddha was venerated and adored, because he was regarded as the means of Theras' success. For example, Bharata and others attributed their achievement of the goal to the Buddha.[175]

BUDDHA AS BHAGAVĀ

The Buddha is the object of worship and is adored owing to his special attribute "Bhagavā" which means worshipful, venerable, blessed and holy. The epithet Bhagavā appears to have its first occurrence in *Dīgha Nikāya* in an oft recurrent formula:

> *bhagavā arahan sammāsambuddho . . . satthā deva manussānam buddho Bhagavā.*[176]

In the form of the above formula, this epithet is also mentioned in other parts of the canon.[177]

According to the *Nikāya*s and the *Dhammapada* Commentary,[178] Buddha is styled as Bhagavā or Lord in his role of the pre-eminent person. In the *Khuddaka Nikāya* books, the epithet Bhagavā means "Blessed"[179] and "partaker of."[180]

In the commentarial works such as the *Khuddakapāṭha Commentary* and *Visuddhimagga*, the epithet is analysed and exegetically discussed. For instance according to the first

---

175. See, *Theragāthā*, verses 175-76; verse. 839: "You cause these people to cross over." (*tuvaṁ anusaye chetvā tiṇṇo tāres' imaṁ pajaṁ*).

176. See, *DN*, I.49.

177. See, *MN*, I.179; *SN*, II.69; V. 343; *Paṭisambhida*, I.174; *Mahāniddesa*, 457.

178. *buddho so bhagavā*; *MN*, I.235; *Petavatthu*, II.9.; *Dh.A.*, III.219.

179. See Childers, *Khuddakapāṭha* (*Journal of Roy. As. Society*, 1869), 2, 4.

180. Fausböll, *Dhammapadam* (Copenhagen, 1855), 4.

source[181] the Buddha is "Blessed" because he has reached the end of the being (*bhavanta-go*), has shown the excellence of *dhamma*-body by abolishing the defects (*bhaggadosatā*); he is both the mundane and supramundane ideal; splendour of all limbs which are perfect in all respects; he is honoured owing to his possession of all virtues and devoid of all vices. The *Visuddhimagga*[182] explains the term "Bhagavā" in many ways in order to facilitate the meditator to recollect Buddha's special qualities. It signifies respect and veneration accorded to the Buddha as the highest of all beings and possessor of special qualities.

> "Blessed" is the best of words,
> "Blessed" is the finest word;
> "Deserving" awe and veneration,
> Blessed is the name therefore.[183]

This work analyses the epithet Bhagavā as a partaker (*bhāgī*) of robes, alms, food, resting place, taste of the law, deliverance, virtue, etc., as he who divided, analysed and classified (*bhaji, vibhaji, paṭivibhaji*) the treasure of *dhamma*;[184] as fortunate (*bhāgyavā*); as associated with blessings (*bhagehi yuttattā*) of six things, viz., lordship, *dhamma*, fame, glory, wish, and endeavour; he possesses the highest kind of lordship in his own mind and also consummated it in all sorts of forms (*sabbākāraparipūraṁ*), endowed with the powers to go anywhere he wishes, to perform any act, to make anyone or anything follow his wishes, to create elements like water, fire at his will and to accomplish anything.[185]

---

181. *The Illustrator of Ultimate Meaning* (*Paramaṭṭhajotikā*) Part I, tr., pp. 116, 118-19 and 140.
182. *The Path of Purification*, tr., pp. 224-29.
183. *Ibid.*, tr., p. 224; chap. vii. 53.
184. *Ibid.*, tr., p. 225; chap. vii. 55.
185. See, *The Path of Purity*, Part II, p. 243; also *The Path of Purification*, p. 228, fn. 27.

The *Visuddhimagga* quotes[186] Dharmapāla, a famous commentator who interprets the word "Bhagavā" in his *Paramatthamañjusā*, the *Visuddhimagga* commentary as follows:

> He is bhattavā (possessor of devotees) because devoted (bhatta) people show devotion (bhatti) on account of his attainments.

Dharmapāla uses the epithet in the sense of "possessor of devotees," expounding it as *bhattā dalhabhattikā assa bahu atthi* (he has many devoted firm devotees).

The *Visuddhimagga* further says[187] that the Buddha is held in great respect by the worldling as well as the intelligent, because of the two conditions, viz., his possession of the hundred characteristics of the virtuous and his attainment in the body of the Law.

Besides the above reasons, the Buddha is unanimously regarded in the canon[188] as the best and highest object of honour for there is none to whom he should greet or rise up or offer seat. He has also never objected whenever he was praised by others,[189] but accepted it without any disapproval.

DEVOTIONAL ATTITUDE OF LAITY AND MONKS IN THE PĀLI CANON

We find tendencies towards Buddha-*bhakti* as early as in the *Vinaya* where in the cordial relation between an *antevāsika* and his *ācāriya* is compared to that of the son and his father.[190] The

---

186. *The Path of Purification*, p. 229, fn. 30; *Visuddhimagga*, Ch. vii. 63 & 65.

187. *The Path of Purity*, Part II, p. 243.

188. See, *Sutta Vibhaṅga of Vinaya*, I., p. 137; See, *Paragika of Vinaya*; *AN*, IV. 173.

189. *Theragāthā Aṭṭhakathā* (*Paramaṭṭhadīpanī*), III (PTS, 1940-59), p. 45f.

190. *ācāriyo, bhikkave, antevāsikamhi puttacittam upaṭṭhapessati, antevāsiko ācāriyamhi pitucittaṁ upaṭṭhapessati* — (s.v.), "Ācāriya," in *Dictionary of Early Buddhist Monastic Terms*, p. 26.

Vinaya also prescribed the devotional attitude of *antevāsika* towards the *ācāriya* by stating that the behaviour of the former should be regarded as improper, if he does not have much affection, faith, respect and amity, etc., towards the latter.[191]

Further, whereas the *Dīgha, Saṁyutta, Aṅguttara Nikāya*s and *Visuddhimagga* enjoined[192] that rightly behaved disciples should honour and revere their teachers and also other recluses and godlymen by observing strict obedience towards them, serving them, waiting upon them rising and saluting them, it is stated in some of the *Khuddaka Nikāya* books[193] that homage, veneration and worship is to be paid to a teacher who expounds the *dhamma*. The *Majjhima Nikāya*[194] and the *Puggala-paññatti*[195] advocate that a possesors of ten blissful qualities, recluses and brāhmaṇas who are righteous in body, mind and speech; those who are of equal in rank and also greater than us in respect of morals, concentration and insight; all virtuous monks irrespective their age are to be revered honoured, served waited upon and worshipped.

Whereas the monks and nuns of the Buddhist order mostly

---

191. *nādhimattaṁ pemaṁ hoti, nādhimatto pasādo hoti, nādhi mattā hiri hoti, nādhimatto gāravo hoti, nādhimattā bhāvanā hoti* — See, *Mahāvagga*, pp. 51-52; 65-67; (s.v.) "Paṇāmanā" in *Dictionary of Early Buddhist Monastic Terms*, pp. 132-33.

192. See, *Siṅgālovāda Sutta* (*DN*, XXXI); *DN*, vol. III, pp. 180-93; See, *SN*, I. 138ff; *SN*, IV.314; *AN*, IV.122; *The Book of the Gradual Sayings* (*AN*), vol. IV, tr., p. 81; *The Book of the Gradual Sayings* (*AN*), vol. III, p. 29; *The Path of Purity*, Part II, pp. 116-18; 134-35.

193. See, *The Suttanipāta*, p. 52; *Sn. Vs.*, 315-16; *Dhammapada Vs.* 106 & 107; *Khuddka-pāṭha*, tr., p. 144:

    asavanā ca bālānam paṇditānañca sevanā ।
    pūjā ca pūjaneyyanan, etan mangalam uttamam ॥

194. See, *MN*, III. 9-12, *Further Dialogues of the Buddha*, pp. 160-62, *MN*, III. 292; *Nagara-vindeyya Sutta* (*MN*, CL).

195. *Designation of Human Types*, tr., pp. 35, 9-10, 38-39, 50-51, 49-50.

devoted their attention to assimilate the essence of the doctrine and to attain *nibbāna* through meditational practices, the Buddhist laity who comprise devout laymen and laywomen (*upāsakas* and *upāsikās*) who have sufficient means to offer gifts and perform acts of charity are more preoccupied in honouring, venerating and worshipping the Buddha and his prominent disciples. In accordance with their function some of the *Nikāyas*[196] and Commentaries[197] defined that *upāsakas* are those who take the three refuges and perform acts of worship.

According to *Vinaya*[198] Tapussa and Bhallika known as *dvevācika upāsakas* are the first laymen who took refuge in the Buddha. They are followed by Yasa's father who became the first that took refuge in the three refuges (*tevācika upāsaka*), Yasa's mother and wife became the first laywomen.[199] It is also recorded in the *Vinaya*[200] that Roja, the Malla expressed ardent love and longing to see the Buddha. It is mentioned in *Dīgha Nikāya*[201] that the great reverence and honour was paid by the nature spirits and *devas* to the Buddha just before his *parinibbāna* soon after which the Mallas too worshipped his body for six days by offering garlands, perfumes accompanied by recitation of hymns, performance of music and dance. King Bimbisāra too is said to have expressed his faith and devotion by praising the Buddha till the end of his life.[202]

---

196. See, *SN*, V.395; *AN*, IV.220.

197. See, *Sumaṅgalavilāsini*, I, p. 234: *upāsatīti upāsako.*

198. *Vinaya Texts*, pt. I, pp. 83-84; See also *Dictionary of Early Buddhist Monastic Terms*, pp. 50-51.

199. *Vinaya Texts*, Part I, tr., p. 109.

200. See, I.B. Horner (tr.), *The Book of the Discipline*, vol. IV, pp. 341-42.

201. *Dialogues of the Buddha*, Part II, tr., p. 150; *DN*, II. 138; *ibid.*, *DN*, II. 159; tr., p. 180.

202. See, *DN*, II, 202 sq: *bhagavantam kittayamānarūpo*. . .

According to *Majjhima* and *Aṅguttara Nikāyus,*[203] king Pasenadi is said to have paid great reverence, devotion and affectionate obeisance, out of gratitude and in order to show his profound humility to the Buddha. The *Majjhima Nikāya* describes his obeisance thus:

> . . . having bowed his head to the feet of the Lord, joyfully covered the Lord's feet with kisses and rubbed them thoroughly with his hands, and announced, "O Sir, I am king Pasenadi of Kosala. . . ."[204]

Whereas brāhmaṇa Janussoni uttered in praise of Buddha the oft recurrent formula *namo tassa bhagavato arhato sammāsambuddhassa,*[205] the aged brāhmaṇa Brahmāyu and the self-proud brāhmaṇa. Mānatthaddha showed their great respect and deep reverence to the Buddha by paying him obeisance in the style of king Pasenadi,[206] Udāyi resorted to homeless life as a consequence of his love and regard for the Buddha.[207]

The *Ghaṭikāra sutta* (*MN*, LXXXI) elucidates that even Kassapa, a past Buddha, was worshipped by the potter Ghaṭikāra by means of unswerving devotion and absolute confidence which was appreciated and approved by the former.[208] Illustrating the age-long tradition of Buddha-

---

203. See, *MN*, II.120; *The Book of the Gradual Sayings* (*AN*), vol. V, p. 46.

204. See, I.B. Horner, *The Middle Length Sayings*, II, XXV; *MN*, II.120: . . . *bhagavato pādesu sirasā nipatitvā bhagavato pādāṁ sukhena ca paricumbati, pāṇīhi ca parisambāhati, nāmaṁ ca sāveti rājāṁ, bhante, pāsenadi kosala;. . .*

205. See, Horner (tr.), *Middle Length Sayings* (PTS), vol. I, pp. 220, 222.

206. See, *Brahmāyu Sutta* (*MN*, XCI); *MN*, vol. II. 144; *SN*, Part II, pp. 177-78; *Brāhmaṇa Saṁyutta* of Sagātha Vagga.

207. See, *SN*, V.89ff: . . . *so khvāham bhagavati pemaṁ ca gāravam ca hiriṇ ca ottappaṁ ca sampassamāno agārsmā anagāriyam pabbajito.*

208. See, *MN*, II.51-54; *Further Dialogues of the Buddha*, vol. II, pp. 26-27.

worship by the *bodhisattas*, the *Nidānakathā* gives an account of *bodhisattva* who born as a lion by his devotion to Paduma Buddha became a future Buddha as a consequence of that merit.[209]

The *Suttanipāta* mentions a devotee's longing to unite with the Buddha through devotional contemplation as follows:

I see him with my mind as it were mine eyes,
By night, by day, incessant, watching over.
I revere him while waiting for the morn.
And thus methinks I am ever with him dwelling
Truely my mind with him is joined, O Brahman.[210]

The work also refers to brāhmaṇa Amagandha's worship of the Buddha in great humility.[211]

In the *Theragāthā*, the Theras' devotion is expressed in a more pronounced way. For example, it is said that Thera Panthaka's mind is filled with deep emotion at the sight of Buddha.[212] A *Theragāthā* verse informs that three hundred monks waited standing wishing to salute the feet of the Buddha.[213] In some of the psalms, highest veneration and homage is paid to the Buddha.[214] The *Theragāthā* records Sunita,

209. Fausböll (tr.), *Buddhist Birth Stories*; See The Commentarial Introduction entitled Nidāna-kathā (The Story of the Lineage), tr., p. 126.

210. See, *Sn. Vs.*, 1142, 44; (q.v.), C.A.F. Rhys Davids, "Love (Buddhist)," *ERE*, vol. VIII, p. 161a.

211. *The Suttanipāta*, tr., p. 42.

212. *Psalms of the Brethern* (Sec. CCXXXI), tr., pp. 242-43.

213. *Theragāthā* (841):

bhikkhavo tisatā ime tiṭṭhantī panjalīkatā ।
pade vīra pasārehi nāgā vandanthu satthuno'ti ॥

214. *Theragāthā*, v. 343: "I venerate the Tathāgata" (*juhāmi dakkhiṇeyyagiṁ namassāmi tathāgataṁ*), *Theragāthā*, V. 480: "I approached him and did homage to the highest of men." (. . . *tatthanaṁ upasaṁkamma vandissaṁ purisuttamaṁ*).

the scavenger, revered and honoured the Buddha by paying obeisance to the latter's feet.[215] Stray references in the canon support the view that even during the Buddha's lifetime even his chief disciples like Ānanda were worshipped. In the *Aṅguttara Nikāya*, a sick nun sends a message which reveals her devotional attitude towards Ānanda.

> Come, thou good fellow! Go to master Ānanda, and on coming to him in my name worship with thy head, the feet of the worthy Ānanda and say: 'Sir, a nun named so and so is sick, . . . she worships with her head the feet of the worthy Ānanda.' . . .[216]

Some of the Pāli commentaries refer to Buddha-worship by monks and nuns. For instance, in *Sumaṅgalavilāsini*,[217] it is stated that during Buddha's lifetime itself, in the first watch of nights *bhikkhus* (monks) used to worship the Buddha in meditation. The *Dhammapada Commentary* records[218] the Buddha-worship by nuns like Kisā-Gotamī.

Acts of Devotion

BUDDHA-PŪJĀ

The word *pūjā* (f.) derived from the root *pūj* which means honour, veneration, and worship occurs with its derivative forms *pūjanā*, *pūjita*, *pūjaneyya* and *pūjanīya* in early Pāli texts like the *Saṁyutta* and *Aṅguttara Nikāya*s and also with its other derivative forms *pūjiya*, *pūjeti*, *pūjako*, *pūjanā* in many of the

---

215. *Theragāthā*, V.623-24: "*. . . vandituṁ upasaṁkamiṁ; vanditvā satthuno pāde ekamantaṁ ṭhito tadā pabbajjaṁ ahamāyāciṁ sabbasatthānam uttamaṁ.*

216. *The Book of the Gradual Sayings* (*AN*), vol. II, tr., p. 148.

217. See, *Sumaṅgalavilāsinī*, pt. I, pp. 45-48; also see *A History of Pāli Literature*, vol. II, p. 415.

218. See, *Dhammapada Commentary*, vol. IV, pp. 156-57; also *op. cit.*, pp. 464-65.

later Pāli canonical books of the *Khuddaka Nikāya*, in the commentaries on the *Dīgha Nikāya*, *Suttanipāta* and *Peṭavatthu*, and in the *Mahāvaṁsa* and *Dīpavaṁsa*.[219]

Whereas *pūjā* means honour in early canonical texts,[220] in the later canonical texts it is conceived as a ceremonial rite, a form of devotional worship and adoration to the Buddha as its object.

In the *Thera-Therigāthā*, *Vimānavatthū*, *Peṭavatthu*, and *Apadāna*, *pūjā* denotes a ritual performance such as worshipping the Buddha by means of various kinds of offerings. According to the *Khuddaka-Paṭha*[221] and *Suttanipāta*[222] worship of the Buddha is conducive for the well-being as well as salvation of beings. In the *Dhammapada pūjā* is regarded as a mental act or attitude. In two verses of the work,[223] Buddha-*pūjā* is explained as the recognition of the lordship of the Buddha and paying homage of reverence to him and his disciples.

In some verses[224] of the *Theragāthā* also, Buddha is depicted

---

219. See, *PTS Dictionary*, p. 471a; Childers, *DPL*, p. 391.

220. See, *MN*, III.11.

221. *Khuddaka-pāṭha*, p. 149.

222. See, *Mahāmaṅgala Sutta of SN*, tr., pp. 43-44; *The Suttanipāta*, tr., p. 39.

223. *Dhammapada verses*, 195-96:

pūjāraha pūjayato buddhayadivāsāvake papanca samatikkhante tinnasokapariddave ।
te tādise pūjayato nibbute akutobhaye na sakkā punnaṁ sankhatuṁ im'etta mapi kenaci ॥

224. *Theragāthā* (*178a*): "The Teacher is worshipped by me, the teaching and the order revered (*satthā ca paricịṇṇo me, dhammo saṁgho ca pūjito*);"
Worshipped of those to be worshipped, Honoured of those to be honoured, Revered of those to be revered. (*pūjito pujaneyyānam sakkareyyana sakkato apacito apacineyyānam tassa icchāmi hātave ti.*)

as an object of worship, honour as reverence. Different acts of piety and religious observances in the *Vimānavatthu* include Faith in the Three jewels, various modes of salutation to the Buddha such as touching his feet, salutating with folded hands and worshipping him by means of diverse offerings of flowers, perfumes, etc. According to some of its narratives by mere fivefold veneration and joyful salutation to the Buddha respectively, a *caṇḍālī* aged woman and Matthakundali, a brāhmaṇa boy were reborn among the *deva*s of thrice-ten.[225]

In the legends of the *Apadāna*, the ideas of piety were further intensified and the formal aspects of religion, viz., *pūjā, vandanā, dāna* and *dakṣiṇā* received a special emphasis which constitute the proper religious sentiments or feelings of devotional love. A claim to *arhant*-ship by homage and other acts of piety is established by *adhikāravāda* which is uphold in this work. These legends also show that the piety of monks and nuns also include Buddha-worship, which ensured salvation to them. In *Buddhāpadāna*, the Buddha is glorified.[226]

According to the *Kathāvatthu* of *Abhidhamma Piṭaka*, it is stated that saint-worship includes the worship of the Buddhas and their apostles.[227]

BUDDHA-ACCANĀ

According to the Pāli lexicons,[228] the English equivalents to the Pāli word *accanā* are oblation, offering, worship. Other forms of the word *accanā*, viz., *accito, accati, accita* denote revere, honour, praise, esteem and celebrate.[229] In the later

---

225. Jean Kennedy (tr.), *Vimānavatthu*, tr., pp. 40-41 and 118-20.

226. See, Perera, "Apadāna," *Ency Bsm*, vol. II, Fas. 1, pp. 2b-3b.

227. See, *Kathāvatthu*, XIII. 2; Thomas, "Saints and Martyrs (Buddhist)," *ERE*, vol. XI, p. 50a.

228. See, Childers, *DPL*, p. 8b; Buddhadatta Maha Thera, *Concise Pāli-English Dictionary*, p. 3a.

229. Childers, *DPL*, p. 9a; *PTS Dictionary*, p. 7b and 8a.

Pāli canonical and commentarial works the Buddha is worshipped by diverse offerings, as a consequence of which the devotees are said to have accrued much merit.

In *Sundarīka Bharadvaja Sutta,*[230] it is enunciated that the *tathāgata* who has destroyed all passions and is liberated in all respects "deserves oblation."

We find in *Thera-Therīgāthā* different accounts of devotional offerings, gifts, and worship by monks and nuns to the Buddhas of the past and as well as to Buddha Śākyamuni, which are conducive to heavenly rebirth, rebirth in the dispensation of Buddhas and happy states of human existence that enabled them to obtain requisite conditions for emancipation.

For example, in *Theragāthā,* it is stated that Thera Khaṇḍasumana as a meritorious consequence of offering a jasmine plant at the tope of Buddha Kassapa in his former birth attained sixfold knowledge in the dispensation of Buddha Gautama.[231] The names of some of the monks in *Theragāthā,* viz., worshipper of foot-prints, water-worshipper, flower-offerer suggest the type of offerings they made to the Buddha.[232]

The *Therīgāthā* records that as a meritorious consequence of their worship accompanied by respective offerings, viz., a spoonful of food, sweet cakes and flowers to Vipassi, a past Buddha, and enshrining his ashes and by offering golden umbrella of jewels, Therīs: Abhaya's mother, Rohiṇī, Sāma and Abhirūpa-Nandā were destined to happy rebirth in various heavens and among human beings and lastly were reborn in the time of Buddha Gautama. Of them, Rohiṇī

230. *The Sutta-nipātha,* tr., pp. 76-77; See verses 14, 18-19 of the *Sutta.*

231. *Psalms of the Brethren,* tr., p. 90.

232. See, Winternitz, *A History of Indian Literature,* vol. II, p. 159.

attained *arhant*-ship.[233] Futher *therīs*, Sundarī, Abhayā, Therikā and Sumedhā respectively made to past Buddhas Vessabhu, Sikhi and Koṇāgamana, etc., offerings of alms, red lotuses, flowers and perfumes and a park for dwelling.[234] *Therīs* Mettikā and Sakulā offered respectively a jewelled girdle and a lamp.[235] Buddha Gautama is said to have been worshipped by *therīs* Bhaddhā Kuṇḍalakesī, Uppalavannā, Khemā and Anopamā.[236] Owing their meritorious acts of worshipping the Buddha by different flower-offerings, two women are said to have reborn among the *devas* of Thrice-Ten and enjoyed celestial pleasures like dwelling in Nandana grove and red-crystal mansion.[237] Similarly by offering scent, wreaths, unguent; fragrant huts to the monastery; food, water, medicine and robes to the Buddha the lay devotees were reborn among the *devas* of Thrice-Ten.[238] By offering his service as a vehicle of transport to the *bodhisattva* (the future Buddha) on the occasion of his great renouncement, the royal horse Kaṇṭhaka was reborn as a *deva* with great *deva*-potency.[239]

The *Peṭavatthu* stories abound in examples in showing that different kinds of offerings made to the Buddha and the order on behalf of the *petas*, either released the *peta* sufferers from their states of suffering or bestowed them with celestial

233. Mrs. Rhys Davids (tr.), *Psalms of the Sisters*, Canto II: XXVI (tr., p. 30); Canto XIII: LXVII (p. 125); Canto III. XXIX (p. 34); Canto II-XIX (p. 22).

234. *Ibid.*, Canto XIII: LXIX (tr., pp. 134-41); Canto II: XXVII (p. 31); Canto I.1 (tr., p. 9); Canto XVI: LXXII (tr., pp. 164-65).

235. *Ibid.*, Canto II, XXIV (tr., p. 28); Canto V: XL IV (tr., p. 60).

236. *Ibid.*, Canto XLVI (tr., pp. 67, 108-09); Canto XI: LXIV (tr., p. 111-12), tr., pp. 81-84; Canto LIV (tr., p. 87).

237. *Ibid.*, tr., pp. 67-70.

238. *Ibid.*, pp. 73-76; pp. 15-16; pp. 71-72.

239. *Ibid.*, pp. 115-17.

comforts.[240] Besides, there are also legends like *Kumāra-peṭavatthu* and *Ubbarīpeṭavatthu* which narrate the Buddha-worship by the laity.[241]

According to *Jātakas*[242] food offered and service paid to the Buddha is to be regarded as good when it is offered with faith (*citta-pasāda*) and it is said that having conceded to king Bimbisāra's request the Buddha gave his hair and nail pairings, while exhorting the king that he may do them honour and customary offerings by keeping them in shrine.

In *Kathāvatthu*,[243] of *Abhidhamma Piṭaka*, on the controverted point whether anything given to the Buddha brings great reward or not, the Theravādins hold that both in this and other worlds there is none equal and better than the Buddha who is "the highest, best, foremost, utter most, supreme, unequalled, incomparable and unique of all two-footed creatures and as he surpasses others in virtue, will and intellect, he is worthy of offerings for those who are desirous of merit." Consequently gifts offered to the Buddha would bring great reward and result in abundant fruit. The *Debates Commentary* added[244] that in view of Theravādins when the gifts offered to even wicked persons accrue rewards in thousandfold, the rewards of offerings of gifts to the Buddha who is the best and foremost of all two-footed creatures will be much more than the former.

The *Khuddakapāṭha Commentary* mentioned[245] an account of

---

240. Law, *The Buddhist Conception of Spirits*, pp. 71-72, 96-98, 80-81.

241. *Ibid.*, pp. 78-79; p. 86.

242. See, *J.*, vol. I, no. 40; *The Jātaka*, vol. I, tr., p. 101; *J.*, vol. II, no. 180; *The Jātaka*, vol. II, tr., p. 59. *The Jātaka*, vol. II, pp. 75-76; *J.*, vol. II, no. 300.

243. *Points of Controversy or Subjects of Discourse*, tr., p. 321.

244. *The Debates Commentary* (Kathāvatthuppakaraṇa Aṭṭhakathā), tr., p. 209.

245. *The Illustrator of Ultimate Meaning*, tr., pp. 140-41.

flower-offering to the Buddha by garland maker Sumana who was prophecied by the former that he will ultimately become a *paccekabuddha* by name Sumanassara after many happy rebirths among gods and men. The Pāli terms *arahā, araho, arahaṁ, arahatā* and *arahati* are meant as a venerable or a holy person who has attained final sanctification, a worthy and deserving person fit to be honoured.[246] Therefore the term *arhant* is attributed to the Buddha for he is worthy to be worshipped with the best offerings. It is stated in some of the *Nikāyas*[247] that an *arhant* is worthy of honour, respect, salutations, offerings, gifts and oblations as he is a peerless field of merit in the world. In the commentary of *Vimānavatthu*,[248] and the *Visuddhimagga*[249] the term *arhant* is explained as he deserves to receive the requisites, i.e., food, robes, etc. (*paccayānaṁ arahattā*). According to the latter source he deserves special worship since he is eligible to receive the best offerings. Hence *deva*s including Brahmā Sahāmpati worshipped him by great offerings. Thus in some of the narratives in the Pāli commentaries of Buddhaghoṣa and Dhammapāla, Buddha is conceived as an object of offerings, which is one of the external acts of worship (*sakkāra pūjā*).

BUDDHA-PATTHANĀ

The Pāli word *patthanā* (San. *prārthanā*) is rendered into English as "aiming at, wish, hope, desire, resolve, request, aspiration and prayer."[250] In the above sense the word *patthanā* is used in

246. See, Childers, *DPL*, pp. 53b and 54a-b.

247. See, *DN*, III. 251; *Dialogues of the Buddha*, Part III, tr., p. 236; *DN*, III. 255; *Dialogues of the Buddha*, Part III, p. 238.

The Book of the Gradual Savings (*AN*), vol. II, tr., pp. 178-79; *The Book of the Gradual Savings* (*AN*), vol. IV, tr., pp. 6-7; 247-48.

248. E. Hondy (ed.), *Vimānavatthū* (with Commy.), pp. 105-06.

249. *The Path of Purity*, Part II, tr., p. 231.

250. See, Childers, *DPL*, pp. 371b-372a; *PTS Dictionary*, p. 407b.

early Pāli canon[251] in the *Saṁyutta* and *Aṅguttara Nikāyas* and *Khuddaka Nikāya* and *Abhidhamma* works, viz., the *Niddesa, Dhammapada, Jātaka, Milindapañha Nettippakaraṇa, Dhammasaṅgani*, and the commentaries on the *Dhammapada Suttanipāta* and *Peṭavatthu*.

Other Pāli forms of the word which are used in the Pāli canon in the sense of "to hope for, long for, wish for, pray for," etc., are *pattheti, patthento, patthayanto, patthetabba, patthita* and *abhipatthita, abhipattheti*. These occur in several later canonical works and their commentaries.[252]

Buddhist prayer is an expression of earnest faith and determined intention to realize *nibbāna* by attaining moral perfection, concentration and wisdom. Many of the Buddhist prayers are expressions of thanks-giving to the Buddha, paying him homage through adoration and exaltation. The solemn vows (*paṇidhāna*) taken by new adherents on the path which is an expression of noble aspiration seems to be the seedbed of Buddhist prayer which in the *Thera-Therīgāthā, Vimānavatthū, Apadāna*, etc., appears to have taken on almost a theistic colouring.

BUDDHA — THAVA AND THUTI

The Pāli word *thometi*, which is a denominative from *thoma* (equivalent of Vedic *stoma*, a hymn of praise) denotes to praise, extol, celebrate, occurs in the first instance in *Dīgha Nikāya*.[253] Other Pāli terms, viz., *thava* (praise, eulogy), *thavati, thaveti* (Sk. eqv. of *stauti, stavayati*), *thuta, thuti, thomamana* which are also meant "to praise, praise of expressing thanks-giving and gratitude, extol, laudation," are mentioned in many of the *Khuddaka Nikāya* books, namely *Suttanipāta, Dhammapada, Jātaka, Cullaniddesa*; in *Abhidhamma* books like *Puggala-paññatti*; and

251. See, *PTS Dictionary*, p. 407b; Childers, *DPL*, p. 372a.

252. *Ibid.*, pp. 407b-408a; p. 67a; Childers, *op. cit.*, pp. 372b; 6a.

253. See, *DN*, I.240.

the *Milindapañha* and *Nettippakaraṇa* and commentaries on the *Suttanipāta, Vimānavatthū, Peṭavatthū* and *Dhammasaṅgani.*[254]

The early Pāli canon contains only some verses of praise addressed to the Buddha scattered here and there which became the precursors of the later Buddhist hymns. In the *Mahājayamaṅgala-Gāthā* and the *Ratna Sutta* contained in the *Khuddakapāṭha* and *Suttanipāta,* several virtues of the Buddha are praised and eulogized.

In the *Puggala-paññatti* also, the praise of the Buddha is advocated.[255] In the *Manorathapūraṇi,* the brāhmaṇa Vangīsa's hymns in praise of the Buddha have been approved and admired by the latter.[256] The *Apadāna* commentary known as *Visuddhajana Vilāsinī* contains Yaśodhara's hymn on the Buddha.

BUDDHA AS OBJECT OF DEVOTION AFTER HIS PARINIBBĀNA

Some of the canonical, post-canonical and commentarial works support the notion, of the continued existence of the Buddha's spiritual presence. This underlies the practice of his being looked upon as an object of veneration and devotion even after his *parinibbāna.* While the *Nikāya* passages already referred to[257] state that the condition of the enlightened one is incomprehensible, it is nowhere stated that the Buddha after his *parinibbāna* had been annihilated.

The *Anāgatavaṁsa,* a post-canonical work which was supposed to have been preached by the Buddha himself at the request of Sāriputta who was keen to know about the

254. See, *PTS Dictionary,* pp. 308b, 309b, 310b; Childers, *DPL,* p. 505a.
255. *Designation of Human Types,* tr., p. 68.
256. *Manorathapūraṇī,* vol. I, pt. I, pp. 266-70; See Law, *A History of Pāli Literature,* vol. II, p. 443.
257. See Supra, Chap. II, Reference Nos. 275-77.

future of the Buddha *sāsana*, provides an account[258] of the gradual decline of the religion divided into five periods of disappearance. Of these five periods when the dispensation of the Buddha will become five thousand years old, the Buddha-relics not receiving reverence and honour will assemble themselves from all places and after performing a twin miracle will become extinct. Of the commentarial works the *Dīgha Nikāya* commentary which mentions about triple *nibbāna* that has been already referred[259] to indicate Buddha's spiritual presence in his relics.

Advantages of Devotion

Unwavering loyalty[260] to the Buddha is variously characterized in the canon as a flood of merit which is conducive to one's profit and happiness;[261] as unsurpassed field of merit;[262] as that which does not subject the possessor to the rebirth in the three realms of woe (i.e., purgatory, womb of animals and *petas*);[263] as conducive to long life, beauty, happiness, good name and

258. See, Weeraratne, "Anāgatavaṁśa," *Ency Bsm*, vol. I, Fasc. 4, pp. 515a-b.

259. See Supra, Chap. II, Ref. No. 278.

260. The word *bhatti* which is meant as service does imply the sense of loyalty. According to *PTS Dictionary*, p. 315b (s.v. "Daḷha"), Daḷhabhattin in the *Dhs. Commy*. is rendered as "firmly devoted to somebody." Therefore unwavering loyalty to the Buddha in the passages referred can only be understood as stead-fast devotion to the Buddha.

261. *The Book of the Kindered Sayings* (*SN*), Part V, tr., p. 336; *The Book of the Gradual Sayings* (*AN*), vol. II, tr., p. 65.

262. *The Book of the Gradual Sayings* (*SN*), vol. I, p. 202.

263. *The Book of the Kindered Sayings* (*SN*), Part V, pp. 325-26; *The Book of the Gradual Sayings* (*AN*), vol. I, p. 202; *The Book of the Kindered Sayings* (*SN*), Part V, tr., pp. 325-26. In this passage addressing Mahānāma, the Buddha assures that a person who possess merely the controlling faculty of faith and affection for the *tathāgata* does not subject himself to downfall and rebirth in hell.

sovereignty among *devas* and human beings;[264] as conducive to rebirth among *devas*,[265] as foremost of the four *deva*-paths, as a means of *deva*-company;[266] and a conducive to concentration of mind.[267]

Further, reverence and devotion to the Buddha helps a disciple in keeping him away from the decline and does not subject him to entertain any doubt with regard to the Buddha and his teaching.[268] In the *Aṅguttara Nikāya* the Buddha prophesied that Ānanda owing to his confidence in the Buddha's cosmical power would obtain seven heavenly births and seven births as a king even if subjected to rebirth, but that as a consequence of his faith in the Buddha he would attain liberation in this very existence.[269] The Introduction to *Junha-Jātaka* further accords with the above assertion, by stating that by his service to the Buddha for twenty-five years Ānanda gained seven blessings which include the blessing of potential Buddhahood.[270] Not only when the Buddha was alive but even after his *parinibbāna*, acts of honour paid to him such as doing homage to the three jewels, it is categorically stated, are of value and fruitful.[271]

---

264. *The Book of the Kindered Sayings* (*SN*), Part V, pp. 335-36.
265. *Alagaddupama Sutta* (*MN*, XXII), *Further Dialogues of the Buddha*, vol. I, p. 100; *MN*, I.141-42: —

 yesam mayi śaddhāmattam pemamattam sabbe te saggaparāyanā ti — See also *MN*, I.444.
266. *The Book of the Kindered Sayings* (*SN*), Part V, tr., pp. 319, 327, 337-38; *Udāna*, Story II.8.
267. *Ibid.*, tr., pp. 335-36.
268. *The Book of the Gradual Sayings* (*AN*), vol. IV, p. 16; *SN*, V.225ff.
269. *AN*, I.227; Poussin & Thomas "Mysticism (Buddhist)," *ERE*, vol. IX, p. 87a.
270. See, *J.*, vol. IV, no. 456; *The Jātaka*, vol. IV, tr., p. 62.
271. Rhys Davids (tr.), *The Questions of King Milinda* (SBE, vol. XXV), *Part I*, pp. 144-51.

FRUITS OF DEVOTION OF LAITY

According to the *Dīgha* and *Saṁyutta Nikāya* passages, the fruits of *upāsaka*s vary from one another. Some attain any of the states from Anagāmi to Gandhabba;[272] some will not be subjected to rebirth in any of the lower planes of existence and some can attain the Sotapattihood.[273]

References are found in some *Aṅguttara Nikāya* passages and in the *Milindapañha* that some laymen and women attained the *arhant*-ship by realizing deathlessness. For example, according to the first source,[274] Sudattagahapati, Cittagahapati, Uggogahapati and a few other laymen are stated to have realized the Immortal. To the inquiry of king Milinda, Nāgasena replied[275] that seven lay people, viz., Sumana the garland maker, Eka-sātaka the brāhmaṇa, Punna the hired servant, the queens, Mallikā and the Mother of Gopāla, Suppiyā the devoted woman and Punna the slave girl, by their acts of devotion obtained the ultimate fruit in their lives, and their fame reached to the *deva*s.

The *Milindapañha* and *Kathāvatthu* unanimously agree that although normally a layman cannot become an *arhant*, there were exceptional cases of laity who were spiritually advanced; but conventionally no layman was recognized as an *arhant* until he renounced his household life.[276]

---

272. *Janavasabha Sutta* (*DN*, XVIII).

273. See, *SN*, V, p. 375; 411.

274. See, *AN*, III, p. 451; T.W. Rhys Davids mentions that a list of twenty laymen attained *arhat*-ship during Buddha's lifetime, according to this passage — See article: "Arhat," *ERE*, vol. I, p. 775a.

275. Rhys Davids (tr.), *The Questions of King Milinda* (*SBE*, vol. XXXV), Part I, tr., p. 172; see also *Paramaṭṭhajotikā*, Part I, pp. 140-41; *Dhp. Aṭṭhakatha*, II.40-47 and *Vimānavatthū Aṭṭhakatha*, 165-69.

276. See, also *Papañcasūdani*, III, p. 196.

Disadvantages of Lack of Devotion

There are also some passages in the canon which refer to the disadvantages of those who are not devoted to the Buddha. For example, according to the *Upālisutta* (*MN*, LVI)[277] when Nigantha Nātaputta could not hear the extollation of the Buddha by Upāli and called the latter's verses of praise as mere eulogy, he vomitted hot blood. According to Buddhaghoṣa's commentary on the *sutta*, as a result of it he died shortly at Pāvā. It is admonished in *Cūḷa-Kamma-Vibhaṅga-Sutta* (*MN*, CXXIV)[278] and also in *Dhammapada* that a person who does not salute those worthy and does not respect, honour and worship them will be subjected to rebirth in either purgatory or in a low family. In the *Puggala-paññatti*, an *Abhidhamma* work, it is said that "a person who is of little faith, devotion and love becomes a wobbler."[279]

---

277. Chalmers (tr.), *Further Dialogues of the Buddha*, vol. I, tr., p. 278; *MN*, I.387.

278. *MN*, III. 205; Chalmers (tr.), *Further Dialogues of the Buddha*, vol. II, pp. 270-71.

279. Law (tr.), *Designation of Human Types*, p. 90.

Epilogue

FROM the above exposition we may conclude that according to Theravāda Conception gods (*deva*) are not immortal beings with any sort of supreme and overriding power over the universe and human destiny, but are superhuman beings who reside in heavenly abodes, which are not, however, everlasting. Gods are not beings who have attained *nirvāṇa* and so they have to learn the truth unto salvation only from the Buddha. But they are the foremost among those who have recognized the Buddhahood of the Buddha and are therefore devoted to him and worship him. As they are inferior to the Buddha in virtue, knowledge and power, they cannot be the objects of the highest type of devotion. Only the Buddha, the *arhant*s and the advanced lay disciples can come into contact with gods, mostly in *samādhi* and infrequently otherwise also. Gods voluntarily offer kindly suggestions and advice with great respect to the disciples in the monastic order, whereas to lay disciples they give as such suggestions and advice equals. While thus they are *kalyāṇamitta*s and in a sense *dhammadūta*s, they should neither be depended upon nor their help invoked by the aspirants of *nibbāna*.

The *Nikāya*s make it clear that by *anussati* of gods, one can obtain knowledge of gods, develop in oneself their qualities and even attain a happy state. But more important than this is that according to the *Nikāya*s *anussati* cleanses the mind, helps one to get rid of hindrances and establishes one in *jhāna*. Buddhaghoṣa, therefore, considers *anussati* as a means to absolute purity; but, nevertheless, while it is an indirect means to higher path, he says, it does not enable one to reach any stage of absorption.

As regards the Theravāda position regarding God, several passages refute the concept of God as creator, active agent, and benevolent ruler. They also show that the conception of God is indistinguishable, unintelligible and inexplicable. Moreover, in Theravāda the doctrines of *aniccā, anatta, paticcasamuppāda, kamma, nibbāna* and the cyclic theory of evolution do not allow any place for God.

Even in the *Vinaya* the Buddha is described as having *sabbaññutā-ñāṇa, iddhi, sabbaseṭṭhatā,* and he is also considered as *ananto*. The *Nikāyas* expounded his omniscience, compassion, various supernormal powers and his supremacy over all beings in the universe. He is also supreme among the highest class of gods — those who attain godhood through purification (*visuddhideva*). There might have been a number of Buddhas but they were so because they had the very same Buddhahood in them. Moreover, the Buddha is *tathāgata* and there is identity between Buddha and *dhamma* on the one hand, and between Buddha and *nibbāna* on the other hand. Moreover, the *Nikāyas* speak of the Buddha as immeasurable and unthinkable. From all this, it seems to be legitimate to assert that for the composers and editors of the *Vinaya* and much more so of the *Nikāyas*, the Buddha was the Numinous Principle, transcendent and infinite. In addition to all this, for all of them the Buddha was Bhagavā.

While all this does not make him the creator, sustainer and destroyer of the universe, nor one who apportions to all rewards according to their virtues (moral action); it must be pointed out that in some of the Indian philosophies considered to be theistic God is not creator or *karmaphalapradātā,* and not even omnipotent, but is only the Ideal, the Teacher or Spectator-Over-Soul. The question may be raised whether the transcendence of the Buddha was accepted by his immediate disciples, and even if so, whether it had his sanction? The Buddha himself asserted his pre-eminence, and that his contemporaries in and outside the monastic order not only did so, but also worshipped him. This is at least what the *Vinaya Piṭaka* indicates and the *Sutta Piṭaka* declares. A critic may still argue that all the passages asserting the Buddha's Transcendence are later and that they had no basis in his teaching, and that they could not have been approved by his loyal direct disciples. But such a critic cannot prove his point unless it is assumed by him that even the earliest Pāli tradition did not completely reflect the Buddha's conception of himself and his first disciples' conception of him.

Saddhā occupies a pivotal place in Theravāda theory and practice. *Saddhā,* which has different shades of meaning such as belief, trust, faith and confidence, is regarded as the essential pre-requisite of the whole spiritual endeavour. It is described in the canon as a virtuous quality, as a spiritual faculty and as the first step in the process of mental purification. It is the pillar on which stands the whole edifice of righteousness. On it depends the development of the rest of the four faculties, i.e., *sati, samādhi, viriya* and *paññā* and their corresponding powers.

As it is the basis of one's inclination to act, without *saddhā* in the Teacher one cannot cultivate it in *dhamma,* and one's attention will not be turned to the consideration of the profound truths taught by the Buddha and the ethical path and meditational techniques enjoined by him. *Saddhā* in the fundamental principles of Buddhist doctrine, viz., *kamma, vipāka, ti-lakkhaṇa, ti-sāraṇa* and *nibbāna,* is an essential condition for realizing the ultimate and according to Buddhism.

Of the different types of *saddhā, ākāravatī saddhā* or *paññāmayī saddhā* (reasoned faith and accompanied by understanding) is given primary place in the Pāli canon. Those who cannot realize *nibbāna* by cultivating it may however practise the shorter and easier method of *aveccappasāda* (absolute or perfect faith in the Buddha and other jewels) which directly leads the adept to mental concentration by eliminating the necessity of observing the *pātimokkha* rules and the usual practice of third and fourth meditations (*jhānas*).

The limitation of *saddhā* has been pointed out in the Pāli canon as well as the commentaries, according to which neither mere *saddhā* nor excessive *saddhā* cultivated by a *saddhānusāri* (he who is conforming by faith) and *saddhāvimutta* (he who is emancipated by faith) can serve as the means to *arhant*-ship for it cannot function effectively in destroying the intoxicants (*āsavas*) completely.

During his lifetime the Buddha is reported to have been the object of *saddhā* as *satthā* and *tathāgata*. He had been shown in the Pāli canon as a great compassionate protector in guiding his disciples and helping them in the progress of their meditation. According to the Pāli canon and its commentaries he was born in the world out of the mercy for the good and welfare of beings. His great compassion is due to his attainment of universal pity; his well-wishing nature and compassion are inestimable.

More significant than this is the *ti-saraṇa* concept which requires *saddhā* in the Buddha who is foremost among the Three Refuges. From the analysis of the canonical and commentarial sources on the evolution of this concept it can be seen that the Buddha is not a just human being who attained purity and wisdom, but is indeed the personification of Enlightenment which is the real object of refuges. The canon makes it clear that the Buddha was considered a unique refuge both during his lifetime as well as after his *parinibbāna*. According to the commentaries on the *Dīgha Nikāya* and the *Khuddakapāṭha*. *Saraṇāgamana* (going for refuge) is an expression of self-devotion to the Buddha and other refuges and communion with them. Taking refuge in the Buddha is stated as conducive to not only *deva*-rebirth and attainment of *sotāpatti*, but also delivers the devoted from all sufferings through the knowledge of the four noble truths.

One of the means of cultivating *aveccappasāda saddhā* is *buddhānussati* (Recollection of the Buddha), whose chief object is to realize the *dhammakāya* of the Buddha. It leads a meditator to mental purification by strengthening faith and mindfulness in the Buddha, as a result of which the former's mind is exalted with gladness and satisfied (*buddhālambanapīti*). It serves as an indirect means of *arhant*-ship by increasing the meditator's insight. The *Nikāya*s of Pāli canon mention a catalogue of advantages of cultivating *saddhā* in the Buddha which include great merit, *deva*-rebirth and *nibbāna* through the attainment of *arhant*-ship.

Lack of *saddhā* in the Buddha is an obstacle to moral and spiritual progress and to the realization of the fruit of *arhant*-ship. Showing irreverence and insolence towards the Buddha or reviling him, whether knowingly or unknowingly, subjects a person to immediate retribution. To harm the Buddha by wounding him was considered an impediment to attainment of emancipation and such a person was also forbidden the higher ordination (*upasampadā*); and ceremonies like Uposatha, Pavāraṇā could not be performed in his presence.

The first occurrence of the word *bhatti* in the sense of decoration and ornamentation has been traced to the *Vinaya*. The word is used in the sense of devotion in the *Theragāthā*. In *Therīgāthā*, it denotes "service or doing service" and in the *Jātaka*, *Dhammasaṅgaṇī* and *Puggala-paññatti*, it means devotion, attachment and fondness. Other Pāli words such as *garukaraṇa*, *namassati* are used in the canon for other accessories of devotion towards the Buddha, and other personages of spiritual eminence.

In some *Majjhima Nikāya* passages, *bhatti* is used in the sense of *saddhā* and in *Aṅguttara Nikāya* passages, the meanings of *bhatti, pema* and *pasāda* are interchanged with *saddhā*. In Buddhaghoṣa's commentaries on the *Dhammasaṅgaṇī* and the *Puggala-paññatti* also special emphasis is laid upon the interrelationship of *saddhā* and *bhatti* and their close identity.

The Buddha was regarded as the object of veneration and devotion as none else shared all the qualities possessed by him as described in the Pāli canon. According to the *Majjhima* and *Aṅguttara Nikāya* passages, he is endowed with all Buddha virtues, and threefold higher knowledge; he is the unsurpassed field of merit; he was born for the welfare and happiness of many beings and hence to see him, to have faith in him, to serve him and to recollect him are regarded as the acts of highest significance. The Buddha is also adored and worshipped owing to his special attribute Bhagavā (Lord, Blessed One, worshipful). Elucidating the epithet 'Bhagavā,' the *Viśuddhimagga* states that Buddha is both the mundane and supramundane ideal, he is the highest of all beings and possessor of six blessings such as lordship, *dhamma*, fame, glory. Dhammapāla, a celebrated commentator, interpreted the epithet in his commentary on the *Visuddhimagga* 'as *bhattavā*,' viz., possessor of devotees who show devotion to him on account of his attainments.

In the *Vinaya* itself the cordial relation between a disciple and his teacher shows the tendency of Buddha-*bhatti*. The *Dīgha, Saṁyutta, Aṅguttara* and *Khuddaka Nikāyas* not only enjoin strict obedience of disciples towards their teachers, but also homage, veneration and worship to the latter. The *Majjhima Nikāya* and *Puggala-paññatti* advocate that all virtuous monks who are equal and greater than us in morality, concentration and insight are to be revered and worshipped. According to the *Nikāyas* and some commentarial works, the followers of the Buddha, viz., his immediate disciples like Ānanda, Vakkali, Vangisa, and his several lay devotees like kings Pasenādi and Bimbisāra paid great homage, devotion and affectionate obeisance to him. From many later canonical works we find that the devotion paid to him was more pronounced; it was expressed through various devotional acts like *pūjā, accanā, patthanā, thava* and *thuti*. Those who believe in God's existence cannot do anything more to express their devotion to Him, if He were to manifest himself in person before them. It is evident from some of the Pāli canonical, post-canonical and commentarial works that it was believed that the Buddha's spiritual presence continued to exist, and therefore he has been looked upon as an object of veneration and devotion even after his *parinibbāna*. His relics, etc., came to be looked upon as repositories of his presence and power in a special way.

Unwavering loyalty and devotion to the Buddha are stated to be not only conducive to worldly benefits like long-life, beauty, happiness, but also to *deva*-rebirth. According to the *Aṅguttara Nikāya*, the *Jātakas* and the *Milindapañha*; both monks like Ānanda and also a good number of *upāsaka*s and *upāsikā*s were destined for liberation and potential Buddhahood, because of their *bhatti*. The disadvantages of a lack of devotion in the Buddha include rebirth in purgatory or in a family of low status.

Even though the Gautama Buddha proclaimed that he had attained enlightenment and that he could show the way to open the door to the immortality by instructing "Strike the mean between Asceticism and sense-indulgence, ultimate meditation, realize selflessness and practice universal friendliness and compassion. That is the way to *nirvāṇa*," yet there were other aspects of his teaching. Love and adoration of the Enlightened One, based upon a deep faith in his teaching and to practise what he taught either a layman, monk or none. This too was emphasized often.

In addition to the terrestrial beings divine and diabolical beings of other sorts were accepted in Theravāda Buddhism. Help and Support of the former for following ethical way was possible; it was equally possible to protect oneself from the harm that might be done by the latter through moral life, holy acts and faith in Buddha's saving power. The Buddha is not a divine being incarnating himself in the world, nor is he a mere human being like us. He is the Enlightened one who surpasses all others, in Virtue, Wisdom, Compassion and Power. He is worthy of worship, devotion and prayer directly and through symbols also. But he is not the creator of heaven and earth or their ruler. Faith in him, worship or devotion of him and his grace can sustain the spiritual wayfarers and according to passages he is capable of bestowing *nirvāṇa* to those who are extremely worthy because of the holy life they lead, loving devotion they have for him and the firm conviction for the *dhamma*/Truth he has taught.

What is the nature of faith and devotion which Theravāda speaks of ? The *tathāgata* even while living is incomprehensible and even after his *parinibbāna* he is so for he is the "Uttermost person, the Supernal person and the attainer of the supernal" (*SN*, III.118). He has the powers, Confidences, Super-knowledges and Buddha *dhammas* (*Niddesa*, I.143) which no one else has. Whoever has settled, rooted by firm faith in the *tathāgata* is his son and he is appropriated by the *dharma* and becomes heir to it (*DN*, III.84). Whoever sees him, sees the *dharma* (*Milindapañha*, 70ff). The *dharma* body and the Brahma Body of the *tathāgata* is *dharma*-become and Brahma-become (*DN*, III.84).

During his lifetime the Buddha was adored through prostrations, salutations, laudations and by offerings of flowers, food and gifts for himself and his Order. His royal devotees had images of him made and figures of him drawn and worshipped them. After his *parinibbāna*, his relics and emblems were worshipped in different ways:

> Circumambulation, litting of lights, burning of incense, offerings of garlands, and precious articles like gems, gold,

etc. Of course during his lifetime and after his *parinibbāna* the Buddha was hymned and hailed as god of gods, Perfection, Wisdom and Compassion personified, and consequently meditating and praying him removes all evil and sin. All these practices and acts of worship are still carried in Theravāda countries of South-East Asia and Ceylon.

Bibliography

Original Texts and Translations

Brandon, S.G.F. (ed.), *A Dictionary of Comparative Religion*, London: Weidensfeld & Nicolson(c), 1970.

Buddhadatta; A.P. (ed.), *Mahāniddesa Aṭṭhakathā* (Saddhammapajjotikā), vol. II, London: PTS, 1931-41.

———, (ed.), *Concise Pali-English Dictionary*, Colombo, The Colombo Apothecaries Co. Ltd., 1968.

———, (ed.), *Vibhaṅga Aṭṭhakathā* (Sammohavinodinī); London: PTS, 1923.

———, (ed.), *English-Pāli Dictionary*, Ceylon: Colombo Apothecaries Co. Ltd., 1955.

Chalmers, Sir Robert (tr.), *Further Dialogues of the Buddha* (tr. from Pali), vols. I & II, London: O.U.P., 1926-27.

Chalmers, R. (tr.), *The Jātaka*, vol. I Delhi: Cosmo Publications, Reprint 1973.

Childers, R.C. (ed.), *A Dictionary of the Pāli Language*, Japan: Rinsen Book Co., Reprint 1976.

Childers (ed.), *Khuddakapāṭha*, London: Journal of Royal Asiatic Society, 1869.

Fausboll, V. (ed.), *Jātaka-I* (with commentary), London: PTS, 1902.

Fausboll, V. (tr.), *The Sutta Nipāta*, SBE, vol. X, part II, Delhi: Motilal Banarsidass, 1977 Reprint.

Feer, L & Rhys Davids, Mrs. (ed.), *Saṁyutta Nikāya* I, London: PTS, 1884-1904.

Fowler, H.W. & Fowler, F.G. (ed.), *The Concise Oxford Dictionary of Current English*, Oxford: Clarendon Press, 4th edn., Reprint, 1956.

Francis, H.T. and Neil, R.A. (tr.), *The Jātaka*, vol. III, Cambridge University Press, 1897.

Francis, H.T. (tr.), *The Jātaka*, vol. V, Cambridge University Press, 1905.

Geiger, W., *The Mahāvaṁśa*, part I, London, PTS, 1958.

Hardy, E. (ed.), *Vimānavatthu Aṭṭhakathā*, London: PTS, 1901.

———, (ed.), *Nettippakaraṇa*, London: PTS, 1902.

Hare, E.M. (tr.), *The Book of the Gradual Sayings* (*Aṅguttara Nikaya*), vols. III & IV, London: PTS, 1934-35.

Horner, I.B, *Buddhavaṁsa Aṭṭhakathā* (Mathuratthavilāsinī), London: PTS, 1946.

———, (tr.), *The Middle Length Sayings*, vols. I-III, London: PTS, 1954-59.

———, *The Milinda's Questions*, vols. I, II, London: PTS, 1969.

———, *The Book of the Discipline*, vol. IV, London: PTS, 1972 Reprint

Jain, B.C. (ed.), *Pāli Kośa Sangaho*, Nagpur: Alok Prakasan, 1st edn., 1974.

Jean Kennedy (tr.), *Vimānavatthu* (The Minor Anthologies of the Pāli Canon, Part IV), London: Luzac & Co., 1942.

Joshi, C.V. (ed.), *Patisambhidamagga Aṭṭhakathā* (Saddhammappakāsinī), II. London: PTS, 1933-47.

Kashyap, Bhikku J. (ed.), *Vinaya I* (*The Maha Vagga*), Nalanda edn., 1956.

Kosambi, D. (ed.), *Abhidhammattha Sangaha*, Sarnath, 1941.

Laurence Urdang and Stuart Berg Fleymer (ed.), *The Random House Dictionary of the English Language*, Bombay: Allied Pub. Pvt. Ltd., 1975 Reprint.

Law, B.C. (tr.), *Designation of Human Types* (Puggalapaññatti), London: PTS, 1922.

———, (tr.), *The Minor Anthologies of the Pāli Canon Part III: Buddhavaṁśa*, London: O.U.P., 1938.

———, (ed.), *Thupavaṁsa* by Vacissara Thera, London: Humphrey Milford, O.U.P. 1935.

Lilley, M.E. (ed.), *Apadāna I*, London: PTS, 1925-27.

Malalasekera, G.P., *Dictionary of Pali Proper Names*, Vols. I & II, London: PTS, 1960.

Maung Tin, *Expositor* (trans. of Aṭṭha-Sālinī), Vols. I & II, London: PTS, 1920-21.

Minayeff, J. (ed.), *Kathāvatthuppakaraṇa Aṭṭhakathā*, J.P.T.S. London, 1889.

Monier-Williams, Sir, *Sanskrit-English Dictionary*, Oxford, New edn., 1899.

———, (ed.), *Buddhavaṁśa*, London: PTS, 1882.

Morris, R. (ed.), *Puggala-Paññatti*, London: PTS, 1883.

Morris, R. and Others (ed.), *Aṅguttara Nikāya*, London: PTS, 1885-1910.

Muller, E. (ed.), *Dhammasaṅgani Aṭṭhakathā*, London: PTS, 1897.

Ñānamoli Bhikku (tr.), *The Illustrator of Ultimate Meaning* (Paramatthajotikā, Part I), Commy. On the Minor Readings by Bhadantacarya Buddha Ghosa, London: PTS, 1960.

———, (tr.), *The Minor Readings* (*Khuddakapāṭha*), London: PTS, 1960.

———, *The Guide* (*Netti-ppakaraṇaṁ*) *according to Kaccana Thera*, London: Luzac & Co. Ltd., PTS., 1962.

———, *The Pitaka Disclosure* (*Peṭakopadesa*) *according to Kaccana Thera*, London: PTS., 1964.

———, (tr.), *The Path of Purification* (*Visuddhimagga*), Colombo: A Semage & Co., 2nd edn., 1964.

Nyanatiloka (ed.), *Buddhist Dictionary*, Ceylon: Free Win & Co. Ltd., 1972.

Oldenberg, H. (ed. & tr.), *The Dīpavaṁsa*, London: Williams & Norgate, 1870.

Oldenberg, H. (ed.), *Vinaya Piṭaka* II, London: PTS, 1879-83.

———, (ed.), *Theragātha*, London: PTS, 1883.

Pe Maung Tin (tr.), *The Path of Purity*, Parts I, II & III tr. of Buddhaghoṣa's *Visuddhimagga*, London: O.U.P., 1922, 1928, 1931.

Poussin, L. De La Vallee and Thomas, E.J., *Mahāniddesa*, I-II, London: PTS, 1916-17.

Rhys Davids, Mrs. (tr.), *Psalms of the Early Buddhists-I*, Psalms of the Sisters, London: PTS, 1900.

———, (tr.), *Psalms of the Early Buddhists-II, Psalms of the Brethren*, London: PTS, 1913.

———, *The Book of Kindered Sayings* (*Saṁyutta Nikāya*), parts I & II, London: 1917; 1922.

Rhys Davids, C.A.F. (tr.), *Dhammasaṅgaṇī* (*Compendium of States of Phenomena*), London: Royal Asiatic Society, 1925.

Rhys Davids, Mrs. (rev. ed. tr.), *Dhammapada* (The Minor Anthologies of the Pali Canon, Part I), London: O.U.P., 1931.

Rhys Davids, T.W. & Oldenberg, H. (tr.), *Vinaya Texts*, Parts I-III, London: PTS, 1881, 1882 & 1885, Delhi: Motilal Banarasidass, 1974-75.

Rhys Davids, T.W. *et al.* (ed.), *Dīgha Nikāya Aṭṭhakathā* (Sumaṅgalavilāsinī), London: PTS, 1886-1932.

Rhys Davids, T.W. (tr.), *The Questions of King Milinda* (SBE, vol. XXXV-XXXVI parts I & II), Delhi: Motilal Banarsidass, 1964, reprint.

———, *Dialogues of the Buddha*, Parts I, II & III (S.B.B. vols. II-IV, London: PTS, 1971-73).

———, *Buddhist Birth Stories* (*Jātaka* Tales), Varanasi: Indological Book House, 1973.

Rhys Davids, T.W. & Stede, W. (ed.), *Pāli-English Dictionary*, New Delhi: Oriental Books Reprint Corporation, First Indian edn., 1975.

Rouse, W.H.D. (tr.), *The Jātaka*, Vols. II, IV & V, Cambridge: Cambridge Univ. Press, 1895, 1901, 1905.

Sakaki, R. (ed.), *Mahavyutpatti*, vol. I, Kyoto, Japan: Suzuki Research Foundation, 1916.

Shwezan Aung & Mrs. Rhys Davids (tr.), *Points of Controversy* (tr. of *Kathā-vatthu*), London: PTS, 1915.

Smith, H. *et al.* (ed.), *Dhammapada Aṭṭhakathā III*, London: PTS, 1906-15.

Smith, H. (ed.), *Suttanipāta Aṭṭhakathā* (Paramatthajotikā II), London: PTS, 1916-18.

Stede, W. (ed.), *Cullaniddesa I-III*, London: PTS, 1918.

Strong, D.M. (tr.), *The Udāna or the solemn utterances of the Buddha*, London: PTS, 1902.

Taylor, A.C. (ed.), *Patisambhidāmagga*, I, London: PTS, 1905-07.

Thittila, U. (tr.), *The Book of Analysis* (*Vibhaṅga*), London: Luzac & Co. Ltd., 1969.

Trenckner, V. *et al.* (ed.), *Majjhima Nikāya, II, III*, London: PTS, 1888-1925.

Trenckner, V. (ed.), *Milindapañha*, London: PTS, 1962.

Upasak, C.S., *Dictionary of Early Buddhist Monastic Terms*, Varanasi: Bharati Prakashan, 1st edn., 1975.

Walleser, M. & Kopp. H. (ed.), *Aṅguttara Nikāya Aṭṭhakathā* (*Manorathapūraṇī*), London: PTS, 1924-56.

Warren, H.C. and Kosambi, D. (ed.), *Visuddhimagga*, Harward Oriental Series, no. 41, 1950.

Warren, H.C., *Buddhism in Translations*, H.O.P., 1953.

Woods, J.H. *et al.* (ed.), *Majjhima Nikāya Aṭṭhakathā* (*Papañcasūdanī*), II, London: PTS, 1922-38.

Woodward, F.L. (ed.), *Udāna Aṭṭhakathā* (*Paramatthadīpanī*), London: PTS, 1926.

———, *Saṁyutta Nikāya Aṭṭhakathā* (*Saratthappakāsinī*), London: PTS, 1929-37.

———, (tr.), *The Book of the Gradual Sayings* (*Aṅguttara Nikāya*), vols. I, II & V. London: PTS, 1932, 1933 & 1936.

———, (tr.), *Itivuttaka : As it was said* (*The Minor Anthologies of the Pāli Canon*, Part II), London: Humphrey Milford, O.U.P., 1935.

———, (ed.), *Theragāthā Aṭṭhakathā* (*Paramatthadīpanī*), I, London: PTS, 1940-59.

———, *Some Sayings of the Buddha*, Oxford, 1925, 1960.

Modern Works

Alicia, Matsunaga, *The Buddhist Philosophy of Assimilation*, Japan: Sophia University, 1969.

Ananda, Guruge (ed.), *Return to Righteousness*, Ceylon: Ministry of Education & Cultural Affairs, 1965.

Barthelmy, Saint-Hilarie, J., *The Buddha and his Religion*, London: Kegan Paul, Trench Trubner & Co. Ltd.

Barua, B.M., *A History of Pre-Buddhist Indian Philosophy*, Calcutta: University of Calcutta, 1918.

Barua, D.K., *An Analytical Study of Four Nikayas*, Calcutta: Rabindra Bharati University, 1971.

Carpenter, J.E., *Theism in Medieval India*, London: Constable & Co. Ltd., 1926.

Conze, E. (ed.), *Buddhist Texts through the Ages*, New York: Philosophical Library, 1954.

———, *Buddhist Thought in India*, London: George Allen and Unwin Ltd., First Publication, 1962.

———, *Thirty years of Buddhist Studies*, Oxford: Bruno Cassirer, 1967.

Dharmasiri, G., *A Buddhist Critique of the Christian Concept of God*, Ceylon: Lakehouse Investments, Ltd., 1974.

Dolly, Facter, *The Doctrine of the Buddha*, New York: Philosophical Library, 1965.

Dutt, Nalinaksha, *Buddhist Sects in India*, Varanasi: Indological Book House, 1977.

Eliot, Sir Charles, *Hinduism and Buddhism*, vols. I, II, III. London: Routledge & Kegan Paul Ltd., 1957.

Fozdar, J.K., *The God of Buddha*, London: The Asia Publishing House Ltd., 1973.

Francis, Story, *The Four Noble Truths*, Wheel Pub. Nos. 34/35, Ceylon: The Buddhist Publication Society, 1968.

———, *Gods and the Universe in the Buddhist Perspective*, Wheel Pub. Nos. 180/181, Ceylon: Buddhist Publication Society, 1972.

Gyomroi, Edith Iudowyk, *The Role of the Miracle in Early Pali Literature*, Unpublished Ph.D. Thesis, University of Ceylon.

Jayatillake, K.N., *Early Buddhist Theory of Knowledge*, London: George Allen & Unwin Ltd., 1963.

———, *Facets of Buddhist Thought*, Ceylon: Buddhist Publication Society, 1971.

———, *The Message of the Buddha*, London: George Allen & Unwin Ltd., First Publication, 1975.

King, Winston L., *Buddhism and Christianity some bridges of Understanding*, London: George Allen & Unwin Ltd., 1963.

Law, B.C., *Heaven and Hell in Buddhist Perspective*, Calcutta: Thacker, Spink & Co., 1925.

———, *A History of Pali Literature*, Part II, London: Kegan Paul, Trench Trubner Co. Ltd., 1933.

———, *Concepts of Buddhism*, Leiden: Kern Institute, 1937.

———, *The Buddhist Conception of Spirits*, Varanasi: Bharatiya Publishing House, 1974.

Ling, Trevor, *Buddha, Marx and God*, New York: St. Martin's Press, 1966.

———, *The Buddha*, London: Maurice Temple Smith Ltd., 1973.

Macdowell, A.A., *The Vedic Mythology*, Varanasi: Indological Book House, 1963.

Marasinghe, M.M.J., *Gods in Early Buddhism*, University of Sri Lanka, 1974.

Monier-Williams, Sir, *Buddhism in its Connexion with Brahmanism and Hinduism and in its contrast with Christianity*, Varanasi: Chowkhamba Sanskrit Series Office, 1964.

Ñānamoli, Thera, *The Three Refuges*, Ceylon: Buddhist Publishing Society, 2nd Imp., 1972.

Nyanaponika, Thera (ed.), *Buddhism and the God-idea*, Ceylon: Buddhist Publications Society, 2nd edn., 1970.

———, *The Threefold Rejuge*, Ceylon: Buddhist Pub. Society, 1965.

Parrinder, Geoffrey, *Avatar and Incarnation*, London: Faber and Faber, 1970.

Poussin, L. De La Vallee, *The Way of Nirvāṇa*, Cambridge, 1917.

Rune, Johnson, E.A., *The Psychology of Nirvāṇa*, London: Allen and Unwin, 1969.

Samuel, Beal, *Chinese Accounts of India*, vols. I-III, Calcutta: Susil Gupta (India) Ltd., 1957-58.

Sushila Pant, *The Origin and Development of Stūpa Architecture in India*, Varanasi: Bharata Manisha, 1976.

Theodre, De Bary, W.M & Others (ed.), *The Buddhist Tradition in India, China & Japan*, New York: Modern Library, 1969.

Watters, Thomas, *Yuanchwang's Travels in India*, Delhi: Munshiram Manoharlal, 1961.

Winternitz, M., *A History of Indian Literature*, vol. II, Delhi: Munshiram Manoharlal, reprint, 1977.

Articles

Alec Robertson, "The Omniscience of the Buddha," *The Maha Bodhi*, Vol. 78, No. 1, January 1970, Calcutta.

Albert, La Roche, "The Person of the Buddha," *The British Buddhist*, vol. 7, no. 2 & 3, London, November-December, 1932.

Allessandro, Costa, "Buddhism: An Agnostic Religion," *Buddhism an Illustrated Review*, vol. II, no. 1, Burma, October, 1905.

Andre, Bareau, "Absolute as the unconditioned," *Encyclopaedia of Buddhism*, vol. I, Fasc. I, Ceylon, 1961.

Anesaki, M., "Ethics and Morality (Buddhist)," *Encyclopaedia of Religion & Ethics*, vol. I, Edinburgh: T&T Clark, 4th Imp., 1960.

Angaraj Chaudhary, "Concept of Pacceka Buddha," *The Mahā Bodhi*, Calcutta, Ocober-December 1975.

Arya Dharma, "The Gods and their Place in Buddhism," *The Mahā Bodhi*, vol. 47, no. 5 & 6, Calcutta, May-June, 1939.

Barua, B.M., "Buddha's Greatness and Role," *The Mahā Bodhi*, vol. 52, nos. 5-6, Calcutta, May-June, 1944.

Barua, Manoj Kumar, "God in Buddhist Philosophy," *The Mahā Bodhi*, vol. 56, no. 7, Calcutta, July 1948.

Bhattacharya, Devaprasad, "Buddhist views on Causation: An Advaitic Study," *Prabhuddha Bharata*, vol. LXXII (July, 1967).

Bhattacharya, H., "Karma," *The Maha Bodhi*, Vol. XXXIII, No. 2, Calcutta, Feb. 1925.

Bond, George D., "Two Theravada Traditions of the Meaning of 'The word of the Buddha'," *The Mahā Bodhi*, Calcutta, October-December 1975.

Chalmers, R., "Tathagata," *The Journal of the Royal Asiatic Society of Great Britain and Ireland*, 1898.

Chizen, Akanuma, "The Buddha," *The Eastern Buddhist*, vol. I, no. 1, Japan, May 1921.

Dasgupta, S.B., "Positive Conception of Nirvāṇa," *World Buddhism*, vol. XXIII, no. 5, Ceylon, December 1974.

De Silva, C.L.A., "The Threefold views," *The Mahā Bodhi*, vol. 48, nos. 5-6, Calcutta, May & June, 1940.

Ellan, J.E., "Practical Buddhism," *The Buddhist Review*, vol. XI, The Buddhist Society of Great Britain and Ireland, London, 1921.

Geden, A.S., "Images and Idols (Buddhist)," in James Hastings (ed.), *Encyclopaedia of Religion and Ethics*, vol. VII, Edinburgh: T&T Clark, 4th Imp., 1959.

Godage, Charles, "The Place of Indra in Early Buddhism," *University of Ceylon Review*, vol. III, no. 1, Ceylon, April, 1945.

Grierson, G.A., "Bhakti Marga," in J. Hastings (ed.), *ERE*, vol. II, Edinburgh: T&T Clark, 1909.

Gymroi, Edith Iudowyk, "Note on the Interpretation of 'Pasidati,' " *University of Ceylon Review*, Ceylon, April, 1943.

———, "The Role of the Miracle in Early Pāli Literature," unpub. PhD. Thesis, University of Ceylon.

Hewavitarne, C.A., "The unknown," *The Mahā Bodhi*, vol. XXII, no. 7, Calcutta, July 1914.

———, "Buddhism and its appeal to the West," *The Mahā Bodhi*, vol. XXI, nos. 2-3, Calcutta, February & March 1913.

Howell, Smith, A.D., "The Christian and Buddhist Conception of Love," *The Buddhist Review*, vol. I, no. 2, 1909.

Jamuna Prasad, "Can there be Religion without God?" *The Indian Philosophical Congress:* Symposium II, 26th Session at Poona, 1951.

Jayawardhana, B., "Brahma," *Encyclopaedia of Buddhism*, vol. III, Fasc. 2, Govt. of Ceylon, 1972.

———, "Cakkavala," *Encyclopaedia of Buddhism*, vol. III, Fasc. 4, Govt. of Ceylon, 1977.

———, "Abhassara," *Encyclopaedia of Buddhism*, vol. I, Fasc. 1, Govt. of Ceylon, 1961.

———, "Brahma Kayika Deva," *Encyclopaedia of Buddhism*, vol. III, Fasc. 2, Govt. of Ceylon, 1972.

Jayawickrama, N.A., "Acariya in Pāli Buddhism," *Encyclopaedia of Buddhism*, vol. I, Fasc. 2. Govt. of Ceylon, 1963.

Joshi L.M., "True Buddhism," *The Mahā Bodhi*, vol. 74, no. 1-2, Calcutta, January-February, 1966.

———. "The Concept of Dhamma in Buddhism," *The Mahā Bodhi*, vol. 75, no. 11, Calcutta, October-November 1967.

Kalipada Mitra, "Nibbanam," *The Journal of the Bihar & Orissa Research Society*, vol. X, part 1 & 2, Patna, December 1924.

Kariyawasam, A.G.S., "Bodhisattva," *Encyclopaedia of Buddhism*, vol. III, Fasc. 2, Ceylon, 1972.

———, "Buddha Nature," *Encyclopaedia of Buddhism*, vol. III, Fasc. 3, Govt. of Ceylon, 1973.

Karunaratna, Upali, "Buddha-Cakkhu," *Encyclopaedia of Buddhism*, vol. III, Fasc. 3, Govt. of Ceylon, 1973.

———, "Buddha-Kṣetra," *Ency Bsm*, Vol. III, Fasc. 3, Govt. of Ceylon, 1973.

———, "Buddhology," *Encyclopaedia of Buddhism*, vol. III, Fasc. 3, Govt. of Ceylon, 1973.

Krishnan, Y., "The Kaya Doctrine in Buddhism," *The Mahā Bodhi*, vol. 60, no. 8, Calcutta, August, 1952.

Kularatne, D.G. D.E.S., "Existence and Creation," *The Mahā Bodhi*, vol. 57, no. 7, Calcutta, July, 1949.

Law, B.C., "Buddhist Conception of Dhamma," *Journal of the Department of Letters*, vol. XXVII, Calcutta University Press, 1935.

———, "Three Rejuges (Trisaraṇa) in Buddhism," *The Maha Bodhi*, Vol. 61, Nos. 5 & 6, Calcutta, May-June, 1953.

Malalasekera, G.P., "Buddhism and Problems of the Modern Age II," *World Buddhism*, vol. XXI, no. 5, Sri Lanka, December, 1972.

———, "Buddha," *Encyclopaedia of Buddhism*, vol. III, Fasc. 3, Govt. of Ceylon, 1973.

Mathuralal Sharma, "Magical Beliefs and Superstitions in Buddhism," *The JBORS*, vol. I, Patna, 1956.

McKechnie, J.F., "God and Gods," *The British Buddhist*, vol. II, London, September 1928.

Mitchell, J.T., "The Theist and Tu Buddhist: An Examination of Some Relative Positions," W.F.B. Review, Vol. XIII, No. 5, Sep-Oct., 1975.

Mudaliyar, M.N. Pieris, "The Place of Miracles in Buddhism," *The Buddhist*, vol. XLIV, no. 1, Ceylon, May 1973.

Murti, T.R.V., "Buddhism and Vedanta," (Symposium III, Part II Symposia), *The Indian Philosophical Congress*, 29th Session at Ceylon, 1954.

Nanajivako Bhikku, "Why is Buddhism a Religion," *Indian Philosophical Annual*, vol. VI, University of Madras, 1970.

Narada, Bhikku, "The Bodhisatta Ideal," *Buddhism in England*, vol. 2, no. 10, London, April 1928.

Narada, Maha Thera, "Buddhism: The Golden Mean," *World Buddhism*, vol. XVIII, no. 10, Ceylon, May, 1970.

Perera, H.R., "Apadana," *Encyclopaedia of Buddhism*, vol. II, Fasc. I, Govt. of Ceylon, 1966.

Poussin and Thomas, "Mysticism (Buddhist)," J. Hastings (ed.), *ERE*, vol. IX, Edinburgh; T&T Clark, 4th imp, 1956.

Poussin, L. De La Vallee, "Nature" (Buddhist), J. Hastings (ed.), *ERE*, vol. IX, Edinburgh; T&T Clark, 4th imp, 1956.

———, "Pratyeka Buddha," J. Hastings (ed.), *ERE*, vol. X, Edinburgh: T&T Clark, 4th imp, 1956.

———, "Abode of the Blest (Buddhist)," J. Hastings (ed.), *ERE*, vol. II, Edinburgh: T&T Clark, 4th imp., 1958.

———, "Bodhisattva," J. Hastings (ed.), *ERE*, vol. II, Edinburgh: T&T Clark, 4th imp, 1958.

———, "Ages of the World (Buddhist)," J. Hastings (ed.), *ERE*, vol. I, Edinburgh: T&T Clark, 4th imp., 1959.

———, "Cosmogony and Cosmology (Buddhist)," J. Hastings (ed.), *ERE*, vol. IV, Edinburgh: T&T Clark, 4th imp., 1959.

Rhys Davids, C.A.F. "Was Original Buddhism Atheistic," *The Hibbert Journal*, vol. XXXVII, London, October 1938-July 1939.

———, "Love (Buddhist)," James Hastings (ed.), *ERE*, vol. VIII, Edinburgh: T&T Clark, 4th imp., 1958.

———, "Desire (Buddhist)," J. Hastings (ed.), *ERE*, vol. IV, Edinburgh: T&T Clark, 4th imp., 1959.

Saddhatissa Mahathera, Ven., "The Three Refuges," *The Mahā Bodhi*, Calcutta, June & July, 1965.

Siddhartha, R., "Buddhism and the God Idea," *The Buddhist Annual of Ceylon*, Vol. III, No. 3, Ceylon, 1929.

Soni, R.L. "God and Buddhism," *The Mahā Bodhi*, vol. 43, no. 3, Calcutta, March, 1935.

Tachibana, S., "What is Karma," *The Buddhist*, vol. IX, no. 12, April, 1930.

Thittila, U., "Saints and Martyrs (Buddhist)," J. Hastings (ed.), *ERE*, vol. XI, Edinburgh. T&T Clark, 4th imp, 1958.

Van Zeyst, H.G.A., "Agnosticism," *Encyclopaedia of Buddhism*, vol. I, Fasc. 2, Govt. of Ceylon, 1963.

———, "Annussati," *Encyclopaedia of Buddhism*, vol. I, Fasc. 4, Govt. of Ceylon, 1965.

———, "Atheism," *Encyclopaedia of Buddhism*, vol. II, Fasc. 2, Govt. of Sri Lanka, 1967.

———, "Buddhanussati," *Encyclopaedia of Buddhism*, vol. III, Fasc. 3, Govt. of Ceylon, 1973.

Varma, V.P., "Early Buddhist Mysticism," *The Mahā Bodhi*, vol. 67, no. 1, Calcutta, January, 1959.

———, "Nirvāṇa in Early Buddhist Philosophy," *The Mahā Bodhi*, vol. 68, no. 7, Calcutta, July, 1960.

Walisinha, Devapriya, "Patisambhidamagga," *The British Buddhist*, vol. III, no. 10, London, July, 1929.

Weeraratne, W.G., "Anagatavamasa," *Encyclopaedia of Buddhism*, vol. I, Fasc. 4, Govt. of Ceylon, 1965.

———, "Anussati Sutta," *Encyclopaedia of Buddhism*, Vol. I, Fasc. 4, Govt. of Ceylon, 1965.

Wijesekara, "Vedic Gandharva and Pāli Gandhabba," *University of Ceylon Review*, April, 1945.

Index of Buddhist Works

Abhidharma Kośa, 33, 68fn, 150

Abhidharma Kośa Vyākhyā, 34fn

Abhidhamma Piṭaka, 48, 82, 87, 136, 166-67, 181, 184

Abhidhammattha Saṅgaha, 10, 10fn

Abhidhānappadīpikā, 2, 32, 32fn, 42, 114

Acchariyabbhutadhamma Sutta, 24, 117, 119

Aggañña Sutta, 52, 58, 63, 66

Alagaddūpama Sutta, 159, 160fn, 189fn

Ambaṭṭha Sutta, 28fn, 90

Anāgatavaṁsa, 187, 188fn

Anamatagga Saṁyutta, 52

Aṅgulimāla Sutta, 97fn

Aṅguttara Nikāya, 9, 39-40, 45, 66, 85, 102-03, 103fn, 110, 119, 121fn, 131, 135, 141, 149, 157, 162-64, 169, 171, 175-79, 186, 189-90, 197-99

Aṅguttara Nikāya Aṭṭhakathā, 118fn, 157fn

Anussati Sutta, 40, 40fn

Apadāna, 114, 124, 124fn, 131, 145, 180-181fn, 186-87

Ariyapariyesana Sutta, 23, 79, 117, 150

Ātānaṭiya Sutta, 24, 30, 33

Aṭṭahasālinī, 74, 125, 165fn, 170

Avyākata Saṁyutta, 132

Ayakūṭa Jātaka, 33fn

Bhaddekaratta Sutta, 20

Bhadra-Ghaṭa Jātaka, 17fn

Bhaya Bherava Sutta, 8fn, 117, 153

Bhikkhuṇī Saṁyutta, 25

Bhūridatta Jātaka, 65, 65fn

Bilāri-Kosiya-Jātaka, 18fn

Brahma Saṁyutta, 22fn, 27fn, 29

Brahmajāla Sutta, 22, 44, 47, 54, 57-58

Brāhmaṇa Saṁyutta, 177

Brahma-Nimantaṇika Sutta, 22fn, 25, 29, 56fn

Brahmāyu Sutta, 90, 177

Buddhāpadāna, 181

Buddhavaṁsa, 75, 75fn, 101, 121, 124
Buddhavaṁsa Aṭṭhakathā, 91fn, 101fn, 109fn, 121fn, 122fn

Cakkavatti Sīhanāda Sutta, 124
Canda Kinnara Jātaka, 17fn
Caṅkī Sutta, 116fn, 144fn
Cariyāpiṭaka, 116
Catukka-nipāta, 13fn
Cātuma Sutta, 27fn
Cetokhila Sutta, 7, 164fn
Cūḷa Māluṅkya Sutta, 69, 70-71
Cūḷa Saccaka Sutta, 79fn
Cūḷa Sakuludāyi Sutta, 62
Cūḷa-Dhamma Samādāna Sutta, 8fn
Cūḷagopālaka Sutta, 144fn, 159
Cūḷa-Kamma-Vibhaṅga Sutta, 191
Cūḷa-Puṇṇama Sutta, 160fn
Cūḷasīhanāda Sutta, 144fn
Cūḷa-Taṇhā Saṅkhaya Sutta, 22
Cūlladhanuggaha Jātaka, 18fn
Cullaniddesa, 108fn, 117, 186
Culla-Suttasoma Jātaka, 18fn

Devadhamma Jātaka, 2fn
Dasuttara Sutta, 134
Devadaha Sutta, 66, 66fn
Devadūta Sutta, 45fn
Dhamacakkappavattana Sutta, 25
Dhammacetiya Sutta, 171
Dhammaddhaja Jātaka, 17fn
Dhammapada, 7, 7fn, 8fn, 24, 76, 86, 98fn, 110fn, 121, 128, 145-46, 149, 155, 157-158, 158fn, 168, 172fn, 175fn, 180, 180fn, 186, 191
Dhammapada Aṭṭhakathā, 76, 77fn, 91fn, 93, 122fn, 146, 158fn, 172, 179, 179fn, 190fn
Dhammasaṅganī Aṭṭhakathā, 123fn
Dhammasaṅganī, 74, 118, 123, 128, 136, 136fn, 146, 146fn, 147, 163, 165, 168, 168fn, 170, 186-87, 197
Dhanjavihaṭha Jātaka, 18fn,
Dhātukathā, 136, 136fn
Dhātuvibhaṅga Sutta, 93fn
Dīgha Nikāya, 13, 29-30, 38, 79, 86, 96-97, 106fn, 109fn, 113, 113fn, 116, 116fn, 119, 122, 124, 130, 134, 139, 149-50, 156, 165, 172, 175-76, 180, 186, 188, 190
Devatā Saṁyutta, 21, 21fn, 30-31, 45fn
Dīghanikāya Aṭṭhakathā, 22, 86fn, 91fn, 101fn, 120fn, 121fn, 132fn, 150, 154, 168fn
Dīpavaṁsa, 180

Gandhabbakāya Saṁyutta, 33
Gedha Sutta, 42fn
Ghaṭikāra Sutta, 177

Gopaka Moggallāna Sutta, 152fn, 170fn
Guttila Jātaka, 17fn

Isigili Sutta, 84fn
Itivuttaka, 12, 13fn, 14, 19, 19fn, 26, 26fn, 103fn, 128, 145-46, 146fn, 149

Janavāsabha Sutta, 8fn, 93fn, 190fn
Jātakanidāna, 118, 121, 124
Junha Jātaka, 189
Jātakas, 18, 33, 34, 60fn, 103fn, 109fn, 117, 118fn, 119, 121fn, 129, 145fn, 149-50, 163, 166, 168, 168fn, 184, 186, 189fn, 197, 199

Kaccāni Jātaka, 17fn
Kaṅha Jātaka, 17fn
Kankavitarana Niddesa, 49
Kaṇṇakatthala Sutta, 3, 18fn, 19fn, 21, 77fn
Kathāvatthu, 13, 13fn, 79, 87-88, 103, 103fn, 108fn, 123, 136, 148, 181, 181fn, 184
Kathāvatthuppakaraṇa Aṭṭhakathā, 106fn, 107fn, 123, 136, 184fn
Keli-śīla-Jātaka, 17fn
Kevaḍḍha Sutta, 23fn, 56fn, 88
Khadiranga Jātaka, 18fn
Khandavagga, 33
Kharaputta Jātaka, 35
Khuddaka Nikāya, 9, 19, 87, 114, 145-46, 167, 175, 180, 186, 198
Khuddaka Vibhaṅga, 53
Khuddakapāṭha, 102fn, 105fn, 112, 112fn, 119fn, 150, 154, 175fn, 180, 180fn, 187, 196
Khuddakapāṭha Comm., 119fn, 151, 172, 184
Kīṭagiri Sutta, 137, 142
Kuddala Jātaka, 18fn
Kulāvaka Jātaka, 16, 17fn
Kumāra-Petavatthu, 184
Kumbha Jātaka, 18fn
Kumbhakara Jātaka, 145
Kurudhamma Jātaka, 17fn
Kūṭadanta Sutta, 154fn

Lakkhaṇa Sutta, 110, 116
Lomassa Kassapa Jātaka, 17fn

Madhuratthavilāsinī, 91
Mahā Niddesa, 73, 79, 79fn, 92fn, 108fn, 114, 151fn, 169
Mahā Niddesa Aṭṭhakathā, 77fn
Mahā Sudassana Sutta, 84,
Mahājayamaṅgala Gāthā, 187
Mahākamma Vibhaṅga Sutta, 82fn
Mahākanha Jātaka, 17fn
Mahāmaṅgala Sutta, 180fn
Mahānāma Sutta, 40, 41, 157
Mahanārada Kassapa Jātaka, 27

Mahāpadāna Sutta, 26fn, 117, 119
Mahāparinibbāna Sutta, 24, 123
Mahā Paduma Jātaka, 18fn, 166fn
Mahā-sakuludāyi Sutta, 161
Mahāsamaya Sutta, 42fn, 46fn, 154fn
Mahāsīhanāda Sutta, 82, 89
Mahā-Vacchagotta Sutta, 85
Mahāvagga, 110, 175
Mahāvaṁsa, 180
Mahāvyutpatti, 114, 114fn
Majjhima Nikāya, 31, 76, 76fn, 77fn, 79, 81fn, 89fn, 106fn, 107fn, 114, 116, 116fn, 117, 119, 121, 131, 134, 141, 145-46, 152, 164, 169, 171, 177, 197-98
Majjhima Nikāya Aṭṭhakathā, 3fn, 78fn, 81fn, 91fn, 121fn, 123fn
Makhādeva Sutta, 84
Mandhātu Jātaka, 17fn
Manorathapūraṇī, 45fn, 94fn, 118fn, 187, 187fn
Māra Saṁyutta, 21fn, 24
Matta-kuṇḍali Jātaka, 26fn
Milindapañha, 57, 78, 87, 100fn, 112-13, 117, 119-20, 125, 125fn, 127fn, 128, 135, 140, 171fn, 186- 87, 189, 199
Mūlapariyāya Sutta, 7, 47

Nagara-vindeyya Sutta, 175fn
Nāna Vibhaṅga, 82
Nettippakaraṇam, 8fn, 12fn, 78fn, 79, 79fn, 89fn, 97fn, 103fn, 128, 135, 135fn, 140, 148, 156, 186-87
Nidāna Vagga, 52fn
Nidānakathā, 109, 109fn, 178, 178fn
Niddesa, 53fn, 80fn, 92, 186
Nimi Jātaka, 18fn, 22

Pañcagati-dīpanī, 10, 10fn
Papañcasūdanī, 122, 191fn
Pārājika, 174
Paramathamañjūsā, 174
Paramatta Jotikā, 1fn, 73fn, 77fn, 83fn, 149fn, 150fn, 151fn, 173fn, 190
Paramatthadīpanī, 32, 95fn
Pāsādika Sutta, 79fn
Pāṭika Sutta, 54, 58
Paṭisambhidāmagga, 73fn, 78, 78fn, 79, 79fn, 86, 100fn, 114, 148, 165, 172fn
Paṭisambhidāmagga Aṭṭhakathā, 79fn
Pāyāsi Sutta, 8
Peṭakopadesa, 7, 7fn, 85fn, 135, 135fn, 140, 156, 156fn, 160, 160fn, 163
Petavatthu, 86, 118, 172fn, 180, 183, 187
Petavatthu Aṭṭhakathā, 8fn
Poṭṭhapāda Sutta, 23fn
Puggala Sutta, 52

Puggala-paññatti Aṭṭhakathā, 170fn

Puggalapaññatti, 79, 102, 102fn, 104fn, 105fn, 107fn, 112, 112fn, 118fn, 123, 136, 142, 163, 165, 168, 168fn, 170, 175, 186-87, 191, 197-98

Ratana Sutta, 112, 187

Raṭṭhapāla Sutta, 8fn

Saddhammapajjotikā, 77

Sadhina Jātaka, 18fn

Sagātha Vagga, 34, 36

Sakkapañha Sutta, 8, 22, 30

Sambadhokasa Sutta, 41

Sammohavinodanī, 48, 91

Sampasādanīya Sutta, 88, 119

Samudda-vanija Jātaka, 166fn

Saṁyutta Nikāya Aṭṭhakathā, 91fn, 101fn, 106fn, 122fn

Saṁyutta Nikāya, 20, 31, 88, 92fn, 106fn, 108fn, 114, 115, 117, 124, 132fn, 134, 141, 148, 155-56, 156fn, 162, 64, 175, 186, 190

Sandaka Sutta, 77

Saṅgārava Sutta, 3-5

Saṅgīti Sutta, 119, 144, 163

Saṅkhāruppatti Sutta, 9

Sāratthappakāsinī, 91fn

Satipaṭṭhāna Saṁyutta, 156

Sela Sutta, 110

Suruci Jātaka, 18fn

Siṅgālovada Sutta, 147, 175fn

Somadatta-Jātakas, 17fn

Sonadaṇḍa Sutta, 90

Sumaṅgalavilāsinī, 59, 86fn, 91fn, 100fn, 130, 132fn, 150fn, 152fn, 176fn, 179, 179fn

Sundarīka Bharadvāja Sutta, 182

Suttanipāta, 30fn, 35fn, 36fn, 78, 86, 100, 102fn, 112, 112fn, 114, 116fn, 117, 134, 146, 146fn, 149, 153, 163, 163fn, 175fn, 178, 178fn, 180, 180fn, 182fn, 186-87

Suttanipāta Aṭṭhakathā, 77fn, 83fn, 86fn, 91fn, 95fn, 100fn, 122fn, 156

Suttapiṭaka, 30, 96, 142

Sutta Vibhaṅga, 174

Tevijja Sutta, 45, 54, 61

Tevijja-Vacchagotta Sutta, 77fn

Theragāthā, 32, 32fn, 94, 99, 106, 114, 118, 120, 128, 145, 145fn, 146, 146fn, 167-68, 171fn, 172, 172fn, 178, 178fn, 180, 180fn, 182, 186, 197

Theragāthā Aṭṭhakathā, 94, 94fn, 95fn, 174fn

Therīgāthā, 32, 32fn, 114, 128, 155, 168, 171fn, 180, 182, 186, 197

Tikanipāta, 61, 66fn

Tinakattha Sutta, 52

Titthayatana Sutta, 61

Ubbaripetavatthu, 184
Udāna, 26fn, 79, 84fn, 85, 85fn, 92fn, 93fn, 99fn, 128
Udāna Aṭṭhakathā, 79fn
Udambarikasihanāda Sutta, 8fn,
Upāli Sutta, 191
Uposatha Sutta, 41

Vaka-Jātaka, 17fnsw
Valāha Saṁyutta, 33
Vana Saṁyutta, 34fn, 35, 36, 36fn
Vatthupama Sutta, 139
Vibhaṅga, 6, 6fn, 7fn, 48, 48fn, 49, 53fn, 146fn, 147, 155, 155fn, 165, 165fn, 167
Vibhaṅga Aṭṭhakathā, 91, 126
Vidurapaṇḍita Jātaka, 18fn, 33, 33fn
Vighasa Jātaka, 18fn
Vīmaṁsaka Sutta, 144fn
Vimāna Vatthu, 9, 87, 114, 117, 128, 168, 180-81, 181fn, 185fn, 186-87
Vimānavatthu Aṭṭhakathā, 168fn, 190fn
Vimuttimagga, 158-59
Vinaya Piṭaka, 23fn, 27, 28fn, 29fn, 30, 35, 35fn, 80fn, 90, 92fn, 93, 93fn, 95fn, 96, 96fn, 97fn, 98fn, 99fn, 110fn, 124, 127, 134fn, 140, 145, 149, 149fn, 150fn, 154fn, 166, 174, 176, 176fn
Visuddhajana Vilāsinī, 187
Visuddhimagga, 15, 39, 49, 49fn, 61fn, 64, 81fn, 83, 84, 84fn, 98, 98fn, 116, 143, 148, 154fn, 156, 157-59, 166, 168fn, 172, 174, 174fn, 185, 198

Yakkha Saṁyutta, 34, 34fn, 36fn

Index of Buddhist Words and Proper Names

Ābhassara, 54, 58, 58fn, 59, 63-64

Abhaya, 183

Abhiññā, 12

Abhipatthita, 186

Abhipattheti, 186

Abhirūpa-Nandā, 95, 182

Abuddhi, 77

Ācāriya, 144-45, 174fn, 175

Accanā, 169, 181, 199

Accati, 181

Accita, 181

Accito, 181

Aciravatī, 62

Ādesanā-pāṭihāriya, 100

Adhicitta, 108

Adhideva, 18fn

Adhigamana, 137fn

Adhimutta, 115

Adhipaññā, 108

Ādhipateyya, 9

Adhisīla, 108

Ādicca-bandhu, 170fn

Agamana Saddhā, 138

Aggadakkhineyya, 154

Aggidatta, 94

Ākāravatī saddhā, 138, 140, 144, 195

Ākāravant, 137fn

Akusalas, 10

Āḷavi-Gotama, 163

Ālavaka, 91, 153, 163

Āmagandha, 178

Amanussa, 33

Amara, 3

Amulika Saddhā, 144

Anāgāmī, 108, 190

Ānanda, 4, 121, 123, 179, 189, 198

Anantagocara, 86

Ananuvejjo, 131

Anāthapiṇḍika, 162fn

Anattā, 12, 51, 57, 67, 102

Anāvaraṇa nāṇa, 81

Andha putthujjana, 137

Aṅgulimāla, 91, 97

Anicca, 12, 51, 66

Anopama, 183

Antarāyika, 166fn, 167fn
Antima-sariro, 171fn
Anumodanā, 14
Anuruddha, 32
Anusāsanī-pāṭihāriya, 100
Anussati, 39, 39fn
Anuttara Samyak-Sambodhi, 107
Anuttariya/s, 100
Apacayati, 169
Apāyabhūmīs, 10
Appatipuggalo, 171fn
Araha, 185
Araham, 185
Arhants, 14, 19, 28, 30-32, 47, 75, 85, 87, 101, 105, 106-08, 131, 142, 149, 158, 161, 167, 181, 185, 190fn, 191,
Arahata, 185
Arahati, 185
Araho, 185
Ārāma devatā, 34, 42, 46
Arittha, 163
Ariyasavaka, 141
Arūpāvacara, 16
Arūpāvacara bhūmis, 11
Asaddhiya, 163
Asankhata, 127
Asaṅkheyya/s, 105, 109
Asaññasattha devas, 13fn
Āsavakkhya-nāṇa, 83, 106
Āsavas, 9, 196
Āsayanusaya nāṇa, 81
Asura, 32
Assaddhā, 137fn, 163
Aupapāduka, 119
Avantiputta, 152fn
Aveccappasāda, 137fn, 139, 155, 186
Avenika dhamma, 100
Avijjā, 8, 47, 86
Avissāsaniya, 163

Bāhuraggi, 44
Bākula, 114
Bhadda-Kappa, 109
Bhaddā Kuṇḍalakesī, 183
Bhaddiya, 44
Bhadrāvudha, 163
Bhagavā, 98, 108fn, 115, 118, 151, 172-74, 198
Bhagavat, 115
Bhagehiyuttatā, 173
Bhaggadosatā, 173
Bhagi, 115
Bhāgyavā, 173
Bhājanaloka, 64
Bhajati, 168-69
Bhajin, 169
Bhallika, 153, 162, 176
Bhatti-kamma, 167fn
Bhattamant, 168
Bhattava, 168, 174, 198
Bhattavant, 168
Bhatti, 167-74, 197-99
Bhavanta-go, 173

Bhikkhu/s, 36, 80, 83, 93, 142
Bhikkhunī/s, 25
Bhuñjatī, 29
Bhūripañña, 86
Bimbisāra, 198
Bodhi, 75-76
Bodhi-sambhāra, 75
Bodhisatta, 74, 75, 85-86, 105, 107, 109, 118-19, 138, 178
Bodhisattva, 18, 118fn, 178
Brahma Sahāmpati, 26-27, 185
Brahma Sanan Kumāra, 26-27
Brahma-bhūta, 55fn
Brahma-kāyika Deva, 44fn
Brahmā/s, 4, 8fn, 16, 19, 20, 22, 23, 23fn, 25, 25fn, 43, 47, 55, 55fn, 121
Brahma-vihāra/s, 56, 148
Brahmāyu, 154, 177
Buddha-cakkhu, 80, 80fn
Buddhaghoṣa, 39 39fn, 49, 61, 73, 78, 98, 124, 148, 153, 159, 170, 185, 191, 193
Buddhakkhetta, 83
Buddhālambanapīti, 158, 197
Buddhanubuddha, 106
Buddhānussati, 155fn, 158-59, 159fn, 197
Buddhatta, 76
Buddha-veneyya, 100
Buddha-vira, 171
Bujjhati, 73-74

Cakkavāḷa, 17fn, 118
Cakkhumant, 86
Cariya, 75
Catu-vesārajja, 89
Cetopariya-ñāṇa, 83
Chaddanta, 91
Chaḷa-bhiññā, 83
Ciñcamāṇavika, 166
Citta, 162
Cittagahapati, 190
Citta-pasāda, 184
Cūlaka, 94
Cuṇḍa, 25

Dasa balāni, 89
Dasa-sīla, 10
Deva/s, 1-33, 193
Devadatta, 27, 87, 97, 166
Devakanna, 3
Devānussati, 38
Devatā/s, 3, 32, 32fn, 33
Devatānussati, 39, 39fn
Devayoni, 32
Dhamma, 20-23, 28, 35, 43, 102, 107-08, 113, 116, 119, 124-25, 125fn, 126-27, 143, 149, 151-52, 157, 164, 173
Dhammabandhu, 126
Dhammabhūta, 126-27
Dhammacakka, 24
Dhammadūtas, 35
Dhammakāya, 126-27, 155, 197
Dhammaniyamata, 126

Dhammarāja, 126
Dhammasāmi, 126
Dhammasayambhu, 126
Dhammatā, 125-26
Dhammeśvara, 126
Dhaniya, 91
Dharmapāla, 174, 185
Dhātu, 126
Dhātu-parinibbāna, 132
Dibba-cakkhu, 12, 80
Dibba-sota, 12, 83
Dighavu, 93
Dīpaṅkara, 86
Dukkha, 12, 51, 70
Dvevācika upāsakas, 176

Ekaggatā, 159
Eka-Sātaka, 190

Gahvaratiriya, 94
Gandhabbā, 8fn, 32-33, 42, 46fn, 190
Gandharvarāj, 32
Gatila Uruvela Kassapa, 90
Gaudambaka, 100
Ghatikāra, 44
Godhika, 94

Hatthaka, 163

Idapaccayatā, 51
Iddhi/s, 88, 104, 194
Iddhipāda, 101
Iddhipatihāriya, 94, 100
Iddhi-vidhi, 83
Indriyaparopariyatta-ñāṇa, 81
Isidatta, 163
Issara, 2, 46, 46fn, 47-49

Jambudīpa, 35, 105
Janmakhetta, 15
Jātikkheta, 119
Jenta, 75, 115
Jhāna, 15, 41, 82, 131, 140, 159, 166, 193, 196
Jīvaka Komarabhacca, 90, 163

Kāccana, 152fn
Kakudha, 93
Kālāma/s, 154
Kaliṅga, 93
Kalyāṇamittā/s, 35, 193
Kalyāṇa-putthujjana, 138
Kāmāvacara, 16, 37
Kāmāvacara bhūmis, 11
Kamma, 14, 18, 51-52, 58, 68, 82, 149, 194
Kamma-niyama, 58
Kandara masuka, 93
Kaṇṭhaka, 183
Kapilavatthu, 31
Kappa, 95
Kappas, 105
Kappina, 32
Karuna Sagara, 86
Karuna Sitala, 86
Kāruṇika, 148

Kassapa, 32, 123
Katta, 59
Khaṇḍadeva, 44
Khaṇḍasumana, 182
Khemā, 95, 183
Kinnara, 32
Kisā-Gotamī, 99, 179
Kokālika, 27, 85
Kolivisa, 90
Koliya, 93
Koṇāgamana, 183
Korakhattiya, 93
Kumbhaṇḍa/s, 33, 35
Kusala-citta, 14
Kusinārā, 99

Lohituppādaka, 166
Lokadhātus, 31
Lokavidu, 85
Lokika Saddhā, 137
Lokika Saraṇa, 153
Lokottaravāda, 118
Lokuttara, 118
Lokuttaratā, 120
Lokuttara Saddhā, 137

Macchikasandika, 163
Magandiya, 75
Mahākappina, 91, 95
Mahākaruṇā, 76, 86
Mahākaruṇasamapatti-ñāṇa, 81
Mahānāma, 188fn
Mahānāma Śakka, 163
Mahāpajāpati Gotamī, 155
Mahāpuruṣa, 116
Mahāsavaka, 84
Mahāvana, 31
Makkhali, 48
Mallika, 190
Mamsa cakkhu, 79
Manatthaddha, 177
Manava-Gamiya, 30
Māra, 8fn, 20-22, 24, 37, 97, 111, 121
Matthakuṇḍali, 181
Mendaka, 163
Mettika, 183
Miccha-diṭṭhi, 47
Migajala, 114
Milinda, 57, 78, 111fn
Moggalāna, 32, 83, 92, 132, 147
Mucilinda, 34

Nāgā/s, 32-33
Nagara devatayo, 32-33
Nāgasena, 57, 87, 120, 128
Nāgavilokana, 122
Nakulapita, 163
Nalagiri, 98
Nāmarūpa, 49
Namassati, 169
Ñāṇa-jāla, 77
Ñāṇa-Sambhāra, 75
Nanda, 90, 95
Nārada, 44

Neyyamandalas, 79
Nibbāna, 43, 47, 51, 55, 68, 87, 94, 124, 128-29, 133, 139, 142, 162, 176, 186, 188, 194-95
Nigantha Nātaputta, 77, 77fn, 191
Nimmātu, 2, 47
Niraya/o, 9-11, 45
Nirvāṇa, 9-10, 15, 25, 42, 98
Nisabha, 94

Okappana Saddhā, 138
Okappati, 137fn
Okappeti, 137fn
Okkappanā, 137fn

Pabbaja, 149
Pabbajanīya Kamma, 113
Pacceka Buddhas, 14-15, 84, 104-05, 108
Paduma, 85
Paduma Buddha, 178
Pakatisavaka, 84
Paṇāma, 169
Pañcamahā pariccaya, 75
Pañcasīla, 10
Paṇidhāna, 186
Paṇipāta, 154
Paññā, 76, 109, 141, 195
Paññā-cakkhu, 80
Paññāvaya Saddhā, 141, 195
Paññā-vimutta, 143
Panthaka, 178
Pārājika, 166
Pārami, 75, 105
Pāramitās, 116
Parinibbāna, 23, 31, 74, 83, 92, 97, 113, 121, 123, 126, 129-30, 132, 152, 187, 189, 196
Pasāda saddhā, 155
Pasadā/o, 139, 170
Pāsenadi, 3, 4, 171, 177, 198
Pasīdati, 138-39
Passika, 94
Pātācara, 99
Paṭiccasamuppāda, 67, 194
Patika, 97
Pāṭimokkha, 196
Paṭisambhidās, 104
Patisaranīya Kamma, 113
Patthanā, 169, 185, 199
Patthayanto, 186
Patthento, 186
Patthetabba, 186
Pattheti, 186
Patthita, 186
Pāvā, 191
Payirupāsati, 169
Pema, 169-70
Pemanīya, 169
Petas, 33, 35, 184
Pettivisaya, 9, 11
Phalagaṇḍa, 44
Pilindavaccha, 84
Pingiya, 44, 114, 163
Piti, 139

Pubbenivasānussati-ñāṇa, 83
Pūjā, 181
Pūjako, 179
Pūjanā, 179
Pūjaneyya, 179
Pūjanīya, 179
Pūjeti, 179
Pūjita, 179
Pūjīya, 179
Pukkusāti, 44, 93
Punabbhava, 137
Punaruppatti, 137
Punna, 190
Punna-sambhāra, 75
Purakkharoti, 169
Purakkhata, 169
Puthujjana, 9, 108

Rohiṇī, 182
Roja, 176
Rukkha-devatā, 32, 34, 42, 46
Rūpa-brahmaloka, 119
Rūpa-kāya, 155
Rupāvacāra, 16
Rūpāvacāra bhūmis, 11

Sabbākāraparipūraṁ, 173
Sabbannu, 79, 86
Sabbannuta-nana, 81, 194
Sabbassavi, 79
Sabbavidu, 86
Saddhā, 9, 133-66, 195-97
Saddhābala, 134, 137, 163
Saddhādika, 54, 109
Saddhānusari, 142-43, 196
Saddhāvimutta, 142, 196
Saddhindriya, 134, 137, 143
Sahalokadhātu, 111
Sahāmpati, 44
Sahassa lokadhātu, 55
Sakadāgāmin, 15
Sakka/s, 14, 16, 18-19, 22, 27-32, 44, 103
Sakkāra pūjā, 185
Sakulā, 183
Śākyamuni, 76, 86, 113, 182
Salha, 93
Sama, 182
Samādhi, 133, 139, 193, 195
Sanankumāra, 44
Samanta-cakkhu, 80-81, 86
Sambodhi, 76
Samma-diṭṭhi, 133
Samma-Sambodhi, 77
Sampakkhandhana, 140
Sampasadana, 140
Samapattis, 104
Samudda-devatā, 32
Saṁvaṭṭa, 58
Samyojana, 139
Sandhana, 163
Saṅgha, 152
Sañjitā, 59
Saṅkhāra, 58
Saragga, 163

Savaka, 106
Saraṇa, 149-50
Saraṇāgamana, 150, 196
Saraṇāgati, 150
Saranattayam, 149
Śāriputta, 89, 92, 111, 117, 132, 139
Sāsana, 126
Sati, 133, 195
Sattaloka, 64
Sattha, 106, 146
Sattharo, 101
Sela, 95, 110, 115
Senaka, 114
Seniya Bimbisāra, 93
Seṭṭho, 59
Sikhi, 183
Sīlabbata-paramasa, 139
Sopaka, 115
Sotāpaññā, 7, 15, 22, 138, 154, 161, 197
Sotapattihood, 190
Śraddhā, 133
Subha, 32, 98
Subrahma, 26
Sudatta, 93
Sudattagahapati, 190
Suddhāvāsa, 26, 119
Sumana, 185, 190
Sumanassara, 185
Sumedhā, 86, 183
Sunakkhatta, 71, 89, 95
Sunaparantas, 94
Sundarī, 183
Sundarī Nanda, 95
Sunīta, 32, 95
Suppabuddha, 93
Suppavāsa, 93
Suppiyā, 98, 190
Sura, 3
Sura Ambaṭṭha, 163

Tajjanīya kamma, 113
Taṇhā, 8
Tapussa, 153, 176
Tapparāyanatā, 153
Tathāgata, 23
Tavakaṇṇika, 163
Tāvatimsa, 16, 123
Tevacika upāsaka, 176
Tevijjā, 12, 83
Thana-kuśala, 92
Thaṇathana-ñāṇa, 92
Thava, 169, 186, 199
Thavati, 186
Thaveti, 186
Therika, 183
Thomamana, 186
Thuna, 99
Thuta, 186
Thuti, 169, 186, 199
Tidasa, 3
Ti-lakkhana, 195
Tiracchāyoni, 9, 11
Ti-saraṇa, 20, 106, 149-52, 154, 195-96

Tissa, 26
Tissamanera, 91
Titthiya, 84
Tudu, 26-27
Tuṣita, 118

Ubbari, 99
Udāyi, 177
Udāyin, 120
Uggatta, 163
Uggavesalika, 163
Uggogahapati, 190
Ukkhepanīya Kamma, 113
Upāka, 44, 75, 158
Upāli, 191
Upapatti devas, 16
Upāsakas, 31, 119
Upasampadā, 149, 166, 197
Upasena, 90
Upatissa Thera, 158-59
Uposatha, 41, 90, 167, 197
Uppalavannā, 183
Uruvela Kassapa, 94
Uttara, 32, 75, 94
Uttarapala, 94
Uttarī manussa, 106
Uttiya, 94

Vaccagotta, 75
Vaci-paṇidhi, 109
Vajirapāṇi, 28
Vajjita, 94
Vajjiyamahita, 163
Vakkali, 20-21, 75, 127, 163, 198
Valāhaka-kāyika, 33
Valliya, 94
Vana-devatā, 32, 34, 46
Vandana, 169
Vangīsa, 115, 187, 198
Vanna, 9
Vasettha, 61, 163
Vasitthi, 99
Vasuki, 32
Vatthu-devatā, 32
Vessabhu, 183
Vicikiccha, 139
Vidhātu, 2, 47
Viḍuḍabha, 4
Vijaya, 163
Vijitasena, 94
Vimutto, 171fn
Vinnanatthitis, 12
Vipassi, 182
Viriyādhika, 109
Visākha, 96
Visayakhetta, 83
Visuddhideva, 117, 194

Yakkha/s, 32-35
Yakkhinis, 34
Yama, 23
Yamaka, 132
Yamakapāṭihīra ñāṇa, 81
Yasa, 9, 95, 149, 176
Yaśodhara, 187